Cheese

JULIET HARBUTT

WILLOW CREEK PRESS
MINOCQUA, WISCONSIN

I would like to dedicate this book to Sarah and Willy Wint for helping me to keep my mind and body intact.

Cheese
By Juliet Harbutt

Published in the USA by Willow Creek Press, Inc. PO Box 147, Minocqua, Wi 54548
For information on other Willow Creek titles, call 1-800-850-9453

First published in Great Britain in 1999 by Mitchell Beazley, an imprint of Octopus Publishing Group Limited, 2-4 Heron Quays, London E14 4JP.

Commissioning Editor: Margaret Little
Managing Editor: Rebecca Spry
Senior Editor: Lucy Bridgers
Design: Pike

Special photography: Laurie Evans
Picture Research: Claire Gouldstone
Production: Karen Farquhar
Index: Anne Barrett

Special thanks to Patricia Michaelson, owner of the wonderful cheese shop, La Fromagerie in London N5, for supplying and preparing cheeses for photography.

ISBN 1 57223 200 5

The author has asserted her moral rights.

Typeset in Linoletter
Printed and bound by Toppan Printing Company in China

Contents

Introduction

Above: The soothing image of life in the country has tempted many city-dwellers into activities such as cheesemaking.

You cannot pick up a newspaper or a magazine without finding a new article or angle on wine – the grapes, the growers, the weather, even the type of oak chips. We are bombarded with information about malolactic fermentation and the mysteries behind taste and the nose. Cheese, like wine, is the fruit of the soil. Yet cheese – one of nature's miracles, made from milk that sustains all mammals throughout their early years – is perceived as a time bomb for arteries, a training ground for dangerous pathogens or simply as a commodity to grate or grill. The complex flavours, marvellous texture and unique fermentation process are often ignored.

How is this possible when cheese contains so much of what we need for a healthy diet and is a truly natural product containing only salt as an additive? And how can milk from the lowly cow produce so many different textures, tastes and aromas when heat and moisture content seem to be the only variables?

The aim of this book is to reveal the magic of cheese; to change our perception of 'milk's leap to immortality' and to place cheese back on its pedestal,

where the Greeks and Romans had it firmly planted. The real story of cheese aches to be told: how it has a 'vintage' every day; how it changes with the seasons; what its origins are and what its history is. Yet cheese is hidden under wrappings and labels telling us its fat content and price, not its taste and flavour. So how do we choose? How do we decide what the texture and flavour will be like and how one cheese compares with another? What little information is provided tends to concentrate on recipes or country of origin.

Styles of cheese

When faced with the vast array of clinically wrapped cheeses now synonymous with supermarket cabinets, or even with the tiny mould-encrusted cheeses piled high on rickety tables under the plane trees on market day in a French village, how do you know which to buy?

Lacking the knowledge to distinguish between the good, the bad and the down right inedible, we hesitate, suspicious of a cheese's underlying character, and run the risk of losing the opportunity of our gastronomic lifetime. What we need is a system on which to build our knowledge, just as we now have for wine. Once winemakers and retailers started to classify and identify wine by grape variety rather than by country or simply colour, we became experts overnight, and tasting notes such as 'hint of blackberries' and 'delightful appley freshness' became commonplace. The same kind of system should, and can, be applied to cheese.

You could divide cheeses up into cow's, goat's and sheep's, but this would be like dividing wine into red, white or rosé – far too general – and it omits the buffalo, camel or yak's milk cheeses. The method I use, based on various European systems, divides cheeses into categories according to the type of rind they grow and their texture. A glance at the rind, a whiff and a surreptitious squeeze will tell you a cheese's texture, character, background, probable traits and foibles, strength of flavour and, with a little practice, its stage of maturity. For it is the amount of moisture or whey in a cheese that determines what type of rind it will form, making the rind an accurate indicator as to the character of the cheese that stares up at you crying 'pick me' from the market stalls of Europe or the supermarkets of the Western world.

There may be the occasional overlap, contradiction or surprise, but the system does allow even a beginner to reduce a seemingly awesome array of cheeses into some semblance of order.

How to use this book

Each chapter outlines the characteristics of a specific type of cheese (eg blue cheese), then one or more classic examples are described (in the case of blue cheeses, Stilton, Roquefort and Gorgonzola), providing a benchmark against which you can measure other similar but lesser-known cheeses (Bleu des Causses, Maytag Blue etc). At the end of each chapter is a list of more cheeses of the same style, including the type of milk and country of origin for each cheese. So if you know what Roquefort or Stilton tastes and feels like, you will be able to use them as a guide to identifying the characteristics of other blues.

Just as you have learnt to recognize a Chardonnay by its hints of luscious, tropical fruit or a fresh fish by the twinkle in its eyes, so you can gain an insight into the traditions, magic and romance of cheese by using the rind as your guide.

I hope this book will be a source of inspiration, a reference book and a travel guide, giving you enough knowledge to be discerning, whether your hunt for cheese is being carried out in the Australian outback, a supermarket or a delicatessen.

KEY AND ICONS

① **Country of origin**

② **Region** Where no region is specified, the cheese is produced country-wide.

③ **Milk source** Symbols are used to indicate the source of the milk, ie cow, goat, sheep or buffalo.

④ **Unpasteurized** Most cheeses are made either with raw or pasteurized milk. However, there are exceptions, particularly when a cheese is made by both artisan producers and in factories. In these cases both a tick and a cross are used.

⑤ **Maturing time** The time taken to reach maturity is an indication of a cheese's strength of flavour and its texture; the older the cheese, the more complex its flavour. Some types, such as fresh, natural rind and hard cheeses, become firmer with age, whereas soft, white-rind, washed-rind and blues become softer.

⑥ **Average weight** To help you envisage what the cheese looks like.

①	**France**	Loire ②
③	Milk source	
④	Unpasteurized	✓
⑤	Maturing time	**10-20 days**
⑥	Average weight	**200g/7oz**
⑦	Vegetarian	✗
⑧	Shape	

⑦ **Vegetarian** Many cheeses use a non-animal rennet suitable for vegetarians. This does not alter the cheese's taste or texture.

⑧ **Shape** To help identify the cheese. Remember when creating a cheeseboard that it is as important to have different shapes as it is to have different textures, colours and milk types.

The beginning

Whether the first cheese was made from yak's milk in Mongolia, camel's milk in Africa or ewe's milk in the Middle East is an ongoing debate, but wherever it happened the cheese will have been made in a similar way. With help from Mother Nature, early man discovered that fresh milk, when left in the warmth of the sun or heated in earthenware pots, would eventually separate into white, fragile, slightly bitter, edible solids and a sharp, watery liquid – with a look not unlike that of milk left out of the fridge overnight.

Next came the realization that warm milk, when stored in sacks of animal skins and constantly joggled on the daily journey to new pastures, would ferment, making the solids firmer and less bitter and giving a longer life. Where the climate, lifestyle and indigenous animals differed, other fermented milk products, such as yoghurt, kumiss (mare's milk) and kephir (milk fermented with yeast), developed.

Those people whose paths took them to the sea or salt plains discovered that mixing the firm curd with salt results in a cheese with a significantly longer life. The discovery of pottery and basket weaving was equally significant, as the curd could be drained, a technique impossible when an open fire, bones and stones were man's only tools. However, there were no written records of cheesemaking until the Greek age, when Homer wrote of a giant shepherd making cheese in Sicily, using wicker baskets or *formos* to drain the curd. *Formos* became *Forma* in Latin and eventually *formaggio*, the Italian for cheese.

By Greek and Roman times, cheesemaking had become sophisticated and diverse. Fresh cheeses were made for home consumption, while hard cheeses were traded around the Mediterranean and travelled in the knapsacks of the Roman legions and of Genghis Khan and his marauding horsemen. As the Roman Empire spread, the art of cheesemaking was taught to the conquered tribes of Europe, and

Above: There are many small, artisan cheesemakers whose only commercial outlets are local markets.

the Roman influence can be seen in the hard cheeses of Switzerland, Britain and Holland.

The fall of the Roman Empire led to the Dark Ages and cheesemaking went through a lean period. Its survival was assured thanks to the monastic orders and itinerant monks, who taught people how to make and eat cheese. During the 11th Century, the Cistercian Monks, who established 500 abbeys across Europe in 30 years, created the first of the pungent, aromatic washed-rind cheeses. Many, such as Cîteaux, are still made by the monks today.

During the Renaissance and Elizabethan times cheese was definitely not politically correct, as many believed the smell was evil and caused illness. Even Shakespeare was rarely complimentary. Fortunately, however, the Normans (originally from France) were, even then, obsessed by cheese and taught the Britons the art of cheesemaking.

Industrialization of cheese

The invention of scientific methods of testing acidity and pasteurizing milk in the late 19th Century was the next major influence on cheesemaking, allowing cheesemakers to substantially reduce waste and improve the quality of their cheeses. However, it also enabled factories to reproduce traditional recipes on a larger scale and gradually, in Britain, Germany and Northern Europe, the art of the cheesemaker, his intuition and instincts, were replaced by mechanization.

In Britain, Germany and Eastern Europe traditional cheesemakers were all but extinct after the Second World War, and production was taken over by large factories or co-operatives. The concept of regionality was all but lost and cheesemaking became the appliance of science and technology. Artisan methods were cast aside and cheese in Britain and the New World had, by the 1970s, become a commodity designed for functionality rather than for its character and flavour.

Modern artisan cheeses

The late 1980s, with its boom economy and sense of optimism, saw the beginning of a revolution in the cheese world, most notably in Britain, America and Australasia. Farmers were looking to diversify and city dwellers, fed up with the madness of life in the fast lane, turned to the country to seek out a more meaningful lifestyle. Bringing with them money, modernity, a strong work ethic, but no agricultural experience, the newcomers saw handmade cheese as an ideal opportunity to make a living. Sheep or goats were the preferred animals for milk, as they were easier to handle than cows, required less land, ate considerably less and were not as terrifying. Recipes from old cookbooks, dairies and ancient

monastic manuscripts were dragged from attics, discovered in libraries or gleaned from letters sent to early settlers in the New World.

These recipes were adapted, adjusted and subjected to the whims, skills and fancies of the cheesemakers. The cheeses were affected by the choice of animals, the climate, the cheesemaker and the wild yeasts and moulds that existed in the dairies, cellars and kitchens. Each of these factors contributed to the diversity of what are known as the Modern British or New Age artisan cheeses.

Against this background the EU is now consciously and unconsciously tearing away the foundations of the traditional cheese industry by its rules and regulations which threaten not only the flavour and texture of cheeses, but also isolated pockets of history where the people still practise transhumance – a way of life inextricably linked to the life cycle of their animals and the seasons.

Above: While travelling around the countryside, it is worth looking out for signs advertizing the sale of local cheeses.

The art & science of cheesemaking

Above: Graders of Parmigiano, like piano tuners, listen to the resonance produced from a gentle tap of their hammer.

The parallel of wine and cheese is never more relevent than when you consider the influence of the climate, terrain, history and geology of a region on the final taste, style and texture of a cheese. Each traditional cheese tells you something about the history of the people who made it and the country where it was made. The method of production, the type of animals, the size and shape of the cheese and even its flavour are dictated by a combination of historical events – the numerous wars of Europe, famines, plagues, changing climates, mountain ranges, the migration patterns of the early nomadic herds and even the discovery of pottery.

For centuries the art of cheesemaking was handed down by word of mouth, and later through recipes carefully recorded by monks. The monks lacked a basic understanding of science, so the recipes contained the same unhelpful comments one still finds in recipes today – 'stir until thick', 'warm, but do not over-heat', 'drain when firm'.

Problems were more often attributed to the menstrual cycle of the dairymaid than to poor hygiene or changing seasons. The failure rate was high, though no doubt consumers had stronger immune systems than we do today. The first major breakthrough came when Fahrenheit developed the thermometer in the 1730s, but most cheesemakers would have been unaware of its existence or even its advantages, and so used their elbow as a guide.

In the 19th Century, when scientists began to unravel the mystery of cheese, cheesemaking became more of a science than an inconsistent art. In 1857, Louis Pasteur (hence 'pasteurization') developed a process of heating milk and so destroying any harmful bacteria without destroying the milk's texture. Unfortunately, pasteurization also destroyed the bacteria that coagulated the milk, and so developing a reliable starter culture became a priority. By 1919, Orla-Jensen had isolated a pure culture of micro-organisms to replace the often unpredictable sour milk and whey starters.

The extraction of rennet had been standardized by Hansen in Denmark in 1870, producing a more consistent curd and cleaner milk. Until then the rennet from the calf vells or stomach had been obtained by drying the vells, cutting them up and then soaking them in water to extract the rennet.

However, the invention of the acidimeter test by Lloyd in 1899 was probably the most significant breakthrough. This enabled cheesemakers to measure the acidity of the whey throughout the process, and so to describe quantifiably what was occurring.

Research continues today, thanks to the ongoing curiosity of the scientific community and the massive research funds used to ensure that the cheese we eat is safe, often at the expense of flavour.

The animals, the milk, the breeds

Milk gives us nourishment essential for life when we are young, and sustenance as we grow up and our diet changes. When converted into cheese, it contains no additional ingredients other than salt and normally rennet. Cheese derives its varied character from the soil, the weather, the seasons and the skill and love of the craftsperson who makes it.

The anonymous, sterile nature of modern shopping has resulted in a generation of people in the Western world losing their perspective on where basic foodstuffs, such as milk, come from. Urban children are often amazed to discover that milk in sterile bottles on supermarket shelves originally comes from cows' mammary glands that suckle their young in an elaborate process of converting grass into milk.

Although the ratio of the various elements of milk varies from species to species and animal to animal, it mainly consists of fat globules, proteins, lactose (milk sugars), minerals and water, with small amounts of pigments, enzymes, vitamins and bacteria. The chart below shows how the ratio varies from species to species.

Bottled milk the world over tends to taste the same, as it is pasteurized. This is not true of cheese, as the dietary habits of an animal will significantly influence a cheese's flavour. Cows and sheep are grazing animals – they eat continuously a diet of mainly short cropped grasses and herbage. Goats, like giraffes, are mainly browsers; they like to eat leaves rather than grasses, hence the reason why it is ill-advized to put a goat in the garden and imagine he will save you from cutting your lawn; instead he will happily avail himself of your precious flowers, and roses will be his first choice.

The breed of cow, goat or sheep can also significantly affect the flavour, and even the texture and colour, of a cheese. The French have recognized the contribution that the different breeds make, and in many regions the breed of animal for a specific cheese is laid down by law.

Above: Goats at Carrus, Corbières –
a region better known for its wines.

THE ELEMENTS FOUND IN THE MILK OF SOME MAMMALS PER 100G

Description	Calories	Protein	Carbohydrate	Fat	Water
Human milk	65.00	1.4	6.6	3.7	87.0
Cow Friesian	66.00	3.1	4.6	3.9	87.8
Cow Jersey	79.00	3.6	4.6	5.1	86.4
Ewe	95.00	5.3	4.9	6.0	83.0
Goat	61.00	3.1	4.2	3.5	88.9
Buffalo	-	3.8	4.5	5.5	-
Camel	-	3.5	5.5	3.0	-
Reindeer	-	8.4	2.4	17.1	-
Semi-skimmed	33.00	3.3	4.8	0.1	91.1

Roquefort must be made with the milk of the native sheep, such as the Lacaune and Manech. Reblochon is made with milk from the small, reddy brown Montbéliard cows indigenous to the region. Their yield is less than that of the Friesian, but the flavour of their milk is more concentrated, imparting a nutty sweetness and an aromatic nature to the cheese. These cheeses are among the finest in the world.

Availability of milk

Another aspect influencing the type of cheese produced and its eventual usage is the seasonal nature of milk. Milk is produced by a mammal to feed its baby, and only under a shepherd's care will an animal continue to yield milk for human consumption for a variable period after the baby has been weaned.

Cheesemakers, however, learnt to make cheeses that could be eaten fresh or preserved, thus ensuring that they and their families had a permanent, if limited, source of protein to supplement their potentially bland diets. Goat's milk is available from January/February, when the kid is taken from its mother, until October/November, whereas the ewe's season is from December to May, providing an overlap for those communities which were fortunate enough to raise both.

During the season, most of the milk would traditionally have been used for drinking, turned into a fermented milk, such as yoghurt, or made into fresh cheeses. The rest would have been preserved in brine in the form of a Feta-type cheese, or firmly pressed and matured in cellars – for two to six months, to provide cheese for the leaner times ahead.

It was these long-lasting, hard cheeses that were used like a superior condiment in the peasant's diet or as the focal point of a menu, such as cheese fondues and gratins in wealthier households.

Top left: British Toggenberg goat. Top right: Jersey cow.
Middle: Charentais cattle in the Saône valley in France.
Bottom: Local breeds of sheep in southern Italy.

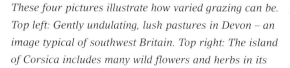

These four pictures illustrate how varied grazing can be. Top left: Gently undulating, lush pastures in Devon – an image typical of southwest Britain. Top right: The island of Corsica includes many wild flowers and herbs in its scrubby grazing. Bottom right: The island of Crete in the southern Mediterranean offers sparse, often parched grazing. Bottom left: The verdant, alpine grazing of Cantal produces some of the finest cheeses in France.

The terroir and flora

Brie was not created by committee nor Stilton coloured by copywriters; rather the white and blue moulds, part of the micro-flora of the regions, probably first appeared on the crust of a shepherd's bread or the walls of the cellars in which the cheeses were stored. The climate and geology of the region of a cheese's origin also determines what an animal eats, and this too affects the final flavour. If you have ever driven past silage, you will know that it does not possess any of the sweet, warm aromas of a bale of hay – imagine how that must taint the milk. Equally important is cleanliness in the milking parlour, dairy, ripening rooms and the place in which you store your cheese. Good hygiene safeguards the subtle influence of the grazing and ensures that the unique characteristics of the breed are untainted by chemicals, bad flavours and pasteurization.

It is this concordant blend of nature's fruits, combined with the skill and lifestyle of the local farmers, that has determined which cheeses have developed in a region. The cheeses of northern Europe reflect the fact that the comfort-loving cow is found grazing the region's lush meadows and temperate climate, munching on the buttercups, daisies and clover, or the brambles, vetches and young shoots of the hedgerows, producing sweet, mellifluous milk with a hint of dandelions. In the north of England, the salt plains produce the slow ripening Cheshire and the bracken and misty valleys of Yorkshire produce the crumbly, wild-honey flavoured Dale cheese such as Wensleydale, Ribblesdale and Swaledale.

This influence of nature upon a nation's cuisine explains why beef, butter and cream are conspicuously absent from the Mediterranean diet – the climate excludes all but the hardy goat and stubborn sheep from the region's craggy cliffs and arid sun-drenched coast line.

The hot, dry, Mediterranean climate, perfect for olives, vines and cereal crops, is hardly ideal for the shade-loving, sedate, dairy cow. But the agile, tenacious goat thrives there, tearing up the sparse, scrubby patches of coast, hill or mountainside. The island of Corsica exemplifies this with a heady mixture of aromatic shrubby bushes (*maquis*), wild thyme and juniper bushes. Its goats produce only one to two litres (1¼-3½ pints) of milk a day, compared with 15 litres (26½ pints) from a cow, but the thick, rich, milk has a distinct, aromatic, sometimes floral taste.

Sheep, such as those native to the plains of La Mancha in Spain, are equally hardy, but prefer flatter land. The Mancha sheep yield even less milk per day to make Manchego, known and loved by the Romans as long ago as the 4th Century. The once-barren plains, scorched by temperatures of up to 50°C (122°F), have been irrigated and are now planted with verdant vineyards and high yield crops where traditionally only the hardy La Mancha sheep survived, grazing on the indigenous shrubs, acorns, *esparto* grasses and wild herbs of the *dahesa* (natural, uncultivated land). Roots from these plants, which are now eaten by the sheep, absorb the minerals from the soil and help produce, even today, the thick aromatic milk that gives Manchego its distinctive character.

The final taste of a cheese, as with wine, is influenced by every bacteria, yeast, mould and molecule of grass, weed or bush that go into the making. The old adage 'variety is the spice of life' therefore is never more relevant than when applied to the variegated pastures and meadows that ensure each cheese achieves its 'leap to immortality'.

The cheesemaking process

The size of traditional cheeses was not determined by the cheesemaker, but rather by the geology and population spread of a region. For example, mountain cheeses were made in huge wheels by small co-operatives, combining all the milk of the local herds. The cheeses would be stored until the end of summer, when the shepherds would bring them down to the valleys to sell. Conversely, farmers from the gently undulating, highly populated plains or lush valleys would bring trays or baskets of their cheeses to the weekly markets. The shape of the cheese was dependent on the cheesemaker converting local materials into vessels to drain the fresh curds. Wooden moulds prevailed in mountain regions, while pottery, woven baskets and plaited belts were more likely in low-lying areas.

Converting liquid milk to solids

Basically to make cheese it is essential to separate milk into its curds and whey (solids and liquids). Curds consist of protein, milk sugars or lactose and fat, and the liquid or whey is mainly water with some protein. To achieve this separation, the milk is warmed to around 30°C (86°F) to provide the perfect environment for the lactic bacteria in the milk to attack the lactose and convert it into lactic acid. In other words, they cause the milk to start to sour.

To speed up the process of acidification and fermentation, a starter culture is added to the milk, consisting of a collection of specially selected bacteria, not dissimilar to those used to make yoghurt. The culture attacks the lactose and converts it into lactic acid. Each bacteria in the culture operates within specific parameters – some like it hot, others kick in when the level of acidity has increased, while others will die off. Some work slowly, while others are exuberant, producing the bubbles or holes in cheeses such as Emmental. These starter bacteria occur naturally in raw milk and cheesemakers can make their own starters from the previous day's milk. But if the milk is pasteurized, the bacteria must be introduced.

To produce a firmer curd, essential for cheesemaking, a coagulant is added after the starter

has stimulated the fermentation process. The most commonly used is rennet, which is an enzyme present in the stomach of all milk-fed animals. Its original purpose is to coagulate mother's milk in the infant's stomach into solids and liquid. The liquid (as we well know) is expelled from the body, while the solids will be gradually digested. Hence, when a young baby is sick it regurgitates what smells and looks like a mixture of yoghurt and cottage cheese.

In ancient times, shepherds realized that the stomach of a young milk-fed animal contained something which caused the coagulation process, and they would carry, in a pouch, a dried stomach that could be soaked in hot water. This liquid, when added to the vat of milk, would cause it to coagulate. Alternatively, fig juice, lemon juice, bay leaves, ladies bed straw and thistle were also used, but the animal rennet was, and still is, the most effective at ensuring that the majority of the solids – protein and fat – are separated out and not left in the whey.

Many cheeses now include a non-animal rennet, making them suitable for vegetarians. This can be fungus-based or created by modifying the DNA structure of a yeast. With the debate as to the safety of genetically modified products, many cheesemakers are returning to the more expensive, but less controversial, animal rennet.

Stage one: Every cheese is made in a different way. This step-by-step guide demonstrates how Cheddar is made. The cheesemaker prepares the starter culture by adding an inoculum of bacteria to a churn of sterile, raw milk. This is left to ripen for 18 hours, then poured into the vat.

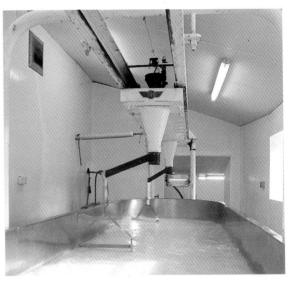

Stage two: The coagulated milk separates into curds and whey. The curds are then cut using two sets of knives set into a frame – like giant combs moving slowly through the vat. One cuts the curd vertically, the other has blades set horizontally, producing sugar-cube-sized curds.

Stage three: Once the curd is cut, the knives are removed and the temperature is gradually raised, scalding the curd and forcing it to release trapped whey. Once the desired acidity level is reached, the whey is drained off and the curd is stirred manually to prevent it from sticking together.

Stage four: The curd and remaining whey is channelled on to a draining table where the base is slightly concave. The fragile curds need to be treated carefully to avoid losing precious fat or protein into the whey. Whey can be fed to pigs or used to make whey cheeses such as Ricotta.

Stage five: The rest of the whey must be gently squeezed out until the curd settles into a coherent mass on the draining table. In factories the curd is often blasted up a tall tower until it has lost sufficient whey. The curd can then be drawn off from the top of the tower and pressed into blocks.

Stage six: To create the unique texture of Cheddar, the mass of curds must be cut into brick-sized blocks, turned by hand and piled two bricks high the length of the vat. The process is repeated every 15–20 minutes, each time increasing the number of bricks on the pile to force out more whey.

Stage seven: Gradually the bricks flatten as more whey is forced out and the all-important acidity is checked constantly to make sure it is rising. The curd is ready for the next stage only when it is coherent, dry, firm and mellow, with the texture of cooked chicken breast when pulled apart.

Stage eight: The thin bricks are then milled to finger-sized pieces and pitched by hand using giant forks to aerate and cool the curd while the salt is mixed in and absorbed. Leicester and Double Gloucester are milled twice to achieve a smoother, more dense consistency.

Stage nine: The dry curds are then scooped by hand into large, perforated, stainless steel moulds lined with cheese cloth, which is folded over the top and then placed end to end in a horizontal press. Even pressure is gradually applied over 12–16 hours, forcing out any residual whey.

Stage ten: The following day each cheese, now weighing around 27.25kg/60lb, must be turned or banged out of its mould, the cloth removed, and then the cheese replaced in the mould to be re-pressed in fresh cloth with increased pressure for a further day – a backbreaking, noisy task.

Stage eleven: The cheeses are unmoulded, sharp or uneven edges removed, and the pristine cheeses are wrapped in clean cloths or bandaged. Sealed with lard or a flour-and-water paste and labelled with the date, the cheeses are placed in a temperature-controlled environment to mature.

Stage twelve: During the first few months the Cheddars are regularly turned to move the moisture evenly through the curd. The natural moulds on the cloth form a barrier against unwanted bacteria and allow the cheeses to mature until the cheesemaker decides they have reached their peak.

Fresh cheeses

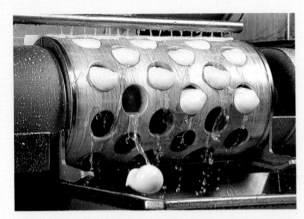

Above: Newly formed balls of Mozzarella tumble from the barrel ready for packaging in a modern dairy in Sicily, Italy.

Fresh cheeses are eaten within a few days of being made, and have little time to develop any complexity of flavour. Most are used in cooking to add texture to a dish and, because the fat is a carrier and enhancer of flavour, it absorbs the oils and essence of the other ingredients. The best examples are superb when used in simple dishes such as Mozzarella with tomatoes, olive oil and basil or a Ricotta and spinach stuffing for ravioli.

The first fresh cheeses made by nomadic tribes would have been originally discovered by accident. The goat's, ewe's, camel's or yak's milk, when warmed by the sun and stored in animal skins, would have soured and separated. The liquid would have been drained away, leaving firm, crumbly white lumps of fat and protein which could then be dried and kept for days. Alternatively, if preserved in oil or brine, they would keep for months, providing much-needed food for the harsh winter months.

Little has changed over the millennia, although in the Western world, cow's milk dominates and sterile plastic sacks have replaced sheep's stomachs. Fresh cheeses have no rind and so their texture and colour looks the same inside and out. Their relatively high moisture content, compared with a hard cheese, means they feel wet and mousse-like and will deteriorate quickly. Those destined for the cheeseboard are frequently wrapped, sprinkled, dusted or rolled in a variety of herbs, spices, leaves or nuts. One of the most exotic is Caprini Freschi Tartufo, a tiny goat's cheese topped with shavings of white truffles, creating a marriage made in heaven.

Fresh cheeses must be eaten within a few days or preserved in salt or oil. Pickled cheeses preserved in brine, such as Feta, are harder and crumbly, and the stretched-curd style, such as Mozzarella, are rubbery and elastic.

The microbes in the milk and the rennet have barely had time to convert the milk sugars to lactic acid, and the fat and protein remain virtually intact. Consequently, the flavour of the fresh cheeses is mild, slightly lemony or acidic, with just a hint of the flora and the subtle inherent differences in the type of animal. It is often hard, therefore, to distinguish between a cow's, goat's or sheep's cheese, and certainly almost impossible to tell the individual breed of an animal.

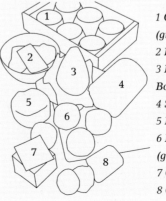

1 *Caprini Freschi Tartufo (group of six; see above)*
2 *Halloumi*
3 *Boulette d'Avesnes (see Boulette de Cambrai)*
4 *Sussex Slipcote*
5 *Boursin*
6 *Innes Button (group of four)*
7 *Gjetost*
8 *Caboc*

Feta

Greece

Milk source	
Unpasteurized	✓
Maturing time	**1-2 months**
Average weight	**1.5kg/3lb 5oz**
Vegetarian	✗
Shape	

The best-known white pickled cheese is Feta, with its soft, crumbly texture and salty, herbaceous flavour. Traditionally made with ewe's milk, Feta is assumed to originate from Greece. Recently, when the Greeks tried to claim it as their own and place it under the protection of the new European PDO (Protected Denomination of Origin) scheme, there was strong opposition, particularly from Denmark. The courts ruled against Greece, saying Feta's origins had been lost in antiquity.

Most Feta is now made in factories from pasteurized cow's milk. However, cheesemakers in Eastern Europe and the Middle East still use methods handed down by word of mouth, based on the recipe first recorded by Homer. I went to Greece on the track of one such cheesemaker.

On the outskirts of a small, isolated homestead in the rugged mountains of the island of Naxos, after a precarious journey along narrow rock-strewn roads held together by the occasional fig, mulberry or battered pine tree, I discovered my contact, Dionysis in the process of milking his exuberant, healthy but gaunt-looking flock. To those of us used to seeing sheep grazing on ankle-deep carpets of grass and clover it would seem these sheep, or less commonly goats, barely eke out a living. Yet their diet of wild herbs, flowers and tenacious grasses produces some of the thickest, most aromatic milk in the world. The scent of the thyme, marjoram and pine is captured and concentrated in the tiny fat globules of the milk and preserved in the form of this simple cheese.

In a cool, white-washed room attached to the stone cottage, Dionysis' mother, Polyxeni, poured a small cup of raw milk, left for 36 hours to generate billions of lactose-loving bacteria, into a large pail of still-warm, fresh milk, carried by Dionysis from the ancient stone milking enclosure. After about 30 minutes, when sufficient lactic acid had been created, the rennet was added and the milk left to curdle while we had a heart-stopping coffee, fresh yoghurt and apricots in the early morning sun. The time this process takes varies according to the temperature, the time of year and how many of Polyxeni's grandchildren are there to distract her.

Once the milk had curdled, Polyxeni cut the soft floppy curd into 3cm/1¼in cubes using what

Left: In isolated mountain regions of Greece small herds of sheep and goats are still hand milked in rough stone huts.

The modernization of Feta

Commercially made Feta is ripened for a few days, cut into blocks and sent to be packaged and given bar codes with descriptions of fat content and other details, but nothing that describes the magic behind this great cheese. The excess whey is often fed back to the sheep or reheated to make Myzithra.

I have often been asked why Feta always tastes better when eaten in Greece or the Middle East where it originates. The answer is simple: before it is eaten, the Feta is soaked in cold water or milk for 10 to 15 minutes to remove the excess salt, so the real flavour of the cheese is not masked. Regrettably this simple process has somehow not been passed on to the rest of the world and as a consequence most of the Feta we eat is over-salty.

Feta is at its best when used in the superb, yet simple Greek salad, or in *spanakopita*, the delicious cheese and spinach pies found all over Greece.

closely resembled a giant wooden comb drawn through the bucket. The curds and whey were then poured into a coarse cloth. Previous generations, including her grandmother's, had used tightly woven draining baskets (which they made themselves from the local reeds) and left the curds to hang from the rafters to drain.

Yesterday's curd, which was now firm and compact yet still moist, was turned out of its cloth, rubbed with salt and hung back up for two days. (Some cheesemakers leave it to ripen on draining tables for up to 15 days and, in parts of Greece and Turkey, the curd is still packed into animal skins.) Polyxeni then cut the cheese into blocks, packed it in barrels of whey and brine and stored it until it would be needed by the family.

Traditionally, cheesemakers who lived farther from the sea, where salt had to be bought, would rub the curd with salt and then store their cheese in olive oil rather than in brine, and a great deal of the Feta that is sold in supermarkets around the world today is presented in this way.

RENNET

Rennet is a solution rich in enzymes called rennin or chymosin, which are found in the walls of the stomach of milk-fed animals such as calves and kids. Its role is to attack milk proteins (casein), causing coagulation – ie the separation of solids (curds) and liquid (whey). The enzymes only speed up the coagulation, so once they have performed their role they are released unchanged from the milk.

Non-animal alternatives (microbial rennets) have been developed using the fungi *Mucor miehei*. These alternatives are successful in soft cheeses, but they can produce off-flavours in hard cheeses. They can be used without affecting the taste or texture of a cheese and, as the resulting chymosin, contain no genetically modified organisms. This fungi has been approved internationally by vegetarian associations and does not need specific labelling.

Certain plants used by cheesemakers for centuries also possess milk-clotting properties, but are too fragile for commercial use.

Ricotta (whey cheese)

Italy

Milk source	
Unpasteurized	✓
Maturing time	**1-5 days**
Average weight	**1.5kg/3lb 5oz**
Vegetarian	✗ ✓
Shape	

Whey cheeses are virtually unknown outside Greece, Italy and Scandinavia, but wherever there is an Italian community you will find a deli selling Ricotta. Ricotta means 're-cooked', and the cheese should be a firm mass of fine, moist, delicate grains. It is best unsalted or barely salted, and unripened, and it is particularly good as a stuffing or in baking, as it retains its lumpy texture when heated. It should not be wet like cottage cheese, or it causes havoc in traditional Italian cooking. Ricotta can also be made with whole milk, resulting in either a smoother, richer cheese or a mixture of whey and milk.

I first came to realise how wonderful Ricotta can be when I had lunch with a wonderful, laughing, Italian woman I had met in a market and her Assisi family. She cooked the Ricotta to perfection.

Before lunch I watched in fascinated horror as my new Italian friend made tiny ravioli stuffed with Ricotta and spinach. 'Gritty spinach coming up', I thought. Instead, the tender, white crumbly cheese retained its shape, allowing the spinach to steam inside its cocoon of pasta. The Ricotta had also absorbed and concentrated the flavour of the delicious fresh spinach, the pinch of nutmeg and the fine dusting of Parmigiano, salt and pepper.

Years later I realized that producers outside Europe, where I had previously tasted Ricotta, often make the great cheeses of Europe based on the design and equipment in their factories rather than on the traditional recipes or on an attempt at authenticity. The end results bear little resemblance to the original.

At its best, Ricotta can be like the cheese I tried recently in Milan, in Peck, one of Italy's finest cheese shops. The cheese was called Fior di Maggio and it felt like a delicate bread and butter pudding – soft, moist and gentle textured, only vaguely grainy – and it melted in the mouth.

The recipe

Real Ricotta is an insight into the practical nature of Italian cheesemakers, for it is made from the 'waste' product, or whey, from Parmigiano Reggiano. It still contains some protein and fat, despite the fact that the cream is traditionally skimmed off to make Mascarpone.

The whey is heated with a few citric acid crystals to encourage the small, white lumps of protein to form. These protein lumps float to the surface and are skimmed off into wicker baskets (now more likely to be shaped plastic moulds) to be cooled rapidly.

The high moisture content of Ricotta means that it must be eaten within a few days of purchase,

smoked version. Whichever you choose, it should be fresh, milky mild, authentic and provide a framework or texture on which to build numerous sweet or savoury Italian dishes.

Similar cheeses

There are many commercial and a few farmhouse Ricottas made outside Italy, ranging from the sublime to the ridiculous. There is also a variety of other whey cheeses which are similar to Ricotta. These hail mainly from Europe, and include Brocciu (France) and Myzithra (Greece).

The Scandinavians use a totally different technique to create this style of cheese. The whey is heated until the milk sugars are caramelized, giving a solid, slightly grainy, deep honey-brown cheese that is more akin to fudge, with a strange aromatic sweetness. The best known examples are Gjetosts (goat's milk) and Mysost (cow's milk).

HOME-MADE RICOTTA

In her wonderful book *Secrets from an Italian Kitchen*, Anna del Conte gives a recipe for home-made Ricotta – ideal if you cannot buy good Ricotta locally. Although not identical to the bought version, home-made Ricotta is better than the long-life, commercial alternatives. Here's the recipe:

1 litre (1¾ pints) full-cream milk
30ml (2 tbsp) lemon juice
2.5ml (½ tsp) salt

Bring the milk to simmering point, stir in the lemon juice and salt, and simmer for 10 minutes, stirring frequently.

Line a sieve with a square of muslin and strain the hot liquid into a basin until it stops dripping. Take up the corners of the muslin containing your Ricotta, give it a good squeeze, and put the Ricotta into a bowl.

Above: As the pure white lumps of protein and fat float to the surface, they are scooped out and drained in baskets.

preferably on the day after it is made, when the sweetness of the milk is just turning sour. Once the cheese loses its pure white, shiny 'wet' look, it is passed its best and it should never be allowed to dry out and become yellow as it will be bitter, sharp and unfit for cooking. It is, however, one of the few cheeses that freezes well.

There are variations of Ricotta, such as *Ricotta Piemontese* (cow's milk), *Ricotta Salata* (dried and salted and ideal for grating), *Ricotta Infornata* (lightly baked) and *Ricotta Romano*, made from ewe's milk from November to June and said to be the best; northern Italians have a liking for a lightly

Mozzarella di Bufala (stretched-curd)

Italy	**Rome**
Milk source	🐃
Unpasteurized	✓
Maturing time	**a few days**
Average weight	**80-150g** **2½-5½oz**
Vegetarian	✗
Shape	◯

The first stretched-curd (or pasta filata*) cheese dates back thousands of years, probably originating from the nomadic tribes of the Middle East and their sheep, and gradually spreading across eastern and central Europe and into the Mediterranean.*

Today stretched-curd cheeses can be found throughout the region, from Kaskaval in Hungary, Kashkaral or Katschkawal in Bulgaria (the best are made with ewe's milk), Gilad in Israel, Halloumi in Cyprus, and the world-famous Mozzarella and Provolone in Italy.

However, using the milk of the water buffalo – possibly introduced as early as the 6th Century – the Italians have made undoubtedly one of the most superb examples of a stretched-curd cheese, Mozzarella di Bufala.

Strictly speaking, aged *pasta filata* cheeses such as Provolone, which can be ripened for years, belong in the Hard Cheese chapter. But as their texture is similar to Mozzarella, and this cheese is so widely known, I have included all *pasta filata* cheeses in the Fresh Cheese chapter.

Each cheese has its own style, yet the basic recipes are similar. Coagulation is usually achieved with rennet, although some use vinegar or soured milk. Once the curds have been cut, hot water is added and some whey is removed, making the curd develop into a plasticized mass which is then dealt with in one of two ways.

Those stretched-curd cheeses from central Europe, such as Kaskaval, are kneaded, traditionally by hand (or even with the knee – hence the expression), but now mainly by machine. Since the cheese is kneaded while still very hot, it must be cooled in moulds before being transferred to the ripening rooms.

Italian examples, such as Provolone, Mozzarella and Caciocavallo, belong to the spun-curd group, and range from the very fresh and delicately flavoured to the sweet but piquant and sharp when fully ripe (particularly if made using kid's rennet).

The recipe

Authentic fresh Mozzarella di Bufala has a high moisture content and should be floppy – quite unlike the rubbery blocks of commercial cow's milk Mozzarella, which are best referred to as 'pizza cheese'. Mozzarella di Bufala has the subtle but pronounced sweet, mossy character and the earthy richness of buffalo milk.

To create Mozzarella di Bufala's unique stretchy quality, the curd is heated in hot water and regularly tested until a piece remains unbroken when stretched to a length of 1m/39in. It is then stretched, spun into balls and thrown into brine to form the skin and set

Left: The popularity of Mozzarella di Bufala has meant that water buffalo can even be found in Britain and Australia.

Other stretched-curd cheeses

India, although home to millions of cows and water buffalo, is not generally thought of as a milk-consuming country. Yet it is the world's largest milk producer. Most is sold as milk, yoghurt and ice-cream, but cheese is increasing in popularity, from the traditional Paneer to the cheese used on McDonald's hamburgers and the occasional Mozzarella.

Some of the best authentic Mozzarella outside of Italy is made by Mahoe, Kapiti and Parkerfield in New Zealand, Sweet Home Farm in Alabama, Rogue River Valley in Oregon and the Todaro Brothers in their deli in New York. Some cheesemakers have even imported herds of water buffalo or borrowed milk from local herds. The Mozzarella Co in Dallas, Texas, is making the first commercially available buffalo Mozzarella in the US, while three herds can be seen grazing against the incongruous background of the English and Welsh countryside in Warwickshire, Devon and Dyfed.

the shape. In Italy it is sold in tubs with whey and eaten within a few days. (Most Mozzarella found outside Italy is made from cow's milk and sealed in plastic sacs, filled with a whey and brine, and has a longer shelf life.)

This method creates layer upon layer of curd, spun, with droplets of whey trapped within the concentric circles. This produces a texture that, when peeled back, resembles cooked chicken breast. Consequently, when Mozzarella di Bufala is sliced, drizzled with olive oil, sprinkled with fresh basil and layered with tomatoes, the layers of moist curd trap and concentrate the combined juices and the result is magnificent. This characteristic, and the fact that when it melts this cheese becomes impossibly elastic, has made it popular the world over.

The pizza is responsible for introducing Mozzarella to the modern world. The cheese is produced in blocks for easy slicing and, although it has the irresistibly stringy texture when cooked, it will never equal fresh Mozzarella in taste or texture. Without the layers and moist texture, the juices of the tomatoes in a pizza rest uncertainly on the slippery surface.

PURRUMBETE BUFFALO MOZZARELLA

My favourite Mozzarella is made by Roger Haldene, a successful businessman and exceptional artist, who once had a wild ambition to introduced water buffalo to his farm, in Victoria, Australia. Three years later, and with broken red tape as long as the Nile, his 55-strong herd can be seen happily grazing the paddocks under the shade of the huge gum trees, and he produces probably the finest Mozzarella outside Italy.

In 1996, Roger sent Nick Haddow, an impassioned young Australian cheesemaker, to southern Italy to learn exactly how Mozzarella should be made. After three months working alongside an artisan producer, Nick returned and the result is a porcelain-white cheese with an authentic perfume, a nutty milky taste and more importantly a superb springy, stringy, wet texture.

The thick, earthy, sweet milk is also made into ice-cream and an exquisite, smooth yoghurt.

Afuega'l Pitu

The fascinating pumpkin or bishop's hat shape of this cheese bears the indentations made where the cloth is knotted at the top. The cheese may be plain, or rubbed with red, hot pimento (paprika). Unaware of its fiery reputation, I tasted this oddly marbled cheese, with its firm, yet grainy texture, under the amused gaze of the local Asturians. Amid hoots of laughter they informed me that its name translates as 'a fire in the throat', although later I was told that the name comes from the expression *'ahoga el pollo'* (drown the chicken) as the cheese is so thick that it sticks in the throat. Whatever the origin of its name, this cheese is worth trying with a robust Spanish wine.

Spain	Asturia
Milk source	
Unpasteurized	✓
Maturing time	2-12 weeks
Average weight	500g/1lb 2oz
Vegetarian	✓
Shape	

Beyaz Peynir (pickled cheese)

No country can claim to have invented Feta, it simply evolved like bread, and there are as many recipes for this cheese as there are for wine. In Turkey, Feta is called Beyaz Peynir and is made in factories, co-operatives and by shepherds throughout European Turkey. Vegetable rennet is generally used to clot the milk and the curds are pressed for a few hours before being roughly chopped and strained again, sometimes in attractive wooden or woven moulds. Once drained, the cheese is cut into slices, salted, placed in tin or plastic containers and covered with brine. It is softer than Greek Feta and most is still made from ewe's milk. It plays a major role in Turkish cuisine.

Turkey	
Milk source	
Unpasteurized	✓
Maturing time	**from 1 month**
Average weight	**various**
Vegetarian	✓
Shape	

Bigoton

The vast majority of French *chèvre* cheeses have been made by generations of cheesemakers using the same recipe, and are named after their shape or the town or region where they are made. Bigoton is therefore unusual, as it is made by only one cheesemaker. Ungoverned by rules and regulations, this tiny oval *chèvre* is dusted with ash and sold as young as one week old, when it has a fresh lemony taste and mousse-like texture that melts like ice-cream in the mouth. I prefer it more mature, when it develops a fine, slightly wrinkled and grey rind and the interior becomes almost runny and wonderfully goaty, though never robust.

France	Loire
Milk source	
Unpasteurized	✓
Maturing time	**from 15 days**
Average weight	**130-150g** **4½-5½oz**
Vegetarian	✗
Shape	

Boulette de Cambrai

This cheese is mostly made in homes rather than commercially. The fresh curd, or a mix of cottage cheese and *fromage frais*, is drained and mixed with parsley, tarragon and chives until the desired texture is obtained, ranging from moist and crumbly to firm and smooth. It is hand moulded into bell shapes and usually eaten a few days after being made. It is mild and aromatic and named after the shape of the cheese and the area of production. It is nowhere near as vicious as the Boulette d'Avesnes which is hot and outrageously spicy, and made with parsley, tarragon, pepper and paprika instead of the chives.

France	Flanders
Milk source	🐄
Unpasteurized	✗
Maturing time	1-5 days
Average weight	200g/7oz
Vegetarian	✗
Shape	⌂

Boursin

It would seem that Monsieur Boursin was destined from birth to become a household name in cheese with the simple, effective, timeless and unforgettable slogan *'du pain, du vin, du Boursin'*. From the start, in 1957, he was committed to quality and consistency, refusing to change the basic range. Now Boursin is available as a low-fat cheese and with flavours certainly not approved of by M Boursin. Boursin is made only from rich Normandy milk and cream. Much of the processing is still only semi-automated to retain the rich smooth texture and flavour of fresh cream, with the fresh light touch and creamy white colour of *fromage frais*.

France	Ile-de-France Normandy
Milk source	🐄
Unpasteurized	✗
Maturing time	from 10 days
Average weight	75, 150g 2¾, 5½oz
Vegetarian	✗
Shape	◯

Brier Run Cheeses

Infused with the flavours of the land, the milk is hand ladled into the moulds for these cheeses. This is essential in order to avoid the harsh, acrid taste sometimes found in goat's milk cheeses and to obtain a creamier, fuller flavour. In the caring hands of Greg and Verena Sava, the milk is converted into some of America's finest goat's cheeses, including Fromage Blanc, Banon, Pyramid and Blue Goat. Set among the scrubby crags and herbaceous pastures of the Appalachian foothills, the Sava's lifestyle sounds quite idyllic, but the reality is that it was over a decade before Greg and Verena had established the business well enough to spend a night away from the farm.

US	West Virginia
Milk source	
Unpasteurized	✗
Maturing time	from 1 week
Average weight	25-900g/1oz-2lb
Vegetarian	✗
Shape	▢ △ ◯

Brocciu, Broccio AOC (whey cheese)

Brocciu is produced in the *départements* of Corse-du-Sud and Haute-Corse and, like Ricotta, it is made from whey or whey mixed with full or skimmed milk which must come from the production of sheep's or goat's milk cheese in the same area. The whey mixture is heated, forcing the protein to come to the surface as tiny white lumps – like grains of rice – which are scooped into moulds, and the Brocciu (or Broccio in French), is eaten within a few days. Some, as with Ricotta Salata, is salted and ripened until it is hard, and sold as *passu* or *sec*. Brocciu is drained in handwoven baskets, each with its own distinctive pattern, and is eaten with fresh or stewed fruit, as a snack with herbs, or in omelettes.

France	Corsica
Milk source	
Unpasteurized	✓
Maturing time	2-5 days
Average weight	500g-1kg 1lb 2oz-2lb 4oz
Vegetarian	✗
Shape	⌣

Burgos

Originally made in Castile-León in winter and spring from the milk of the Churra – a local breed of sheep – Burgos is now made all year round in factories throughout Spain from pasteurized cow's milk. The fresh curd is pressed into ceramic (or more likely plastic) moulds, creating corrugated grooves down the sides and small ridged wedges on the top and bottom. Ready to eat within hours, it is pure white with a smooth, compact, moist, yet rubbery consistency, and retains the taste of fresh, sweet milk with just a hint of acidity and salt. The cheese is produced around the city of Burgos and is not unlike Mozzarella. It is used in numerous local dishes, or as a dessert with walnuts and honey.

Spain	
Milk source	
Unpasteurized	✓✗
Maturing time	1-5 days
Average weight	1-2kg 2lb 4oz-4lb 8oz
Vegetarian	✗
Shape	⬭

Caboc

Made with cream-enriched milk, Caboc is a small log. It is mild, slightly sour and feels like butter in the mouth (in fact, it comprizes a staggering 59 per cent fat); while the rind of toasted pinhead oats give it a nutty, yeasty flavour. Like so many great recipes, it survived by being passed on, generation to generation, although it had all but disappeared until its revival in 1962 by Susannah Stone. She is a direct descendant of the creator, Mariota de Ile, daughter of The MacDonald, Lord of the Isles, who was forced to flee to Ireland to avoid abduction by the Campbells. When Mariota returned to her homeland she brought with her the recipe for Caboc.

Scotland	Ross and Cromarty
Milk source	
Unpasteurized	✗
Maturing time	5 days
Average weight	110g/3¾oz
Vegetarian	✓
Shape	⬭

Caciocavallo (stretched-curd)

A typical stretched-curd *pasta filata* cheese from southern Italy, Caciocavallo is best made with the milk of the local Podolian cows, who are browsers rather than grazers, enjoying sweet leaves and berries of wild brier-roses, hawthorn, juniper and blackthorn. The cheese is still mostly farm made, and at three months it is sweet and supple and eaten as a table cheese. Some are matured for up to two years and can be grated. Bright golden yellow and close textured, the aroma is intense, while the taste is full but mellow. Oily and smooth and shaped like a fat skittle, it is tied with a cord and hung up to dry. Similar cheeses are made around the Mediterranean and date back to pre-Roman times.

Italy	South
Milk source	
Unpasteurized	✗
Maturing time	3-4 months
Average weight	2-3kg 4½lb-6lb 8oz
Vegetarian	✗
Shape	🍐

Cancoillotte

With the appearance of *crème fraîche* but a cheesy taste and salty bite, Cancoillotte is referred to on modern packaging as 'super butter'. Each family has its own recipe adding white wine, herbs or garlic to the basic ingredient – Metton – a well-matured local skimmed-milk cheese. The cheese is heated gently with 30 per cent of its weight of salty water and, once combined, butter is added (again around 30 per cent of the weight of the cheese) and stirred. When the mixture is smooth it has the consistency of liquid honey and simple flavours – delicious spread on toast, fresh bread or dolloped on steamed vegetables. A local speciality well worth seeking out, and similar to Spanish Tupi.

France	Franche-Comté
Milk source	
Unpasteurized	✗
Maturing time	a few days
Average weight	150g/5½oz
Vegetarian	✗
Shape	🏺

Capriole Banon

Creative writing instructor turned cheesemaker, Judy Schad, has formed a formidable partnership with nature with her herd of alpine goats. Like the new wave of young chefs of America, Judy has created a range of exciting cheeses by concentrating on maturing them to accentuate the character of the milk. As diverse in style as her writing, the cheeses range from fresh logs to hard Festiva, similar to California Jack, flavoured with pine-nuts, basil and sundried tomatoes. It is, however, the Capriole Banon that is her greatest success – chestnut leaves macerated in brandy and white wine encompass the soft creamy curd, imparting a heady mix of aromas and flavours.

US	Indiana
Milk source	
Unpasteurized	✗
Maturing time	from 2 weeks
Average weight	185g/6½oz
Vegetarian	✗
Shape	⬯

Cerney

The village of Cerney in Gloucestershire is home to Cerney cheeses –
the creation of Lady Angus who introduced goats to this traditionally
dairy-farming area. Although Cerney comes in many guises, each has a
mild, zingy, citrus taste and light *fromage frais* texture, with a charismatic
goaty finish. First came Cerney Pyramid, with a fine dusting of ash that
stands out against the pure white of the goat's milk. Under cheesemaker
Marion Conisbee-Smith's inspired guidance some rather more exotic
flavours have emerged including Cerney Ginger (with chunks of finely
chopped, spicy ginger), Cerney Peppers, and a range of cheeses liberally
doused with strong fruit-based liqueurs.

England	Gloucestershire
Milk source	
Unpasteurized	✓
Maturing time	7-10 days
Average weight	250g/9oz
Vegetarian	✓
Shape	

Chèvre de Provence

Liz Parnell has an alchemist's touch when it comes to converting
nature's raw materials into delicate, subtle, lemony fresh goat's cheeses.
The tiny disk-shaped Chèvre de Provence is marinated in oil and
herbs, gradually absorbing the herbaceous, cut-grass fragrance of the
oil and aromatic character of the fresh herbs. To achieve the light yet
luscious texture of the *fromage frais*, it is made by hand and slowly
drained to retain a high-in-moisture style of cheese that slides over the
palate like ice-cream. American cheese-lover Simon Johnson declares
'I can say without hesitation that her Fromage Blanc and Chèvre de
Provence are American Treasures'. Hear, hear.

US	Alabama
Milk source	
Unpasteurized	✗
Maturing time	1-3 months
Average weight	100g/3½oz
Vegetarian	✓
Shape	

Cream cheese

Next in popularity to cottage cheese, this is an unripened cheese
made with single or double cream. Only low-fat varieties require
rennet and most can be made at home by adding a starter culture to
tepid milk and leaving it for 12 to 24 hours to slowly coagulate. Pour
the curds into a cloth, knot it, and hang up the curds to drain. At two to
three hour intervals scrape the curd into the centre of the cloth, mix
together well, and re-hang or lightly press to assist drainage. Once
firm, add salt, pack the cheese into pots and eat within two to three
days. Some commercial cream cheeses contain stabilizers in order to
increase the keeping qualities of the cheese.

Worldwide	
Milk source	
Unpasteurized	✗
Maturing time	from 2 days
Average weight	various
Vegetarian	✗
Shape	

Crescenza

The best examples of Crescenza reputedly come from around Milan and Pavia. These are luscious, almost wet cheeses with a fresh clean acidity (not unlike yoghurt) and the smell of warm cow. They are wrapped in simple white greaseproof paper and should be eaten very fresh: within 10 days. The quality, however, varies considerably, ranging from rubbery and sweet to jelly-like or mushy with a sour, synthetic taste, and the low-fat varieties can be grainy. Used more and more in modern Italian cooking. Crescenza is a member of the *stracchino* family, a generic name for cheeses from Lombardy that are soft and square-shaped, such as Taleggio or Robiola.

Italy	Lombardy
Milk source	
Unpasteurized	✗
Maturing time	**from 10 days**
Average weight	**1-2kg** **2lb 4oz-4lb 8oz**
Vegetarian	✓ ✗
Shape	

Crowdie

Thought to have been introduced by the Vikings around the 8th Century, Crowdie (*Gruth* in Gaelic) is produced from skimmed milk. Slightly sour, creamy, yet crumbly, it gently collapses on the palate and spreads well on warm home-made bread or Scottish oat cakes. Susannah Stone's company, Highland Fine Cheeses, was founded in 1963, after she found herself with more of her home-made Crowdie than the family could cope with. Susannah took the excess to her local grocer in *lieu* of unpaid grocery bills and has not looked back since. Her *Gruth Dhu* (Black Crowdie) is a blend of Crowdie and double cream, formed into oval shapes and covered in toasted pinhead oats and crushed peppercorns.

Scotland	Ross and Cromarty
Milk source	
Unpasteurized	✗
Maturing time	**a few days**
Average weight	**125g/4½oz**
Vegetarian	✓
Shape	

Cuajada

Not unlike the old-fashioned English junket, Cuajada is made by adding rennet to fresh milk, which is gently heated and then poured into small earthenware pots were it sets, forming a soft, white floppy junket or milk jelly. It is irresistible drizzled with local honey or served in place of yoghurt with fruit. Cuajada originally comes from the Basque Country and northern Navarra where the local thistle, rather than animal rennet, was used to coagulate the milk. This would give the cheese a milder taste and a more floppy consistency compared with those you find today, which are made with animal rennet and produced in homes and factories all over Spain.

Spain	Navarra and Basque region
Milk source	
Unpasteurized	✓ ✗
Maturing time	**3-4 days**
Average weight	**various**
Vegetarian	✓
Shape	

Dancing Winds Fresh Goat

An intolerance for lactose can drive a cheese-lover to the brink, or in Mary Doerr's case to experimenting and making her own goat's milk cheeses. Through trial and error she made a fortuitous discovery, that no-salt, low-fat *chèvre* can be delicious, and so she targets the health market. The farming is organic, and traditional European methods are used which give the cheese a gentle goaty herbaceous character and citrus freshness. This also provides a superb background for the herbs and spices used to enhance the Dancing Winds range of cheeses. The cheeses are sold mainly at St-Paul's farmers' market, by mail order and direct from the on-farm store.

US	Minnesota
Milk source	
Unpasteurized	✗
Maturing time	from a few days
Average weight	various
Vegetarian	✓
Shape	various

Fantome

Anne Topham started cheesemaking in 1980. Self-taught, she kept the style of the cheeses and her farming methods simple and traditional. The goats graze freely, the cheese is handmade and the whey, along with any less than perfect cheeses, is feed to the appreciative pigs. Anne's goats graze on the rich limestone soil and her cheeses reflect the seasonal changes in the grazing that only nature can control. The range of melt-in-the-mouth fresh goat's cheese is superb, Fantome being the finest. It also includes Boulet (football shaped), sometimes marinated in oil and herbs, and various other small disc-shaped fresh cheeses available plain, or sprinkled with fresh herbs or ash.

US	Wisconsin
Milk source	
Unpasteurized	✗
Maturing time	from a week
Average weight	various
Vegetarian	✗
Shape	

Farmer cheese

Originally made for home consumption using milk from the family cow, this is a simple cheese, similar to those made by the early Romans. The milk is curdled, tied in a cloth and drained until the curd is nearly solid. Salt and sometimes pepper is added, then the cheese is put in trays to 'set' and cut into various sizes. The cheese is grainy, without the lumpiness of cottage cheese, but not as rich and smooth as cream cheese. It is usually eaten fresh with fruit, salads or in place of the higher fat cream cheese (it is also referred to in other countries as curd cheese). Farmer cheese can be slightly sour and slices rather than crumbles.

US	
Milk source	
Unpasteurized	✗
Maturing time	a few days
Average weight	various
Vegetarian	✗
Shape	

Fromage frais

Fromage frais (fresh cheese) describes a group of cheeses that is
unripened and has a high moisture content and mousse-like texture.
Mild and lactic with a citrus zing on the finish, similar to yoghurt,
fromage frais dates back thousands of years, when a starter culture
(similar to that used to make yoghurt), rather than rennet was used to
coagulate the milk. The fat content varies from very low – *maigre* (five
per cent) to *allégé*, *double* and *triple crème* (75 per cent) versions. Both
artisan and creamery versions are available throughout France, and
include Fromage Blanc, Petit Swiss, Faiselle de Chèvre, Chèvre Frais,
Brousse du Rove and Fontainebleau.

France	
Milk source	
Unpasteurized	✓✗
Maturing time	**15 days**
Average weight	**150-300g** **5½-10½oz**
Vegetarian	✗
Shape	

Galotyri

I first encountered this ancient cheese after a lengthy walk clambering
up long-forgotten ravines in search of a cheesemaker. I was greeted
with a local rosé, a chunk of bread and a mass of soft, shiny curds
piled into a small ceramic bowl that looked like it had come from
Byzantine times. Mixed with wild thyme, the cheese tasted like heaven.
The following morning I watched as my hostess boiled up the morning
milk, added salt, and once it had curdled, beat the curd, strained it and
hung it in a goat's skin to drain. A mix of small lumps and creamy soft
curd – eaten fresh it was sour yet not sharp and had a hint of
fermenting fruit and white wine.

Greece	**Ithilos and** **Thassily**
Milk source	
Unpasteurized	✗
Maturing time	**a few hours**
Average weight	**250-500g** **9oz-1lb 2oz**
Vegetarian	✗
Shape	

Gjetost (whey cheese)

Norway's most popular cheese was traditionally made in homes as a
means of using the precious whey proteins left over from cheesemaking.
Personally, I think you had to be born to appreciate Gjetost, for it is like
no other cheese I have tasted. Traditionally made from the milk of hardy
local goats (*gjet* means goat) it is now mostly factory made with a blend of
cow's and goat's milk. The whey is heated until the milk sugars (lactose)
caramelize, turning a deep honey-brown colour. Sweet, with a strange
aromatic quality, and looking just like caramel-coloured fudge, it should
be eaten in slithers as a snack or at breakfast. Mysost is milder and made
from pure cow's milk, while pure-goat Ekta Gjetost is stronger.

Norway	
Milk source	
Unpasteurized	✓
Maturing time	**15 days**
Average weight	**4½-5½oz** **130-150g**
Vegetarian	✗
Shape	

Halloumi (stretched-curd)

The early nomadic Bedouin tribes of the Middle East learnt to preserve their milk by kneading the curd rather than pressing it, forcing out the whey and producing an elastic, fibrous curd that, when stored in brine would keep for months. Today various forms of this stretched-curd cheese can be found – some are plaited while others are twisted into balls or flattened into squares. Halloumi is sold in small blocks with a thin layer of fresh mint that heightens the rather bland, milky taste of the cheese. It is more dense than Mozzarella and is one of a handful of cheeses that hold their shape when heated – fry it with no oil or even barbecue it and the outside becomes crisp while the inside melts like Mozzarella.

Cyprus	
Milk source	
Unpasteurized	✓
Maturing time	**a few days**
Average weight	**200g/7oz**
Vegetarian	✓
Shape	

Hipi Iti

In 1985, Kapiti Cheese was set up by Ross McCallum, a man of vision, who was convinced that the pastures and climate of New Zealand could produce unique cheeses rather than emulate those of Europe. It was another five years, however, before the first New Zealand sheep's milk cheese, Hipi Iti, appeared. Although sheep had played a major role in New Zealand's economy for centuries, no-one had introduced one of the milking breeds until the late 1980s. Preserved in oil and fresh herbs, Hipi Iti ('little sheep' in Maori) is similar to Feta, but softer and only slightly salty, with a sweet, burnt caramel finish – a characteristic of ewe's milk.

New Zealand	Wellington
Milk source	
Unpasteurized	✗
Maturing time	**2 months**
Average weight	**90g/3¼oz**
Vegetarian	✓
Shape	

Hollow Road Cheeses

The resurgence of interest in farmstead cheeses in America can be attributed to several wonderful women cheesemakers, including Joan Snyder, previously an investment banker. Each of her Hollow Road cheeses, from the fresh logs to the creamy square Camembert, offers an insight into the character of ewe's milk cheeses and the dedication required to produce delicious, sweet, clean milk. Following the principles of organic farming, Joan and cheesemaking partner Ken Kleinpeter have carved out a place in American history with their range of cheeses, all of which have the rich, burnt caramel sweetness and nutty finish so typical of fresh goat's cheese.

US	New York
Milk source	
Unpasteurized	✗
Maturing time	**from a few days**
Average weight	**various**
Vegetarian	✗
Shape	**various**

Innes Button

Innes Button, a tiny goat's cheese, stunned the judges at the first British Cheese Awards in 1994, with its delicate mousse-like texture and subtle yet distinctive aromatic goaty character, and was voted Supreme Champion. It dissolves on the palate, leaving a trail of almonds, wild honey, lemon, white wine and tangerine. The cheese is the result of meticulous care, following the traditional methods of the French artisan producers with a touch of English eccentricity – classical music is piped into the milking parlour to relax the goats. Attractively presented in rustic wooden boxes, Innes Buttons are also sold sprinkled with pink peppercorns, fresh herbs or dusted with paprika.

England	**Staffordshire**
Milk source	
Unpasteurized	✓
Maturing time	5-10 days
Average weight	50g/1¾oz
Vegetarian	✗
Shape	⬭

Juustoleipä

Despite the seemingly inhospitable climate, dairy farming is a thriving industry in Finland – although, like many of the great European cheeses, most Finnish cheeses are made in ultra-modern co-operatives. Juustoleipa, both farm- and factory-made, dates back to the time when reindeer milk was commonly used for its production. Freshly formed curds were drained and pressed into flat wooden platters with a wide rim. The cheese was then toasted in front of a fire until the outer layer was slightly charred, hence the name 'cheese bread'. A speciality of Finland and Lapland, it is generally served for breakfast or as a dessert with jam, and is crunchy with a hint of burnt onions. Also known as Leipäjuusto.

Finland	
Milk source	🐂 🦌
Unpasteurized	✓
Maturing time	from a few days
Average weight	various
Vegetarian	✗
Shape	⬭

Kasseri (stretched-curd)

Kasseri is used in Greece in much the same way as Mozzarella or Provolone is used in Italy. The rugged, mountainous terrain and climate, however, dictates that unlike Mozzarella, it has always been made with ewe's milk or mixed with goat's milk when ewe's milk is in short supply. Made with a minimum of 80 per cent ewe's milk, this stretched-curd cheese is a young version of Kefalotyri. It has been immersed in hot brine, creating a rubbery, stringy texture. Kasseri is quite salty and pungent, with a dry feel in the mouth and an underlying sweetness from the ewe's milk, but the aromatic goat's milk tends to dominate. A classic partner for filo pastry or spinach.

Greece	
Milk source	🐑
Unpasteurized	✓
Maturing time	1 month
Average weight	1-9kg/2¼-20lb
Vegetarian	✗
Shape	

Kervella Chèvre Frais

Far from the madding crowd in Gidgegannup, near some of the finest beaches and vineyards in the world, Gabriella Kervella introduced fresh goat's cheese to Australians some 10 years ago. Loved by Australia's foodies and top chefs alike, her success lies mainly in the quality of her herd – a mix of Anglo-Nubian and Saanen goats – carefully bred to adapt to the vagaries of the local climate. Fed only on organic pastures balanced with minerals, they produce sweet, slightly aromatic milk which Gabriella lovingly converts into her cheeses. The fresh mousse-like Kervella Chèvre Frais, a classic French-style rindless goat's cheese log, melts in the mouth, with just a hint of almonds and a suggestion of goat's milk on the finish.

Australia	WA
Milk source	
Unpasteurized	✗
Maturing time	a few days
Average weight	various
Vegetarian	✗
Shape	various

Labneh

Made using one of the earliest forms of cheesemaking, Labneh is mainly made in homes rather than dairies, by draining soured milk or yoghurt overnight in a cloth. Traditionally, the Bedouin tribes would use a goat's or sheep's skin. This would then be pressed into earthenware pots, or rolled into balls, sometimes with the addition of a delicious fragrant coating of wild thyme (*zaatar*) and toasted sesame seeds, or mixed with lemon juice, fresh mint and olive oil and served with *falafel*. Given the intense heat of Lebanon, the cheeses would be preserved in oil or brine. Similar cheeses are found throughout the Middle East, particularly in Syria.

Lebanon	
Milk source	
Unpasteurized	✓
Maturing time	a few days
Average weight	various
Vegetarian	✗
Shape	

Laura Chenel's Chèvre

Ranging from Fromage Blanc to an aged Tomme, each of Laura Chenel's *chèvres* reflects the freshness and aromatic character of the grazing, the milk and the careful handling. Inspired by the French artisan cheesemakers with whom she worked in 1979, and disenchanted by city life, Laura turned to the land for a sense of purpose. She took the plunge with a few goats, but it took 10 years before she was ready to sell her *chèvre* commercially. Located in the wine-growing county of Mendocino, her cheeses are now eagerly sought by chefs and visitors to the region, and still appear on the menu of Chez Panisse in Berkeley – Laura's first customer.

US	California
Milk source	
Unpasteurized	✗
Maturing time	from a few days
Average weight	various
Vegetarian	✗
Shape	various

Liptauer

Litoi, a simple curd cheese made by shepherds in the Tatra mountains for centuries, forms the base of Liptauer cheese – a cauldron of fiery flavours. Handed down from generation to generation, there have been discussions as to the right balance and mix of ingredients going on for centuries. All but the most stubborn people, however, would agree that this white, soft, potted cheese must contain a mixture of the following – onions, chives, caraway seeds, capers, anchovies, pickled cucumber, garlic, salt and generous lashings of paprika. The art, it would seem, is to achieve a level of ferocity greater than your neighbour's Liptauer. It apparently works equally well as a thirst enhancer and a hangover cure.

Hungary

Milk source	
Unpasteurized	✓
Maturing time	**from 1 week**
Average weight	**various**
Vegetarian	✗
Shape	

Little Rainbow Chèvre

Barbara Reed first started to experiment with cheesemaking in 1981 when looking after a friend's goat. Initially she made cheese for her son, who was allergic to cow's milk, but she soon diversified her range. Whether you prefer the moist, smooth, citrus-fresh cheese or the drier, aged unpasteurized style, each exudes the personality of the cheese-maker, and the varied diet of the delightfully roguish goats. The rich sweetness of the milk has helped to destroy the myths that goat's milk is harsh and only for the most sophisticated. The Little Rainbow Chèvre range is mainly sold at New York's Greenmarket, and the cheeses have become a talking point on many a New Yorker's cheeseboard.

US **New York**

Milk source	
Unpasteurized	✓ ✗
Maturing time	**from a few days**
Average weight	**various**
Vegetarian	✗
Shape	**various**

Munajuusto or Ilves

This rather eccentric cheese is made by whisking eggs into ripened buttermilk, which is then added to fresh milk and heated gently until the curds form. Once cool, the soft curds are ladled into cloth or hand-woven baskets to drain. The following day the curd is salted, placed in a clean cloth and gently pressed using a plate. Shaped into a flat, smooth 'cake', it is then sprinkled with sugar and, like Juustoleipa (*see* page 35), is roasted in front of a fire or grilled on both sides. The result is a firm yet moist sunshine-yellow cheese speckled with some burnt sugar splotches; in fact, a little like a baked cheesecake. The factory version is sold as Ilves.

Finland

Milk source	
Unpasteurized	✗
Maturing time	**2-10 days**
Average weight	**various**
Vegetarian	✗
Shape	

Murazzano

Like many Italian cheeses, Murazzano's history is clouded by local myths, but it was first mentioned by Pliny the elder in his *Naturalis Historia* where it was described as a ewe's milk cheese from Liguria. What makes this Piedmontese Robiola (*see* page 40) so appealing is its supple texture and fresh, milky sweetness with a hint of caramel – a characteristic of ewe's milk cheese. These smooth, round white cheeses are made with a blend of ewe's and up to 60 per cent cow's milk, and only milk from the native Langhe breed of cow can be used (who feed on fresh hay and fodder). A local speciality, Bruz di Murazzano is made by fermenting pieces of Murazzano in ewe's milk and local *grappa* (brandy).

Italy	Cuneo
Milk source	
Unpasteurized	✓ ✗
Maturing time	**4-5 days**
Average weight	**150-250g** **5½-9oz**
Vegetarian	✗
Shape	

Myzithra or Mitzithra (whey cheese)

Mild and refreshing, with a fine crumbly texture, Myzithra was traditionally made from the whey of Feta or Kefalotyri (a 'male' or 'first' cheese), to which some fresh milk was added (then referred to as a 'female' or 'second' cheese). The whey is heated, causing the remaining proteins and fat to float to the surface as tiny particles and, as with ricotta, then drained in cloth. Once cool, it is ready to eat. Made in many forms, it is mixed with cream or milk to make it richer and smoother, or salted and dried to use as a hard, grating cheese. It is mainly round, rindless and shows the imprint of the cloth. It makes deliciously light but flavoursome pastries. A sour Myzithra, Xinomyzithra, is made in Crete.

Greece	
Milk source	
Unpasteurized	✓
Maturing time	**1 day-months**
Average weight	**500g-2kg** **1lb 2oz-4½lb**
Vegetarian	✗
Shape	

Paneer

It is hard to imagine that India is now the world's largest milk producer, when the cow is stereotyped as a sacred animal or an emaciated beast of burden tirelessly ploughing the waterlogged fields for rice. In the last 20 years' milk production has increased dramatically to supply the enormous population with yoghurt, ghee, ice-cream and the cheese, Paneer. Made by curdling hot milk with fresh lemon juice or vinegar, the fine lumpy curd is then strained in muslin, rinsed in water and pressed for 10 to 15 minutes. This firm, pale yellow cheese should be eaten within a few days of being made, and can be deep-fried, marinated in masala, barbecued in a tandoori or used in innumerable vegetable dishes.

India	
Milk source	
Unpasteurized	✗
Maturing time	**a few days**
Average weight	**various**
Vegetarian	✓
Shape	

Pant ys Gawn

A small, delightful goat's cheese that has done much to dispel the British misconception that goat's cheeses are aggressive, bordering on demonic, in character. Made in small rounds or logs, Pant ys Gawn is ideal for the cheeseboard, has a moist, *fromage frais* texture and a mild, fresh citrus tang, with just a hint of tarragon from the aromatic goat's milk. Sold when only a few days old yet, with clever packaging, they have a remarkably long shelf life. Varieties include mixed herbs, black cracked pepper and garlic and chives. Abergavenny Fine Foods also makes a traditional Caerphilly, St-David's (a spicy semi-soft cheese), and a number of blended or speciality cheeses.

Wales	Gwent
Milk source	
Unpasteurized	✗
Maturing time	from 4 days
Average weight	100g/3½oz
Vegetarian	✓
Shape	

Perroche

Randolph Hodgson of the Neal's Yard Dairy and his *protégé*, Charlie Westhead, have converted many with their delicious, unpasteurized fresh goat's milk cheeses. These small truncated cones of pure white, soft mousse-like curd provide a stark background for the fresh tarragon, rosemary or dill in which they are rolled. The slightly aromatic, zesty milk absorbs the sweet herbaceous oils of the herbs. They have a high moisture content and a short shelf life – each one is a masterpiece and they are consistent gold medal winners at the British Cheese Awards. They also make Wealden, Finn, *fromage frais*, *crème fraîche* and yoghurt.

England	Hereford
Milk source	
Unpasteurized	✓
Maturing time	2-8 days
Average weight	various
Vegetarian	✓
Shape	

Provolone DOC (stretched-curd)

Provolone, made with stretched-curd, is the large, fat, sausage-shaped cheese you see hanging by thick cord from the ceilings of Italian delis around the world, surrounded by salamis, strings of dried peppers and Parma hams. Provolone Dolce (mild), aged for two to three months, has a thin waxed rind and is supple, mild and smooth, becoming stringy when cooked. Piccante (piquant), generally coagulated with kid's rennet for a stronger flavour, is aged for 6 to 24 months. Darker in colour with a tough rind and a stronger spicy flavour, it is ideal at the end of a meal or grated over pasta. The weight and shape vary – the Giganti can be over three metres long and usually made for trade fairs.

Italy	Lombardy
Milk source	
Unpasteurized	✗
Maturing time	3-24 months
Average weight	200g-50kg 7½oz-110lb
Vegetarian	✗
Shape	various

Queso Fresco

When the Spanish conquered Mexico in 1521 they brought with them
their religion, cuisine and animals such as cattle, pigs and chickens.
The monks set about spreading the word of God, but were also
responsible for introducing cheese to the Mexicans, and it was rapidly
assimilated into their daily diet. Queso Fresco (fresh cheese) is soft
and breakable rather than crumbly like Feta, with a slightly grainy feel.
Mild, slightly salty with a fresh acidity, it is an essential ingredient for
enchiladas and burritos. Queso Fresco was based on the Spanish
cheese Burgos, being originally made from goat's milk, but now milk
from the more prolific cow is used.

Mexico

Milk source	
Unpasteurized	✗
Maturing time	a few days
Average weight	various
Vegetarian	✗
Shape	

Rigotte

Similar in texture to Feta, Rigotte was traditionally made when milk was
abundant. The excess cheese, preserved in oil rather than salt, was sold
or kept for family use during the lean winter months. Initially firm and
slightly grainy with a lemony freshness, Rigotte develops a slight
bitterness with age. If it is encouraged to dry out it becomes quite tart and
develops the classic pale blue-grey moulds of natural rind cheeses
(especially in humid conditions). It also may be rubbed with *roccou*
(annatto), giving it a reddy-orange rind. When marinated in oils flavoured
with thyme, rosemary, oregano and peppers, it absorbs the flavours and
the result is reminiscent of *saucisson* (cured sausage).

France

Auvergne
and Lyonnais

Milk source	
Unpasteurized	✓
Maturing time	10 days
Average weight	70-90g 2½-3¼oz
Vegetarian	✗
Shape	

Robiola di Roccaverano DOC

Roccaverano, a typically Italian hillside town, clings to the rocky outcrops,
where for centuries goat's milk has been transformed into a fresh cheese,
now made commercially from a mix of goat's, ewe's and up to 85 per cent
cow's milk. Traditionally, the goats supplemented their grazing with
brambles and wild thyme – giving a characteristic to Robiola which many
locals believe has been diluted with the introduction of cow's milk. When
fresh, this cheese is sweet and moist, but after 20 days, it develops a
reddish sticky rind and becomes supple, creamy and sharper, underlining
the aromatic taste characteristic of goat's milk. Similar cheeses made
nearby cannot use the name since its protection under law in 1989.

Italy

Lombardy

Milk source	
Unpasteurized	✓ ✗
Maturing time	3-20 days
Average weight	200g/7oz
Vegetarian	✗
Shape	

Le Roulé

The finely chopped forest green herbs provide a splash of colour against the pure, white fresh cheese, and its unusual swirl or Swiss roll pattern inevitably attracts the consumer's eye. Soft and moist, it melts in the mouth, releasing the distinct, refreshing taste of fresh herbs and garlic. Not dissimilar to Boursin, but with a lighter texture, it can be found in supermarkets and delicatessens around the world, despite its tendency to collapse even when cut with the finest wire. Since its highly successful launch in the mid-1980s, a variety of new sizes and flavours have been created – salmon and dill, strawberry, Roulé Light and mini-Roulé.

France	Loire
Milk source	
Unpasteurized	✗
Maturing time	1-3 weeks
Average weight	various
Vegetarian	✓
Shape	⬭

Saratoga Goat's Cheeses

What inspired Dee Lever to become a cheesemaker would have sent the average person to an early grave. Left partially paralysed by a horrendous car crash Dee, with support from husband Mike and her friends, set about learning how to make cheese. With painstaking care and an innate talent for drawing the best out of her cheese, Dee has created a symphony of tiny, delicate, moussey cheeses (all dipped in wax to stop them drying out), including Piccolo, Encore, Sonata, Minuet and Opus. My favourite is the Piccolo, which won two top prizes at the New Zealand Cheese Awards in 1996. Mild, fresh and gently aromatic, with a complexity of flavours, they have won the hearts of New Zealand's young chefs.

New Zealand	Masterton
Milk source	
Unpasteurized	✗
Maturing time	from a few days
Average weight	100-150g 3½-5½oz
Vegetarian	✓
Shape	⬓

Scamorza (stretched-curd)

This stretched-curd cheese is shaped like a little round ball tied at the top, and looks like a money bag. It was traditionally made by the producers of Caciocavallo (*see* page 29) when the scirocco wind was blowing, creating unfavourable conditions for ripening their cheeses. Using virtually the same recipe, but ready to eat within 48 hours, Scamorza provided an almost instant income. Drier than Mozzarella, with a similar rubbery, stringy texture, it lacks the depth of flavour gained from slow ripening, but gives body to numerous local dishes. Scamorza Affumicate (smoked), now made commercially, was originally made by artisan cheesemakers, who hung the cheeses to dry in the rafters.

Italy	Southern
Milk source	
Unpasteurized	✗
Maturing time	2-3 days
Average weight	various
Vegetarian	✗
Shape	🝙

Sea Stars Goat's Cheese

Surrounded by huge square chunks of hard Cheddar-like cheeses, these tiny goat's cheeses stand out in supermarket cabinets like the stars they are. A truly original concept, each cheese is decorated with colourful edible flowers or petals. Simple but effective, it attracts the buyer's attention to these delicate, moist, lemony fresh cheeses that possess just a hint of goat's milk. Nancy Gaffney fell into cheesemaking when she was asked to look after Fanny, a goat with attitude who bred at an alarming rate, and Nancy has since won awards for her cheeses. Nancy also makes *fromage blanc* and *chèvre* tortas – layers of creamy *chèvre* with either sundried tomatoes and basil or pistachio and dried apricots.

US	California
Milk source	
Unpasteurized	✗
Maturing time	from a few days
Average weight	100-200g 3½-7oz
Vegetarian	✗
Shape	

Sussex Slipcote

Slipcote is named, not after a town, but for its unusual habit of slipping out of its rind as it matures. Made throughout Britain since the Middle Ages it was described in *Law's Grocer's Manual* (c 1895) as 'a rich and soft kind of cheese made of milk warm from the cow, and often with cream added. It closely resembles white butter.' Now only made by Sussex High Weald, to a recipe that dates back to Shakespeare's days (carefully ladling the curds into the moulds to retain as much of the whey as possible), it is creamy, mousse-like, with a refreshing citrus acidity and a touch of sweetness from the ewe's milk. Available in three varieties: plain, garlic and herb, or cracked peppercorns.

Britain	Sussex
Milk source	
Unpasteurized	✓
Maturing time	10 days
Average weight	100g, 2kg 3½oz, 4½lb
Vegetarian	✓
Shape	

Tomme d'Aligot (Aligot)

This is basically just lightly pressed unsalted curd. Moist, supple, open-textured, pale ivory in colour with a sweet-sour lactic aroma and a mild nutty taste, it must be eaten fresh. It is the fresh curd taken from the draining tables of Cantal, Salers or Languiole, and is one of the oldest French cheeses which has been made in mountain dairies (*burons*) for centuries. Tomme d'Aligot is a cooking cheese which becomes stringy when heated (though not as stringy as Mozzarella) and is ideal in soups, grilling and pastries. A speciality of the region is Aligot mashed into hot potatoes and seasoned with garlic, the juices and fat from local grilled, spicy sausages and salt and pepper – delicious and filling.

France	Auvergne
Milk source	
Unpasteurized	✓
Maturing time	1-2 days
Average weight	7-20kg 15½-44lb
Vegetarian	✗
Shape	

Tupi

Tupi is both the name of the cheese and the small earthenware pot in which it is fermented and sold. The curds from young or damaged cheeses are broken into a pot, mixed with fresh milk, local brandy and aniseed or olive oil, stirred, and left for two months or until the final stages of fermentation, when the *bollida* (bubble) announced it was ready. An idiosyncratic recipe, the final taste is always strong, lingering and aggressive. It spreads superbly on crusty Spanish bread, but demands a hefty wine or sherry to smooth its rough edges. It is mainly made at home and is rarely sold, except in local markets and the famous market, La Bocqueria, off Bacelona's Ramblas.

Spain	Catalonia
Milk source	
Unpasteurized	✓
Maturing time	2 months
Average weight	100-250g 3½-9oz
Vegetarian	✗
Shape	

Vulscombe

The number of British goat's milk cheeses has grown from around 20 in 1984 to more than 120 in 1998, thanks to pioneers such as Joyce and Graham Townsend. Small and round, garnished with a fresh bay leaf or peppercorns, this pure white curd has a striking, elegant appearance. Solid, like firm *fromage frais*, Vulscombe has a fresh lemon sorbet taste and just the merest hint of goat's milk – the result of coagulation by the curd's acidity, rather than by rennet. Joyce and Graham's goat herd quickly expanded to over 100, but with the increasing demand for their cheese the couple decided to sell the herd and concentrate on cheesemaking. They now make more than 25,000 cheeses a year.

England	Devon
Milk source	
Unpasteurized	✓
Maturing time	1-3 weeks
Average weight	185g/6½oz
Vegetarian	✓
Shape	

Windy Hamlet Fresh Goat Cheeses

Like many of the American farmhouse cheesemakers, Dorothy Benedict produces both fresh and aged goat's cheeses in the Windy Hamlet range. When young, the cheeses have the classic acidity of good clean goat's milk, with a suggestion of white wine and tarragon; with age they develop a soft white rind tinged with bluish-green and take on a mushroomy aroma. The Crottin has a drier, more nutty character. Dorothy first became involved with goats when she bought some pigmy goats as companions for her favourite dressage horse on its retirement. Soon the herd grew into 125 fun-loving, milk-yielding goats of mixed breeds. And so the Windy Hamlet cheeses were born.

US	Massachusetts
Milk source	
Unpasteurized	✗
Maturing time	from a few days
Average weight	175-900g 6oz-2lb
Vegetarian	✗
Shape	various

Fresh

Cheese name	Country of origin	Region	Milk source
Aligot *see* Tomme d'Aligot	France	Auvergne	Cow
Anari	Cyprus		Cow & goat
Anthotiro (Anthotyros)	Greece		Ewe & goat
Asadero	Mexico	South	Cow
Bandal	India		Buffalo or cow
Bel Gioioso Provolone	US	Wisconsin	Cow
Beli sir u Kriskama	Serbia		Cow & ewe
Boilie	Ireland	Co Cavan	Goat
Boule des Moines	France	Burgundy	Cow
Brinza or Burduf Brinza	Romania		Ewe
Brousse	France	Provence	Ewe
Bryndza	Slovakia		Ewe
Bûchette Sariette	France	Languedoc-Roussillon	Goat
Caeoli	England	Hereford & Worcester	Goat
Caprini	Italy	Piedmont	Goat
Castlefarm Heather	Ireland	Co Limerick	Goat
Cerney Banon	England	Gloucestershire	Goat
Chabis	England	East Sussex	Goat
Chèvre Frais	France		Goat
Cornish Pepper	England	Cornwall	Cow
Cottage Cheese	Worldwide		Cow
Crannog	Scotland	Dumfries & Galloway	Cow
Curthwait	England	Cumbria	Goat
Cypress Grove Aged Chèvre	US	California	Goat
Dacca	India	West Bengal	Cow or buffalo
Davatty	England	Devon	Ewe
Domiati	Egypt		Buffalo or cow
Faisselle de Chèvre	France	Poitou, Loire	Goat
Fontainebleau	France	lle-de-France	Cow
Fresh Portuguese	US	Massachusetts	Cow
Fromage Blanc	France	*see* Fromage Frais	Cow
Fromage du Larzac	France	Midi-Pyrénées	Ewe
Fromage Fort du Lyonnais	France	Lyonnais	Cow & goat
Fromagerie Belle Chèvre	US	Alabama	Goat
Galloway Goat's Milk Gems	Scotland	Dumfries & Galloway	Goat
Gournay Frais	France	Normandy	Cow
Greystone Chevratel	US	Pennsylvania	Goat
Gruth Dhu	Scotland	Ross & Cromarty	Cow
llves *see* Munajuusto	Finland		Cow or reindeer
Italian Peasant	South Africa	Boland	Cow
Junglandis (Jove's Balls)	England	Hereford & Worcester	Goat

Kashkaval or Katschkawalj	Bulgaria		Ewe
Knockalara	Ireland	Co Waterford	Ewe
Kugelkäse	Austria	Danube	Cow
La Friche	US	Minnesota	Ewe
Lingot du Berry	France	Berry	Goat
Liptoi	Hungary		Ewe
Mandjeskaas	Belgium		Cow
Manouri	Greece	Crete, Macedonia	Ewe or goat
Mato	Spain	Catalonia	Goat & cow
Mesost	Sweden	Various	Cow
Metton	France	Franche-Comté	Cow
Mozzarella	US	Texas	Buffalo
Nanterrow	England	Cornwall	Ewe
Olde York	England	North Yorkshire	Ewe
Peekskill Pyramid	US	New York	Cow
Petit-Suisse	France		Cow
Purrumbete Mozzarella	Australia		Buffalo
Quark	Germany		Cow
Queso Blanco (White cheese)	Mexico		Cow
Queso de Murcia DO	Spain	Murcia	Goat
Rangiuru Cheeses	New Zealand	Rangiuru	Goat
Redwood Hill Cheese	US	California	Goat
Rosary Plain	England	Wiltshire	Goat
Roubilliac	England	Hertfordshire	Goat
Sérac	France	Rhône-Alpes	Ewe & goat
Siraz	Serbia		Cow
Sirene	Bulgaria		Cow & ewe
Stamp Collection 'Priscilla'	England	East Sussex	Ewe
Surti	India	Bombay	Buffalo
Tafayer	Lebanon	Various	Cow or ewe
Tartare	France	Perigord	Cow
Tasmanian Highland Chèvre Log	Australia	Tasmania	Goat
Telemea	Romania		Ewe, buffalo or cow
Tellicherry Crottin	US	Maine	Goat
Todara Mozzarella	US	New York	Cow
Trois-Epis	France	Various	Cow
Turtle Creek Chèvre	US	Florida	Goat
Vemmont Chèvre	US	Vermont	Goat & cow
Wealdon Round	England	Hereford & Worcester	Cow
Xynotyro	Greece		Ewe & goat
Yarra Valley Pyramid	Australia	Victoria	Goat
Yorkshire Feta	England	North Yorkshire	Ewe

Natural rind cheeses

Above: Natural rind cheeses are best bought from local cheese shops or markets close to their source.

Some fresh cheeses, in particular goat's milk cheeses, turn into natural rind or aged cheeses if left to drain and dry out in cellars. The wet, protein-rich surface attracts an orchestra of moulds and wild yeasts – first the fuzzy, white penicillin (*Penicillium candidum*), then patches of blue, followed by grey, yellow and even red. Each of these moulds and yeasts contributes to the ripening process and, with salt rubbed or sprinkled onto the surface, helps to dry out the cheese. In the hands of a competent retailer or *affineur*, the cheeses age gracefully and can be sold at varying stages of ripeness, depending on the tastes of the customer.

Regrettably, most English-speaking consumers are suspicious of mould, as many British and American goat's cheesemakers have discovered to their cost and frustration. Finding that the beautiful tufted blue mould has been rejected by all but the most enthusiastic consumers, goat's cheesemakers have been forced to scrub down and sterilize their cellars and introduce, through spraying and inoculation, the more acceptable white mould. Hence it is almost impossible to buy a natural rind

goat's cheese outside France. Natural rind cheeses are available in almost any shape, from pyramids to thumb-sized bells, and can be covered in ash, paprika, herbs or pepper. Here is an outline of the stages through which these cheeses pass.

Stage one: Up to 10 days old, the cheese is fresh, moist and has no rind except for a sprinkling of salt, sometimes mixed with wood ash. The flavour is mild and lemony, with a hint of herbs from the goat's milk on the finish.

Stage two: Stored in a cool room or cellar, the young cheese will start to lose moisture. A soft, thin, almost opaque rind will develop and the surface will attract a variety of micro-flora. The first white tufts of *Penicillium candidum* (the mould on Camembert) will start to appear within ten days.

Stage three: Gradually, at around 9 to 12 days, a delicate blue mould will appear and, over the next few weeks, it will spread over the rind. The cheese will start to shrink, causing the wrinkles to deepen. Eventually the surface will be encrusted with this mould and the cheese will become firmer, sometimes almost brittle, with a nutty, pungent aroma and taste.

1 *Pérail*
2 *Pouligny-St-Pierre*
3 *Fleur du Maquis*
4 *Rouelle (see Cendré de Niort)*
5 *Coeur Poitevin (see Mothais)*
6 *Cendré de Niort*
7 *Banon*
8 *Rocamadour (boxed)*
9 *Mothais*
10 *St-Marcellin*

Crottin de Chavignol AOC

France	Loire
Milk source	🐐
Unpasteurized	✓
Maturing time	**1-5 weeks**
Average weight	**60-100g** **2-3½oz**
Vegetarian	✗
Shape	⬭

*The Loire region has not only been home to the kings of France and their legendary châteaux, but also to wonderful fruity, crisp wines and to many nutty, aromatic French goat's cheeses (*chèvres*). Here you can sample rare local cheeses, and visit cheesemakers whose goats still have names, not numbers, and whose cheeses owe their character to a blend of history, man's ingenuity and the unique climate.*

The Saracens introduced goats to the area around the 12th Century and since then each village has created its own individual shape – from logs, pyramids, hearts and rounds to bells, figs and tiny balls. The best-known is Crottin de Chavignol, central to the delicious Chèvre Salade – a Crottin sliced in half, grilled on fresh slices of baguette, served on a bed of dressed frisée lettuce or finely sliced cucumber.

The topography of the Loire is rolling hillsides covered in woodlands, wild flowers and green pastures dotted with herds of goats and vineyards fed by huge rivers. But the climate frequently conspires to hide many of its treasures behind a constant vale of insipid drizzle and mist.

Most Crottin de Chavignol, or Chavignol found outside France, is very young. Yet one of the curious things about these cheeses is their ability to age gracefully under the care of a competent retailer or *affineur*. They can be sold at varying stages of ripeness, depending on the tastes of the clientele.

Most artisan cheesemakers have little space to mature their cheeses and so sell them on to an *affineur*. The cellars of these *affineurs* positively hum with the activities of billions of bacteria and moulds working their way through an alphabet of cheeses stacked in every nook and cranny, on straw, wooden racks, in baskets and earthenware pots, all at varying stages of ripeness. Each cheese demands a different temperature and humidity to give of its best. Nurtured for weeks, or even months, they emerge on the shelves to tempt even the most jaded palate.

If, however, Crottin de Chavignol is abused when young by a careless retailer or thoughtless wholesaler, or kept too cold for too long, it will age without maturity, becoming hard and bitter.

At 10 days the cheese is soft with a mild, lemony fresh, slightly salty flavour and just a hint of goat's milk, while the rind is barely formed and the interior is pure white, moist and slightly grainy. Within two weeks the rind has thickened and wrinkled and attracts a fine dusting of the virulent white penicillium mould overlaid with a delicate pale blue mould, while the interior is more compact and the colour of old ivory.

Over the next few weeks the cheese continues to dry, going from 140g/5oz to around 60g/2¼oz, creating deeper wrinkles, and the blue-grey mould gradually spreads over the entire surface. After four months the

*Above: Each tiny cheese is checked and rubbed by hand
with salt, before being stored in caves or cellars to mature.*

moulds blacken, the interior is hard, yellow, almost
brittle and the flavour has gone from rich and nutty
to aromatic and distinctly goaty to intense, sharp,
powerful. The reason for the cheese's name 'Crottin
de Chavignol', which translates as 'horse droppings of
Chavignol' becomes obvious at this stage. However, at
this level of ripeness this cheese is an acquired taste
that even the locals believe requires courage to attempt.

Traditionally, herds were small and Crottin de
Chavignol was made mainly by individual households,
with any excess being sold in local markets. A few
fermier (farmhouse) or artisanal producers exist, but
most of the cheeses are now made in large factories,
using traditional methods, to meet the worldwide
demand of more than seven million in 1997.

The AOC guarantee

Along with 34 other French cheeses, Crottin de
Chavignol comes under the control of the
Appellation d'Origine Contrôlée (AOC) system.
This regulates the area in which the cheese can be
made, its size, shape, the type of rennet used and
the minimum age at which the cheese can be sold.

Considered fairly effective, if draconian, for
French wines, the AOC system is not thought to go
far enough for cheese – particularly in instances where
cheeses made outside of the defined area can still use

the name of an AOC cheese (they cannot carry the
AOC logo, a minor point for anyone unfamiliar with
the rules). Many people believe the breed of animal
should also be specified to prevent the invasion of
the Friesian cow, whose high-yield, bland milk has
infiltrated many cheese-producing regions in France
and Northern Italy in the last 20 years.

The AOC rules for Crottin de Chavignol specify
that only fresh milk can be used, and the coagulation
must be mainly from acidity using a starter, so only
a little rennet is permitted. The curd must be drained
before being put into moulds. About 6-10 litres/10½-
17½ pints of goat's milk are needed to make the
140g/5oz cheese that will eventually weigh around
60g/2¼oz at one month. The ripening process must
last for at least 10 days, and the cheese's size must
be 4-5cm/1½-2in diameter; 3-4cm/1¼-1½in high, with
45 per cent fat content (or 37 per cent minimum per
cheese *fermier*).

AOC CHEESES OF FRANCE

Cow	Comté
Abondance	Fourme d'Ambert
Beaufort	Epoisses de Bourgogne
Bleu d'Auvergne	Langres
Bleu des Causses	Languiole
Bleu du Haut-Jura	Livarot
Bleu du Vercors	Maroilles
Sassenage	Mont d'Or
Brie de Meaux	Munster
Brie de Melun	Neufchâtel
Cantal	Pont l'Evêque
Camembert de	Reblochon
Normandie	St-Nectaire
Chaource	Salers
Goat	Pouligny-St-Pierre
Brocciu (goat/ewe)	Rocamadour/Cabécou
Chabichou du Poitou	Selles-sur-Cher
Crottin de Chavignol	Ste-Maure de Touraine
Picodon	Valençay
Ewe	Ossau-Iraty-Brebis-
Roquefort	Pyrénées

Arômes au Gène de Marc

The French, renowned for turning any event into a culinary advantage, even call into service the skins and pips left over from pressing grapes. Small, round immature cheeses, such as Rigotte, St-Marcellin, Pelardon or Picodon are packed into earthenware pots and macerated or cured for two to three months with the fermenting grape skins and pips and topped up with the local brandy or *marc*. Mainly for home consumption, these creamy, bitter-sweet, yeasty cheeses can be found in markets and cheese shops from October through to January. Once the mould sets in, however, they become hard and flaky with a strident flavour – an acquired taste but excellent with a glass or two of *marc*.

France	Rhône
Milk source	🐄 🐐
Unpasteurized	✓
Maturing time	4 weeks
Average weight	80-120g 2¾-4¼oz
Vegetarian	✗
Shape	⬭

Banon

Chestnut leaves soaked in wine or *eau-de-vie* are tied with raffia around this cheese to prevent the interior from drying out, and to provide a home for a medley of moulds. These work magic on the curd, creating a small parcel of exquisite earthy aromas. Young Banon is moist, nutty and reminiscent of white wine, but with age the rind softens until the cheese runs out of the now disintegrating, mould-encrusted leaves, revealing layers of character – vegetal, yeasty, rich, sharp, tart and nutty. The best cheeses are made with goat's or ewe's milk, available at the weekly market in Banon. Woods, lavender fields, wild thyme and vineyards provide a backdrop to this hilltop village and to the local grazing.

France	Provence
Milk source	🐄 🐐
Unpasteurized	✓
Maturing time	2-8 weeks
Average weight	80-100g 2¾-3½oz
Vegetarian	✗
Shape	⬭

Blue Age Rollingstone Chèvre

Exchanging their potter's wheels and artist's brushes for milking machines and curd cutters seems to have been a natural progression for Charles and Karen Evans, who have made cheesemaking almost an art form. Blue Age is an unusual surfaced-ripened cheese with blotches of thick blue mould on the outside. Inside, the curd has softened to a creamy smooth finish, while the taste is quite sharp with a spicy tang from the blue mould and a hint of hawthorn and tarragon. Other cheeses made by Charles and Karen, too numerable to mention, include the Idaho Goatster and tiny *chèvre* decorated with colourful edible flowers.

US	Idaho
Milk source	🐐
Unpasteurized	✗
Maturing time	3-4 weeks
Average weight	250g/9oz
Vegetarian	✗
Shape	various

Bouton de Culotte

One cannot imagine calling an English or American cheese 'trouser buttons' yet Bouton de Culotte sounds charming in French. This is a small, brittle and round cheese. When young it is nutty and firm, but the locals prefer it hard, brittle and almost rancid with age. Some also form the base of *fromage fort*, a very French dish in which the young curd is packed into earthenware pots with salt and pepper, covered with wine or *marc* and left to ferment. Cream and herbs may also be added to the dish and, just before serving, more wine or *marc* is stirred into the brew; it is then spread on crusty bread or used to stuff an onion. The result is a wonderful, eye-watering, mouth-puckering experience.

France	Burgundy
Milk source	🐐
Unpasteurized	✓
Maturing time	2 weeks
Average weight	20-40g ¾-1½oz
Vegetarian	✗
Shape	⬭

Bouton d'Oc

The pear-shaped Bouton d'Oc is a mere 3cm (just over an inch) in diameter at the base, 1cm (less than half an inch) at the top and barely 3.5cm (an inch and a half) high. They tend to be sold by the dozen and ripen very quickly because of their tiny size. Pick one of the cheeses up by the half toothpick protruding from the top and the delicious fine textured, creamy cheese is gone in a mouthful. If you manage to seek out these delightful little cheeses, Bouton d'Oc are ideal served with drinks. Le Bicorne is the shape of Napoleon's hat, Bichoux de Cevenols are tiny truncated cones on a string, the slightly larger Valençay is a pyramid and Clochette a small bell.

France	Pyrénées
Milk source	🐐
Unpasteurized	✗
Maturing time	10 days
Average weight	15g/½oz
Vegetarian	✗
Shape	△

Bûchette d'Anjou

Bûchette d'Anjou translates simply as 'a small log from Anjou' – an area in the Loire Valley also known for its fresh, fruity rosé wines. These characteristics are shared by the cheese, so they make good companions. Unlike Crottin, the cheese is moist and best when fresh and creamy, tasting of just a hint of goat's milk. Numerous *bûchettes*, named after local villages, use local herbs such as savoury, rosemary and thyme and include the Buchette de Banon which is garnished with *pebre d'ai* (donkey's pepper). Bûchette d'Anjou is sprinkled with ash, which imparts a taste reminiscent of asparagus and wild herbs to the creamy soft mature cheese, and offers an attractive contrast to the pure white cheese.

France	Loire
Milk source	🐐
Unpasteurized	✓
Maturing time	2-3 weeks
Average weight	85-100g 3-3½oz
Vegetarian	✗
Shape	⬭

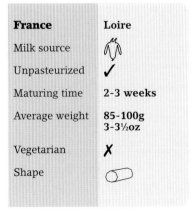

Cendré de Niort

Cendré traditionally referred to the method of maturing cheeses in a box of wood ash rather than the more decorative modern method of mixing coarse salt with powdered charcoal and sprinkling it over fresh cheeses. Most Cendrés originate in the wine-growing regions, using the charred trimmings of the vines. When milk was abundant, the cheeses were buried in wood ash to preserve them until they were needed during the *vendange* (grape harvest) to feed the hungry pickers. Today, every cheese shop in France carries a range of these attractive, creamy, slightly tangy, often unusually shaped cheeses. Lesser known varieties include Rouelle (with a hole in the centre) and La Taupinière (mole hill).

France	Poitou-Charentes
Milk source	
Unpasteurized	✗
Maturing time	**10 days**
Average weight	**various**
Vegetarian	✗
Shape	

Chabichou du Poitou AOC

Like Rocamadour (page 55), the soft curds are created by slowly ripening the milk with small amounts of rennet, so coagulation is mainly from lactic bacteria rather than the action of the enzyme rennet. The curds are ladled into cylindrical moulds embossed with CDP on the base, dating back to the 18th Century. This cheese is rarely aged for as long as the smaller, more compact Crottin, so the texture is smoother and more moist and the flavour is milder, though still goaty with a fresh ground-nut finish. Many cheeses previously referred to as Chabichou must now be called simply *chèvre*, or named after a local village, as they are made outside the legally defined areas for AOC.

France	Poitou-Charentes
Milk source	
Unpasteurized	✓
Maturing time	**10-20 days**
Average weight	**150g/5oz**
Vegetarian	✗
Shape	

Chèvrefeuille

Périgord is a haven for goats, with its rugged terrain and magnificent chestnut trees, whose leaves are often used to wrap the local *chèvre* cheeses or to line the small wooden boxes used for displaying them. Chèvrefeuille are covered with chopped fresh thyme, tarragon and marjoram, providing a brilliant contrast to the shiny white interior and the gentle acidity and aromatic character of the goat's milk. With age, the texture is more creamy and the cheese is infused with the herbaceous oils. Similar cheeses can be found in a range of shapes – *cloche* (bell), *figue* (fig), *buchette* (log), *coeur* (heart) and tiny rounds, truncated cones, squares or balls used as *amuses bouches* in restaurants across France.

France	Périgord
Milk source	
Unpasteurized	✓
Maturing time	**2-4 weeks**
Average weight	**200g/7oz**
Vegetarian	✗
Shape	

Fleur du Maquis

When young, Fleur du Maquis is firm yet moist and lemony fresh; with age it becomes encrusted with the blue-grey mould, softening to a luscious, toe-curling, burnt-caramel and nutty tang. The aroma is a heady mix of wild thyme, rosemary, juniper berries and the *maquis* (Corsican landscape), with the scent of soil, sun and sea. Like all Corsican cheeses it exudes an aromatic quality due to the exceptional natural grazing and the ancestry of the native goats and sheep. The cheeses are made mainly by artisans, often in isolated shepherds' huts, using recipes handed down through generations. Each cheese, I was assured, was the particular favourite of Corsica's most famous son, Napoleon.

France	Corsica
Milk source	
Unpasteurized	✓
Maturing time	**1 month**
Average weight	**600-700g** **1lb 5oz-1lb 9oz**
Vegetarian	✗
Shape	

Hubbardston Blue Cow

The word 'blue' in Hubbardston Blue Cow refers not to an internal blue mould, but to the thick furry coat of blue-grey mould beneath which lurks one of America's great cheese secrets. A consistent winner at the American Cheese Society festival, this cheese is made by Letty Kilmoyer, whose plans to make a soft white cheese were dashed by the determination of Mother Nature, who ultimately dictates which moulds will grow. The unconventional blue coat speeds up the ripening process, softening the curd to a point at which it literally runs to greet you and slides across the palate releasing hints of almonds, celery and herbs, finishing with a strong tangy bite. Letty also makes fine goat's cheese.

US	Massachusetts
Milk source	
Unpasteurized	✗
Maturing time	4-6 weeks
Average weight	140g/5oz
Vegetarian	✗
Shape	

Mothais

Mothais is unusual because, unlike most natural rind cheeses, where the cheesemaker encourages the cheese to dry out, it is ripened in cellars where the humidity is close to 100 per cent. Consequently the rind is sticky, moist and wrinkled with a faint pinkish hue that develops a dusting of white mould overlaid by a few patches of blue mould. The interior is creamier than Crottin and the taste, though less pronounced, reflects the complex natural grazing (grasses and flowers) of this region. Wrapped in a chestnut or plane leaf, Mothais is an attractive addition to any cheeseboard. Similar cheeses include the heart shaped Coeur Poitevin and Santranges.

France	Poitou-Charentes
Milk source	
Unpasteurized	✗
Maturing time	3-4 weeks
Average weight	250g/9oz
Vegetarian	✗
Shape	

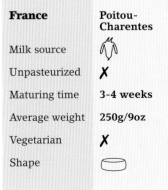

Pérail

The thin crusty rind is pale ivory with a pinkish hue, and bears the marks of straw mats. Dusted with a fine white mould, it resembles an old-fashioned powder puff; while beneath the surface the moist young curd is firm and slightly grainy. Pérail is similar to a young Crottin, but the surface area is much greater and the moulds work vigorously on the curd alongside the internal bacteria, creating a texture like ice-cream. As it melts in the mouth it releases the subtle nature of the ewe's milk and the local flora; sweet, like *crème-caramel*, with a nutty finish and underlying fresh acidity reminiscent of brambles and wild flowers. It has similar characteristics to the more famous cheese from this area, Roquefort.

France	Rouergue
Milk source	🐑
Unpasteurized	✓
Maturing time	1-3 weeks
Average weight	130g/4¾oz
Vegetarian	✓
Shape	⬭

Persillé

The term 'blue' generally refers to cow's milk cheeses that develop streaks of internal blue mould. However, in Savoie, *persillé* is a generic term used to describe mainly goat's cheeses that develop a bluish hue within the *pâte* or interior, though few of these cheeses truly merit the term as they tend to be sold too young. The characteristic blue-grey moulds compete with colourful and vigorous moulds, yeasts and cheese-mites, creating a drier, flakier cheese, which is often pungent, sharp and salty. Persillé des Aravis, more akin to Reblochon, is brushed frequently to encourage the growth of a protective coat, while Persillé de Tignes and Persillé de la Tarentaise have a flaky texture and dry, brown crusty rinds.

France	Savoie
Milk source	🐐
Unpasteurized	✓
Maturing time	4-12 weeks
Average weight	250-550g 9oz-1lb 4oz
Vegetarian	✗
Shape	⬭

Pouligny-St-Pierre AOC

As with most natural cheeses, the fresh milk for Pouligny St-Pierre is coagulated by lactic bacteria with only a little rennet. This produces soft white floppy curds that are never pressed, but instead allowed to drain, with just the weight of the curds to squeeze out excess moisture. This cheese has an elegant pyramid shape and reddish-orange rind, coated with splodges of white, pale-blue and grey moulds. Ripened on straw mats for a minimum of two weeks, it is infinitely more interesting after four to five weeks, when the local flora (*moisissure*) has had a chance to display its multifaceted nature. *Fermier* (or farmhouse cheeses) carry a green label, while a red label denotes *laitier* (creamery-made).

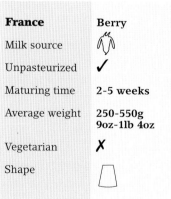

France	Berry
Milk source	🐐
Unpasteurized	✓
Maturing time	2-5 weeks
Average weight	250-550g 9oz-1lb 4oz
Vegetarian	✗
Shape	⏢

Queso del Montsec DO

The rustic-looking, reddish-yellow rind of Montsec is coated with wood ash and has patches of white and grey moulds. The cheese has a dense, fairly grainy texture that softens around the edges feeling very creamy in the mouth yet with a definite bite. The distinctive taste of goat's milk provides a strong herbaceous finish. Like Garrotxa (*see* page 126), it was invented by a group of young urban professionals who embarked on an agricultural career. Goats rather than cows were chosen, requiring less fodder, less space and, for the inexperienced, being easier to manoeuvre. Combining traditional cheesemaking skills with marketing and commercial expertise, the makers launched Montsec in 1978.

Spain	Catalonia
Milk source	
Unpasteurized	✓
Maturing time	**2-3 months**
Average weight	**1kg/2lb 4oz**
Vegetarian	✗
Shape	

Rocamadour or Cabécou de Rocamadour AOC

These mouth-sized goat's cheeses must be made with raw milk, using only small amounts of rennet. They must also be allowed to coagulate slowly for at least 20 hours, compared with the usual 30 to 60 minutes for natural rind cheeses. This ensures the development of a smooth, creamy texture and fresh, acid taste, and the cheeses become firmer, nutty and more aromatic with age. With their creamy white wrinkled rind, sometimes decorated with sprigs of herbs or bacon, the cheeses are irresistible served with crisp, *frisée* lettuce, *croûtons* and local wine.

France	Lot
Milk source	
Unpasteurized	✓
Maturing time	**15 days**
Average weight	**30-60g/1-2¼oz**
Vegetarian	✗
Shape	

Selles-sur-Cher AOC

Named after a village on the river Cher, where it was first sold, Selles-sur-Cher is now protected under the AOC system. This is a classic Loire cheese found in local cheese shops in various stages of maturity, from young and fresh to strong, nutty and salty with a distinct goaty tang. The texture is initially hard when bitten into but then the cheese melts in the mouth luxuriously. A mix of charcoal made from local vines and coarse salt is sprinkled over the fresh cheese, adding to its visual appeal as well as aiding the draining of the whey. This concept was probably introduced as early as the 8th Century, when Saracen invaders from Spain brought goats and cheesemaking skills into France.

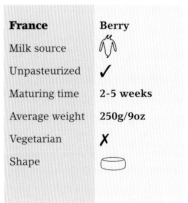

France	Berry
Milk source	
Unpasteurized	✓
Maturing time	**2-5 weeks**
Average weight	**250g/9oz**
Vegetarian	✗
Shape	

St-Marcellin

Most artisan French cheeses are found only in the region where they are made, but the small, thin disk-shaped St-Marcellin are found in most reputable cheese shops across France. Stacked on counters or plied on straw, their thin yellow crusts, dusted with white and delicate pale blue moulds, barely contain the interiors. Oozing over each other, distorting their shape, they create an irresistible mass, like freshly made cookies. Pleasantly bitter, green-grassy in taste, with hints of crisp white wine and yeast, they are as popular today as they were when served at the royal table in the Louvre as early as 1461, when they would have been made from goat's milk rather than cow's milk as most are today.

France	Loire
Milk source	
Unpasteurized	✓
Maturing time	**10-20 days**
Average weight	**200-500g** **7oz-1lb 2oz**
Vegetarian	✗
Shape	

Ste-Maure de Touraine AOC

Ste-Maure is plain or rolled in wood ash and the white interior is grainy and moist in texture until the moulds grow and draw out the moisture, making the cheese firmer and more dense. It has a delightfully musty, slightly goaty smell and a lemony flavour which intensifies with age. Whether made on small farms or in large factories, Ste-Maure de Touraine must comply with the AOC regulations, which dictate that the freshly formed curd is scooped by hand into log-shaped moulds, with one end marginally wider than the other to make tipping them on to trays to dry easier. Some farmhouse cheeses have a piece of straw, *paille*, running through the centre – pull it out or use it to pick up the cheese.

France	Loire
Milk source	
Unpasteurized	✓
Maturing time	**2-4 weeks**
Average weight	**150g/5oz**
Vegetarian	✗
Shape	

Tymsboro

While most British, American and Australasian cheesemakers battle to eliminate the grey-blue mould from their cheese rooms, Mary Holbrook continues to make one of Britain's finest cheeses. This aversion to mould, except the pure white Camembert-type, deprives English-speaking countries of so many cheeses. Tymsboro is a lopsided pyramid, dusted with charcoal which is just visible under its fine white-grey crust. Like Camembert, the interior is runny around the edges and firm, like Crottin, in the centre. The taste is lemony fresh and hints at elderflowers, wild marjoram and fresh apples with a tangy finish – a reflection of the natural grazing in the picturesque Mendip hills, near Bath.

England	Somerset
Milk source	
Unpasteurized	✓
Maturing time	**2-4 weeks**
Average weight	**250g/9oz**
Vegetarian	✗
Shape	

Natural Rind

Cheese name	Country of origin	Region	Milk source
Arômes au Vin Blanc	France	Rhône-Alpes	Cow
Autun	France	Midi-Pyrénées	Goat
Baratte	France	Burgundy	Goat
Bressan	France	Rhône-Alpes	Goat with some cow
Brin d'Amour *see* Fleur de Maquis			
Brique Ardechoise	France	Rhône-Alpes	Goat
Brique du Forez	France	Auvergne	Cow & goat
Cabécou de Rocamadour AOC *see* Rocamadour			
Cabradi Madurat	Spain	Catalonia	Goat
Cailloux du Rhône	France	Rhône-Alpes	Cow or goat
Chabifeuille	France	Berry	Goat
Chabis see Chabicou	France	Burgundy	Cow or goat
Clacbitou Fermier	France	Burgundy	Goat
Classic Blue	US	Massachusetts	Goat
Clochette	France	Poitou-Charentes	Goat
Coeur de Berry	France	Central	Goat
Coeur Poitevin	France	Poitou-Charentes	Goat
Cotswold Crottin	England	Oxfordshire	Goat
Figue	France	Aquitaine	Goat
Grabetto	Australia	Victoria	Goat
La Taupinière	France	Poitou-Charentes	Goat
Le Cornilly	France	Berry	Goat
Mâconnais	France	Burgundy	Cow & goat
Monte Enebro	Spain	Avila	Goat
Pavé Blésois	France	Loire	Cow
Pélardon	France	Languedoc-Roussillon	Cow
Penamellera	Spain	Asturias	Cow, goat or ewe
Persillé des Aravis	France	Savoie	Goat
Picodon de L'Ardèche/de la Drôme	France	Rhône-Alpes	AOC Goat
Poivre d'Ane	France	Côte d'Azur	Cow, ewe or goat
Rouelle	France	Loire	Goat
Sancerre	France	Loire	Goat
Santranges	France	Berry	Cow
Squire Tarbox Inn	US	Maine	Goat
St-Felicien Fermier	France	Burgundy	Cow
Tarentais	France	Savoie	Goat
Tomme de Romans	France	Dauphine	Cow
Tomme du Vercors	France	Dauphine	Cow
Valençay	France	Berry	Goat
Wabash Cannonballs	US	Indiana	Goat

Soft, white-rind cheeses

Above: Floppy curd is very gently ladled into Camembert moulds to retain as much of the moisture as possible.

Soft, white-rind cheeses conjure up images of butter-yellow, soft centres oozing provocatively out of their rinds. The best-known varieties are Brie and Camembert, and thousands of variations of these two cheeses are made in France and around the world. But there are actually at least 80 soft, white-rind cheeses made from cow's, goat's or ewe's milk. The voluptuous, almost liquid texture of these cheeses does not indicate a prohibitively high fat content – on the contrary, it is due to the high water or whey content.

After the milk has been separated with rennet, the soft, floppy, jelly-like curd is scooped into high sided hoops or moulds. These are filled, then left in a humid room to allow the weight of the curd to gently squeeze out more of the whey. Once the desired level of moisture is reached, the moulds are removed and the soft curd is placed on straw mats in another room, to which *Penicillium candidum* and other moulds have been introduced.

Gradually the moulds, attracted to the moist, protein-rich surface of the cheese, start to form, spreading in patches until the surface of the cheese is enveloped, protecting the inside from drying out.

Hence, soft, white-rind cheeses are sometimes referred to as 'mould-ripened' cheeses. Initially the mould resembles luxurious white velvet but, as the cheese is turned to ensure it evenly ripens, the mould is flattened into a crusty rind. As more colourful moulds, yeasts and pigments join in the creative process, each helps to break down the curd.

The invasion of these colourful artists is not, however, welcomed by all cheesemakers. Many fight a constant battle to keep the rind free of all but the purest white penicillin mould. The results are more stable, less robust, pasteurized versions of cheese that range from sweet and mushroomy to bland and unremarkable except for their creamy, smooth texture. Without the help of the myriad bacteria and moulds, they can never replicate the unforgettable feel and taste of a raw-milk Brie or Camembert.

The stage at which these cheeses are eaten is a matter of taste. Some people prefer young cheeses with their dry, chalky centre and sharp slightly salty tang; others enjoy the soft, runny, custard-like texture and stronger, more distinct flavour that comes with maturity. (Brie-style cheeses with a blue internal mould, such as Cambozola, are listed under Blue Cheeses, on pages 144–163).

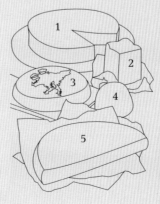

1 *Brie de Melun AOC*
2 *Gratte-Paille*
3 *Le Fougerus* (see *Dreux à la Feuille*)
4 *Gaperon*
5 *Cooleeney* (see *Brie de Meaux*)

Camembert de Normandie AOC

France	Normandy
Milk source	
Unpasteurised	✓
Maturing time	**3-6 weeks**
Average weight	**250g/9oz**
Vegetarian	✗
Shape	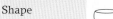

Only the cheesemakers in Calvados, Eure, Manche, Orne and the Seine-Maritime are permitted to call their Camemberts 'Camembert de Normandie AOC'. Ankle-deep pastures and numerous streams dominate this gentle undulating region of France, with its mild and humid maritime climate. It is the quality of these ancient pastures, along with careful breeding and the use of the indigenous cows, that gives this region's cheeses their special character.

The finest Camembert de Normandie has a flavour reminiscent of wild-mushroom soup, and a yeasty, almost meaty taste. Inside the thin crusty rind lies perfection – a delicious cheese with a voluptuous, creamy consistency.

Camembert, like Brie, is self-draining – only the weight of the moisture-filled curds, piled high in small, perforated moulds, is used to press out excess whey. Four to five scoops of soft curds are gently ladled into deep, open-ended, round moulds, placed side by side on large draining tables.

Once the cheeses are firm enough to stand on their own, they are turned out of their moulds and carefully moved to special drying rooms. Insufficient drying results in a runny cheese rather than one with a supple, creamy texture. Here, each Camembert is turned every 48 hours to move the moisture evenly through the curd and to allow the fine penicillin mould to gradually spread across every surface. Maturation takes a minimum of 21 days, compared with 28 days for Brie. However, the best examples are matured for longer than this, and sold only when the curds have completely broken down, forming the homogeneous, smooth, custard-like consistency that is typical of ripe Camembert.

Like many artisan cheesemakers in France, Camembert producers sell their immature cheeses on to *affineurs*, freeing up their cellar space and increasing their cash flow. Each *affineur* has his own vision of what makes a perfect Camembert, and so there are more than 2,000 brands; 500 from Normandy, the rest from elsewhere in France, but the best are from the Auge region between Torques and Dive.

The finest Camemberts have a fragrant aroma and taste of wild-mushroom soup. They have

Left: Rennet is poured into each large bucket of milk to coagulate it into curds and whey.

smooth, voluptuous consistency. Don't be put off by the reddish-brown pigments and thin, crusty rinds; inside you will find perfection. But look out for cheeses that are dry, cracked and dull-looking, or that have sweaty, soapy-looking rinds.

The modernization of Camembert

According to the great cheese master, Patrick Rance, Camembert started life around 1790 as a meagre, dry, yellow-brown cheese made for family consumption by Marie Harel, a young farmer's wife. Fortunately for cheese-lovers, the Harel family gave shelter to a young priest from the Brie region, on the run during the French Revolution of 1789. Having closely watched his parishioners make cheese, he was able to return the Harel's kindness by imparting his knowledge. This helped them turn the small, rather bitter cheese into a delicious, softer, infinitely more palatable and memorable experience.

It would, however, be some years before Camembert received its official name. In 1855, Marie Harel's daughter presented a cheese to Napoleon II, and he asked where it was from. When she said 'Camembert' he replied 'Camembert it shall be called'.

However, three other major events had to take place before Camembert took on the form we know today. Firstly the development of railway in the late 1800s expanded the market for cheese. Secondly, and more significantly for Camembert, came the invention of the small wooden cheese box that proved ideal to protect the cheese on its journeys to the markets of Paris and the rest of Europe. The third milestone, in around the 1920s, was the discovery of how to isolate white penicillin moulds and introduce them into the ripening rooms. These virulent white moulds could fight off the less aggressive grey and blue moulds that had tainted the young cheese, and protect the interior from drying out. *Et voilà*, the voluptuous texture and mushroom aroma of a classic Camembert was finally achieved.

Factories and dairies around the world and even in France have tried to emulate Camembert de Normandie but, as with fine wine, it is the climatic conditions and *terroir* that make Normandy Camembert unique.

IDENTIFYING THE PERFECT CAMEMBERT

The rind should be fine and off-white rather than like thick white velvet, and the presence of some reddish-brown pigmentation indicates the cheese is nearly ripe. Too much pigmentation, especially around the edges, means it is on the downhill slope.

The aroma should be mushroomy with a yeasty, almost meaty taste. A whiff of ammonia is acceptable; a strong discernible smell of it means that the cheese has gone too far.

However, the feel gives you the final confirmation as to a Camembert's character. Begin at the edges and work your thumbs towards the centre. It should feel supple from edge to centre and should not feel runny or uneven. Do not boast of eating only runny Camembert – the runniness is due to secondary fermentation that destroys the true flavour of soft white cheese.

Brie de Meaux AOC

France	**Ile-de-France**
Milk source	🐂
Unpasteurized	✓
Maturing time	**4-8 weeks**
Average weight	**2.5kg/5½lb**
Vegetarian	✗
Shape	⬭

Although most modern examples of Brie and Camembert are very similar, the classic Brie de Meaux stands out, with its smooth, voluptuous, but not quite runny texture and its taste of creamy-wild-mushroom soup with a dash of sherry.

Like fine wine, Brie de Meaux owes its complexity and inherent character to the unique combination of climate and micro-flora of the region in which it is produced – Ile-de-France – as well as to the foibles of the cheesemaker.

Brie de Meaux has a well-established history. The earliest record of the cheese is from AD774, when Emperor Charlemagne, having tasted the cheese in the town of Brie, arranged to have two batches of it supplied annually to his home in Aix.

To the southeast of Paris is the Ile-de-France – with its tall, silver-grey poplars, stony river beds and industrial developments. This is the home of the classic Brie, Brie de Meaux, and its lesser-known cousin Brie de Melun (sharper and saltier due to a different type of coagulation, *see page 65*).

To qualify for the Brie de Meaux AOC label the milk must be unpasteurized and the soft, floppy curd must be ladled by hand into moulds to prevent the fat and protein being lost into the whey. But perhaps the most influential factor is that each Brie

de Meaux must be ripened slowly and carefully at specific temperatures and humidity levels. This enables the milk's heritage to be unveiled – the minerals in the soil, the wild herbage and numerous varieties of grass, or whatever was in season and took the fancy of the herd.

The cheeses spend a minimum of four weeks cellars, where a multitude of wild moulds and yeasts see the purity of the white *Penicillium* rind as a blank canvas on which they work their art, appearing as colourful blotches and splashes of red, orange, blue, grey, yellow and even purple. Most Brie de Meaux, however, are not matured by the cheesemakers. The cheeses are sold, while still young, to an *affineur*. It is his name, not the producer's, that normally appears on the label.

Each *affineur* has his own vision as to what constitutes the ideal Brie de Meaux. Like great winemakers, *affineurs* manipulate the humidity, the temperature, even the type of straw mats on which the cheeses sit. The results are as distinctive as wines from individual vineyards in Burgundy.

However, while AOC regulations prevent total bastardization of this magnificent cheese, the breed of cows whose milk is traditionally used to make the cheese has been virtually phased out. Their rich, thick milk has been replaced with that of the Friesian, bred to produce volume rather than voluptuous cheese. And much of the native grazing has been replaced with ploughed fields. Exquisite, farm-produced Brie de Meaux is still available, but rare. Today critics say that Brie de Meaux's future is threatened by commercialism, pasteurization and a preoccupation with safety and standardization.

The modernization of Brie

As the domain of the supermarkets has expanded, the watchful eye of the cheesemonger and his wooden shelves have been replaced by the sales assistant and a cold cabinet.

The problem for supermarkets is that Brie de Meaux, like all traditionally made raw milk Bries, can develop an unpleasant, acrid, ammonia taste and aroma if kept too cold for too long, and particularly when wrapped in the ubiquitous plastic wrap. Consequently, a new style of Brie has been developed – one that is milder, more stable, less assertive, with a long shelf life and able to withstand refrigeration for long periods.

First the French cheese giants, responsible for producing around 70 per cent of the world's Brie, changed the size; in the case of Brie de Meaux, 3kg/6½lb cheeses were unmanageable for supermarkets. Then Bries enriched with cream, a technique already used for many smaller, traditional cheeses of the area, were introduced. First came the 52-per-cent-cream Brie, then the 60-per-cent. The resulting cheese feels wickedly rich in the mouth with a distinct but subtle mushrooms-in-butter taste.

Stabilized Brie has also been developed – ideal for supermarkets as it matures quickly and remains almost in a state of suspended animation until required by the consumer. It is produced in large factories in France, Argentina, South Africa, Australia and New Zealand.

Modern 'Brie' (and indeed 'Camembert') is really any cheese bearing the soft white *Penicillium* mould, and its appeal is mainly its creamy texture as the flavour is mild and undemanding.

Above: Cheeses being matured by an affineur. *The role of the* affineur *– who must intimately understand the ripening process – is crucial to the ultimate quality of the cheese.*

QUALITY AND BUYING TIPS
Like the girl with the curl in the middle of her forehead, when it's good, it's very very good and when it's bad it's awful. Look for cheeses with dry, cracked rind. You will know when you have found the perfect Brie de Meaux – it is smooth, voluptuous and not quite runny. The aroma is of mushrooms with a slight hint of ammonia, and the taste is of creamy, wild-mushroom soup with a dash of sherry.

WINE WITH BRIE
Ideally fruity red burgundy (Pinot Noir) or an aromatic Bordeaux from Pomerol or St-Emilion (Merlot and Cabernet Franc). Also try Pinot Noir from New Zealand or Oregon. Bordeaux should be aged or the young tannin masks the richness of the Brie and over-emphasises any ammonia on the rind.

SIMILAR CHEESES
Cooleeney from County Tipperary in Ireland and other unpasteurized Bries.

Bath Cheese

Many cheese aficionados once believed the British soil and climate to be unsuitable for making soft cheeses – a myth firmly put to bed by the Padfields. They discovered the recipe for a cheese, first made 100 years ago in Bath, but trial and error quickly told them that the recipe was inaccurate. However, with a little ingenuity, Bath II was born in 1992. It comes beautifully wrapped, with an abridged version of its origin and a wax seal. Initially a little grainy, with a mild, slightly tart, salty finish, the thick, furry rind conceals a 'condensed milk' interior with hints of marinated mushroom and warm milk, balanced with a peppery, dandelion bite. The Padfields also make Kelston Park and York Cheese.

England	Somerset
Milk source	
Unpasteurized	✓
Maturing time	3-4 weeks
Average weight	225g/8oz
Vegetarian	✗
Shape	▱

Bondard (Bonde, Bondon)

The aromas and tastes of youthful Bondard are of field mushrooms, with a salty, mouth-tingling, dry sherry finish. Beneath the thick, white rind the cream-enriched curd is soft and slightly grainy towards the centre, with the feel of butter dissolving on the palate. If ripened for up to two months, Bondard develops a sharp, salty bite and red pigments on the rind; most, however, is consumed within two to four weeks. Named after the bung or *bonde* used in old Normandy cider barrels, these cheeses were originally made for home consumption. Many examples were traditionally called Neufchâtel, but are now made outside the designated AOC zones and can no longer use the name Neufchâtel.

France	Normandy
Milk source	🐄
Unpasteurized	✓
Maturing time	2-8 weeks
Average weight	200g/7oz
Vegetarian	✗
Shape	⬭

Bougon

When I first heard of this cheese I was curious to known how it had earned its name *bougon* which means grumpy in French. In fact, like most French cheeses, it is named after the town where it is made. Bougon is a soft goat's milk cheese, pure white and more runny than Brie or Camembert, with a mild but still distinctly goaty taste, best described as a blend of tarragon, thyme and white wine. It is made in the shape of pyramids, logs and mini-rounds. Similar cheeses have been made for centuries in various forms and areas of France, but Bougon has only recently been produced commercially, the best-known brand being La Mothe-St-Heray.

France	Poitou-Charentes
Milk source	
Unpasteurized	✗
Maturing time	2-3 weeks
Average weight	80g/3oz
Vegetarian	✗
Shape	⬯

Bouquet des Moines

Undisputed champion of chocolate, and bordered by two of the world's greatest cheesemaking countries (France and Holland), Belgium has never been particularly famous for its cheeses. Yet its climate has for centuries produced rich, creamy milk. Best-known among Belgium's cheeses are the strong, washed-rind Trappist cheeses such as Herve, but the popular velvety rinded Bouquet des Moines has a character entirely of its own. Slightly saltier than most soft-white cheeses, it has a pleasant, if undemanding, flavour of mushrooms in butter, with a gooey, cold-custard texture and a hint of sweetness on the finish.

Belgium	Herve
Milk source	🐄
Unpasteurized	✗
Maturing time	3-4 weeks
Average weight	150g/5½oz
Vegetarian	✗
Shape	⬭

Boursault (cream-enriched)

In an age when consumers and producers go to ludicrous lengths (*see* page 167) to reduce fat intake, sales of double-cream cheeses such as Boursault continue to grow. The rind is softer and thinner than that of most commercial Brie, and exudes a sweet, mushroomy aroma. The high cream content means this cheese is more stable and keeps for longer in the fridge. This is a smooth and creamy cheese, yet solid like ice-cream, but with careful ageing it becomes almost runny. It is buttery with a nutty finish, and has enough acidity to balance the richness; one of the best enriched cheeses. Invented by Henri Boursault in 1953, it is also known as Lucullus, and is similar to Délice de St-Cyr (a larger version).

France	Ile-de-France and Normandy
Milk source	🐄
Unpasteurized	✗
Maturing time	3-4 weeks
Average weight	200g/7oz
Vegetarian	✗
Shape	⬭

Brie de Melun AOC

Brie de Melun comes from the same region as Brie de Meaux, but is sharper, stronger, more robust and salty due to different methods of coagulation. Rennet is used to coagulate Meaux, whereas Melun relies entirely on the action of lactose-loving bacteria. As with Brie de Meaux, the care and attention of the *affineur* is as crucial to the quality of the cheeses as the role of the cheesemakers themselves. When the yellow mould has just a touch of red – *ferment de rouge* – the cheeses have reached perfection. When young and fresh, they are mild and slightly sour with a salty finish; after eight to nine weeks they turn supple (but not too soft), pungent and meaty.

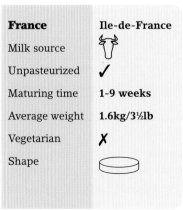

France	Ile-de-France
Milk source	🐄
Unpasteurized	✓
Maturing time	1-9 weeks
Average weight	1.6kg/3½lb
Vegetarian	✗
Shape	⬭

Brillat-Savarin (cream-enriched)

A triple-cream cheese, buttery and slightly sour, it melts in the
mouth like vanilla ice-cream when young, and becomes richer and
more tangy as it develops its thick, velvety white crust. This cheese
would have been appreciated by the famous French magistrate
born in 1755, after whom it was named. Brillat-Savarin was a rather
volatile figure and he would not have hit the history books had he not
published a gastronomic tome, *La Physiologie du Goût*, demonstrating
a lifetime committed to the joy and taste of good food. As a result his
name is used to give authenticity to this wickedly rich cheese, which
was created in the 1930s.

France	Normandy
Milk source	
Unpasteurized	✗
Maturing time	3 weeks
Average weight	500g/1lb 2oz
Vegetarian	✗
Shape	

Capricorn Goat

The only soft white cheeses available in Britain 12 years ago were
imported from France. No-one would have believed it possible to make,
let alone sell, a Camembert-style goat's cheese that would appeal to
the suspicious British palate. Yet demand is increasing and Capricorn
Goat can now be found throughout the British Isles. The milk comes
from 11 farms which, between them, now have over 2,000 goats.
A small cylinder, with a delicate soft white rind, it can be eaten young
when slightly chalky or aged when the edges become almost runny.
Mild, but distinctly goaty, its fresh, creamy character develops with
age a pleasant bitterness reminiscent of chicory and nuts.

England	Somerset
Milk source	
Unpasteurized	✗
Maturing time	4-6 weeks
Average weight	125g, 1.1kg 4½oz, 2½lb
Vegetarian	✓
Shape	

Chaource AOC

Chaource is made in a narrow area between the Aube and Yonne rivers,
among sheltered valleys and north-facing slopes. The curds are left to
develop for 24 hours – significantly longer than most soft-white rinded
cheeses – so the grainy, moist texture and high acidity is more like French
chèvre that uses the same method. Each cheese must be hand-ladled,
drained, salted and left to dry for a minimum of 14 days on rye-straw
mats to meet AOC regulations. Some prefer Chaource fresh and slightly
tart, with a barely-formed rind; others prefer to wait until red ferments
appear on the thick, slightly bitter rind, with hints of mushrooms and the
piquant, fruity, sharp interior – a contrast to the buttery texture.

France	Champagne
Milk source	
Unpasteurized	✓ ✗
Maturing time	2-8 weeks
Average weight	250-450g 9oz-1lb
Vegetarian	✗
Shape	

Chèvre Log or Bûchette

Sold in supermarkets worldwide, Chèvre Log ranges from the sublime
to the ridiculous, thanks to the misconception that cheese, if kept cold
enough, will not age. On leaving the factory it is wrapped in a plastic
'straw mat' which becomes imbedded in the thick white rind, creating an
attractive corrugated effect. Regrettably, the 'straw' is normally replaced
with plastic wrap by the time it gets to the supermarket. The bi-products
of fermentation cannot escape and the rind becomes bitter, shiny and
reeks of ammonia. Chèvre Log should have a fresh, fruity acidity with
a touch of almonds. The texture is dense with a fine grain, becoming
slightly sticky in the mouth, and the aromatic goaty taste intensifies.

France	Loire
Milk source	🐐
Unpasteurized	✓
Maturing time	**10-45 days**
Average weight	**3kg/6½lb**
Vegetarian	✗
Shape	⬭

Coach Farm Cheese

The family responsible for this cheese are dedicated to excellence at
every stage of production – from the varied diet of the goats, to the
wrapping that ensures the cheeses arrive on your table with their
subtle, aromatic sweetness intact. Whether the cheeses are sold young,
mild and lemony, or mature, with a fine penicillin rind and firm yet
flaky texture that melts in the mouth, they beg to be devoured. The
finish is a distinct yet subtle aromatic flavour. This is one of the most
widely distributed cheeses in America with both styles being available
in a variety of flavours, including 'Pyramid', where the lemon-fresh
cheese is interspersed with hot, aromatic, green peppercorns.

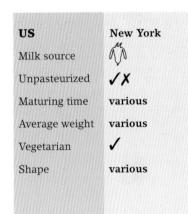

US	New York
Milk source	🐐
Unpasteurized	✓✗
Maturing time	**various**
Average weight	**various**
Vegetarian	✓
Shape	**various**

Coeur de Camembert au Calvados

The art of matching wine with food is a pleasurable occupation, but
since they are unlikely partners, it sometimes seems to be taking things
to the extreme. It must be said, however, that it has its possibilities. This
cheese, a semi-cured Camembert with its rind barely formed, is soaked
in Calvados (a locally distilled apple brandy). Toasted breadcrumbs are
then pressed into the cheese with a half walnut for garnish, *et voilà,* it's
ready to go. The soft, savoury cheese absorbs the heady spirit with its
faintly appley aroma, creating an unusual and certainly popular
combination. To me it is like pouring a fine port into a ripe Stilton:
sacrilege. However, one man's meat is another man's poison.

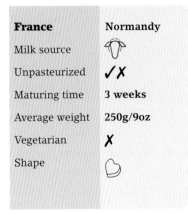

France	Normandy
Milk source	🐄
Unpasteurized	✓✗
Maturing time	**3 weeks**
Average weight	**250g/9oz**
Vegetarian	✗
Shape	♡

Coulommiers

Coulommiers, a smaller version of Brie, was traditionally made from the milk of the family cow. In the 19th Century, small production gradually died out as women became more educated, turning to less time-consuming tasks, and the small farms merged into large commercial units. At the same time, the native dairy breeds of cow were gradually replaced with beef herds and the high-milk-yielding Friesian. Coulommiers is similar to Brie de Meaux, with its mushroomy aroma and voluptuous texture, but is generally milder – unless you discover one of the few artisan cheeses still in production. Also known as Brie de Coulommiers or Petit Brie.

France	Ile-de-France
Milk source	
Unpasteurized	✓
Maturing time	**1 month**
Average weight	**400-500g approx 1lb**
Vegetarian	✗
Shape	

Dreux à la Feuille (Feuille de Dreux)

Chestnut trees, with their magnifent candle-like flowers, dominate the French countryside. Centuries ago, an entrepreneurial cheesemaker, looking for a means of protecting his cheeses during ripening, and to differentiate them from other Brie-type cheeses of the area, decided to wrap his cheese in chestnut leaves. Gradually, as the leaves turn from firm, forest-green to a brittle, rich, copper-brown colour, they imbue the cheese with a taste and aroma reminiscent of woodlands in the autumn. Dreux à la Feuille is slightly thinner and firmer than Brie, but still with a characteristic mushroomy aroma and full-bodied flavour. A similar cheese, Le Fougerus, is decorated with a fern leaf.

France	Touraine
Milk source	
Unpasteurized	✓
Maturing time	**2-3 weeks**
Average weight	**300-350g 10½-12oz**
Vegetarian	✗
Shape	

Evansdale Farmhouse Brie

Colin Dennison, a self-taught cheesemaker has a boundless curiosity and a strong dose of New Zealand attitude (if you need something doing, do it yourself). Colin is one of a new generation of cheesemakers which has created a range of uniquely New Zealand cheeses. Evansdale Farmhouse Brie is one of New Zealand's finest soft white cheeses (Supreme Champion at the 1998 New Zealand Cheese Awards). Deeper than traditional Brie, it has a soft white rind and a smooth, creamy texture that melts in the mouth and gradually releases its flavour of mushrooms, melted butter and green grass. Rarely found outside Dunedin, it is available by mail-order or from the farm itself.

New Zealand	Dunedin
Milk source	
Unpasteurized	✗
Maturing time	**6 weeks**
Average weight	**2.5kg/5½lb**
Vegetarian	✗
Shape	

Explorateur (cream-enriched)

This small cylinder, with its delicate white-downed surface, was invented in the 1950s and named in honour of Explorer, the first US satellite to be launched. Enriched with cream, it appeals to the French, who love rich food. It is still one of the most popular of the triple-cream cheeses found in cheese shops and supermarkets around the world. Its delicate aroma of mushrooms gives way to a rich, buttery taste and a slightly sharp, salty finish. The extra cream gives it a firm, almost solid texture, with a slightly grainy feel that dissolves in the mouth. If kept too cold and for too long the rind becomes damp and bitter and the taste sharp and aggressive.

France	Ile-de-France
Milk source	🐄
Unpasteurized	✗
Maturing time	3 weeks
Average weight	250-450g or 1.6kg/9oz-1lb or 3½lb
Vegetarian	✗
Shape	⬭

Flower Marie

Kevin and Alison Blunt of Greenacres Farm are part of the new wave of British cheesemakers who have turned their backs on professional careers to take up cheesemaking. Despite spending the first five years in a caravan while the goats lived in comparative luxury in cosy barns, they clearly have a passion for their new life and this comes across in the quality of their goat's and ewe's milk cheeses. There is a gentle fragrance of freshly peeled mushrooms from the soft, pink-tinged rind that protects the dense interior. As it melts in the mouth, the subtle, caramel sweetness of ewe's milk behind the lemony freshness is unveiled. Their goat's cheese, Golden Cross, is equally wonderful.

England	East Sussex
Milk source	🐑
Unpasteurized	✓
Maturing time	5-6 weeks
Average weight	210g or 1.6kg 7½oz or 3½lb
Vegetarian	✓
Shape	⬦

Gaperon

The unusual spongy feel and outspoken character of the garlic and spicy peppercorns dominate this otherwise mild, milky cheese. Traditionally, Gaperon was made at home by the farmer's wife using the liquid left after the cream had been seperated and beaten into butter (ie buttermilk). The garlic and peppercorns were kneaded into the fresh curds and pressed into small, basin-shaped moulds. Once drained they would be tied with raffia and hung in the kitchen to dry, developing a fine white dusting of mould. The number made was once said to signify a farmer's wealth and therefore influence the marriage prospects of his daughters. Today, most are made in small creameries from skimmed milk.

France	Auvergne
Milk source	🐄
Unpasteurized	✗
Maturing time	2 months
Average weight	250-350g 9-12oz
Vegetarian	✗
Shape	⌣

Gratte-Paille (cream-enriched)

Nearly twice the thickness of Camembert and enriched with cream, this cheese takes much longer to ripen. As a result, most are still grainy or slightly chalky in the centre, becoming smooth, dense, rich, oily and mushroomy towards the outside. With age, the rind becomes dry and reddish, and the interior develops a slight (though pleasant) sharpness. Invented in the 1970s, Gratte-Paille's name comes from *gratter* (to scrape off) and *paille* (straw), as when bales of straw were taken through the narrow streets to the cattle, pieces of straw would become wedged in the walls along the way. Some are still sold on straw mats to lend authenticity. Similar cheeses include Brillat-Savarin and Pierre Robert.

France	Ile-de-France
Milk source	
Unpasteurized	✗
Maturing time	3 weeks
Average weight	300-350g 10½-12oz
Vegetarian	✗
Shape	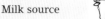

Humbolt Fog

The recipe for Mary Keehn's success has been distinctive packaging, attractive shapes and a close relationship with her milk suppliers. Her cheeses are French in style, fresh and moist, almost mousse-like, with a pleasant acidity and herbaceous finish. With careful ageing, Mary draws out the cheeses' individual characters as the white mould develops. Humbolt Fog deserves a special mention, with its central layer and outer covering of ash, over which the white mould spreads. When cut, the contrasting layers resemble the early morning fog that drifts across Humbolt county and through the redwoods. Other cheeses include Pee Wee Pyramids, Bermuda Triangle, Fromage Frais and a Chèvre Tomme.

US	California
Milk source	
Unpasteurized	✗
Maturing time	3-4 weeks
Average weight	250g/8oz
Vegetarian	✓
Shape	⬭

Le Coutances (cream-enriched)

In supermarkets, where space is at a premium and catching the consumer's eye is paramount, the little wood-like box that houses Le Coutances has a simple, rustic appeal. This cheese is also an excellent example of how traditional cheesemaking techniques can be adapted to modern technology to create cheeses that have their own character, rather than trying to replicate or emulate artisan cheeses. Le Coutances is a double-cream cheese and looks like a small Chasource – the thick rind smells distinctly mushroomy. The texture is more dense and creamy, with an acidic, slightly bitter tang, and even quite a green, 'cats pee' character on the finish.

France	Normandy
Milk source	
Unpasteurized	✗
Maturing time	3-4 weeks
Average weight	200g/7oz
Vegetarian	✗
Shape	⬭

Neufchâtel AOC

From the Pays de Bray region of Normandy, the method of production for Neufchâtel has changed little since its inception. Unlike other soft white cheeses, the curds are lightly pressed, then inoculated with the penicillin mould by the kneading in of broken pieces of cheese that have already developed the bloom of penicillin. Typically, Neufchâtel is quite grainy and some say at its best when the rind develops a reddish pigmentation. The smell is of ammonia, while the taste is bitter, salty and almost acrid. Neufchâtels range in shape from the heart-shaped Coeur de Neufchâtel – produced in vast quanitites for Valentine's Day – to the small cylinder, perhaps the strongest and most vicious of the Neufchâtel family.

France	Normandy
Milk source	🐄
Unpasteurized	✗
Maturing time	10-21 days
Average weight	100-200g 3½-7oz
Vegetarian	✗
Shape	various

Olivet Cendré

Like other ash-coated cheeses, Olivet Cendré was traditionally made during the summer, when milk was plentiful, and then preserved or buried in vine or wood-ash for three months. This significantly slowed down its maturation compared with other soft white cheeses, and ensured it was available when demand was at its peak, particularly during hay-making or the grape harvest. Olivet Cendré is similar to Camembert, but slightly firmer, less voluptuous in texture, and with a strong, rather spicy tang. However, you need to dust off the thick layer of ash, or it is like eating Camembert on a windy day at the beach. Other similar cheeses include Vendôme Cendré, Checy and Cendrés of Champagne.

France	Orléannais
Milk source	🐄
Unpasteurized	✓
Maturing time	3 months
Average weight	250g/9oz
Vegetarian	✗
Shape	⬭

Palet de Babligny

The Lyonnais region is famous for its gastronomy, with Lyon as its capital – home to several notable cheese shops, where most of the local cheeses can be found in superb condition. It is in this region where the tiny cheese Palet de Babligny is made by a Monsieur L'Essor. According to Patrick Rance, it is 'unlike any other cheese I have ever tasted'. Covered in a fine powder of white penicillin mould that discolours with age, the interior is hard and flaky, with a taste like mature, fruity Cheddar. Yet it melts like chocolate in the mouth and has a hint of meadow flowers, hay and *chèvre*. It is not widely available, but well worth seeking out.

France	Lyonnais
Milk source	🐄
Unpasteurized	✓
Maturing time	2-3 weeks
Average weight	100g/3½oz
Vegetarian	✗
Shape	⬭

Pavé d'Affinois

Most of this cheese is sold too young, when it is grainy, mild and
virtually tasteless, except for a hint of mushrooms and fresh milk.
However, after two to three weeks in a warm, humid cellar, the interior
literally melts, retaining a firm, slightly chalky centre the size of
a quail's egg. It practically runs when cut and is reminiscent of mild
Brie and Granny Smith apples. Made in vast factories, this is one
of the first cheeses to be made using ultrafiltration – a way of extracting
a higher yield of solids from milk than through traditional methods. No
rennet is required, only a culture to encourage the lactic fermentation.
It has penetrated the market very successfully.

France	Lyonnais
Milk source	
Unpasteurized	✗
Maturing time	**2-4 weeks**
Average weight	**150g/5½oz**
Vegetarian	✓
Shape	

Pithiviers au Foin

Traditionally this cheese was made in summer – like Olivet Cendré –
when milk was plentiful. It was stored in hay until the autumn, when
it was an essential part of the grape pickers' diet. Today, Pithiviers au
Foin is simply rolled in grass or hay and sold within a few weeks of
being made. Slightly thinner than Camembert, it has a fine, white rind
that develops a dusting of pastel-coloured pink, yellow and grey-blue
moulds beneath the fine strands of grass or hay. Its vaguely sweet,
milk-caramel taste has a subtle aroma of fresh hay and mushrooms.
It is produced near the small market town of Bondaroy, and most are
made in creameries rather than on small farms.

France	Orléannais
Milk source	
Unpasteurized	✓
Maturing time	**3-4 weeks**
Average weight	**250g/9oz**
Vegetarian	✗
Shape	

St-Killian

Ireland's pastures have produced wonderful milk for centuries,
but few monasteries (who introduced soft cheeses), or even recipes
have survived the religious and political upheavals. However, in the
late 1980s, with a resurgence of interest in cheese, came a renewed
demand and desire to make softer cheeses. St-Killian, from
Carrigbryne Farm, has become Ireland's biggest-selling farmhouse
cheese. It is a small hexagonal Camembert-style cheese with a thick
white rind that can be a little whiffy in its aroma of mushrooms and
damp cellars. But the soft, nearly liquid interior is beguilingly rich
and tastes like warm butter, with a slightly green, grassy bite.

Ireland	County Wexford
Milk source	
Unpasteurized	✗
Maturing time	**6 weeks**
Average weight	**250g/9oz**
Vegetarian	✓
Shape	

Sharpham

Sharpham Estate consists of 500 acres of pastures, vineyards, orchards, woodlands and gardens, set in the beautiful River Dart valley. There are 70 acres of permanent pastures and meadow land, providing grazing and hay for the Jersey herd, which undoubtedly gives the estate's milk a unique flavour. Vegetarian rennet and carefully chosen starter cultures are used with meticulous attention to hygiene, while traditional methods of hand cutting and moulding the curd are followed. The Brie-type cheese is so smooth and thick it feels like Devonshire clotted cream, with just a hint of acidity and a whiff of mushrooms. Sharpham also makes English wine and is well worth a visit.

England	Devon
Milk source	🐄
Unpasteurized	✓
Maturing time	6-8 weeks
Average weight	250g, 450g, 900g/9oz, 1lb, 2lb
Vegetarian	✓
Shape	⬭ ▱

Whitestone Farmhouse

Bob Berry turned to cheesemaking in the mid-1980s. He embarked on a mission to produce a cheese from Friesian cows that reflects the unique grazing of Oamaru, with its limestone outcrops, diverse grasslands and windswept coast. Frustration and triumph followed in equal measure. Whitestone Farmhouse was declared New Zealand's Best Original Cheese in 1995. Its fine penicillin rind has the fragrance of cut grass and the texture has the springy elasticity of young Caerphilly, while the centre is still moist and crumbly, becoming softer towards the rind. There is a 'sea-breeze' freshness with a fruity tang, reminiscent of feijoa (an aromatic New Zealand fruit) on the finish.

New Zealand	Oamaru
Milk source	🐄
Unpasteurized	✗
Maturing time	4-6 weeks
Average weight	800g or 1.5kg 1¼ or 3lb
Vegetarian	✓
Shape	⬭

Woodside Edith Cheese

In the beautiful Adelaide Hills, Paula Jenkins and Simon Burr, like most New World cheesemakers, produce a variety of cheeses. These range from a traditionally made cloth-wrapped Cheddar to the delicate, mousse-like Goat's Curd. However, it is their Edith that has attracted most attention. It has a thick, velvety coat, marbled with ash, and a delicate smooth texture, derived from the laborious task of hand-ladling the curd into the moulds. Named after the cheesemaker in France who first inspired Paula to make cheese, Edith has captured the hearts of Australian chefs. Further diversification is in the making from this dynamic duo.

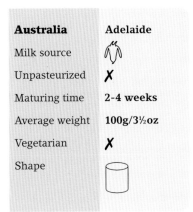

Australia	Adelaide
Milk source	🐐
Unpasteurized	✗
Maturing time	2-4 weeks
Average weight	100g/3½oz
Vegetarian	✗
Shape	⬭

Soft-white rind

Cheese name	Country of origin	Region	Milk source
Aakronia Camembert	New Zealand	North Auckland	Cow
Adele	New Zealand	Motueka	Cow
Aorangi	New Zealand	Paraparaumu	Cow
Blanche de Paris	New Zealand	Taranaki	Cow
Blissful Buffalo	England	Cornwall	Buffalo
Bosworth	England	Staffordshire	Goat
Bouton d'Or Camembert	New Zealand	North Auckland	Cow
Brie de Melun Blue	France	lle-de-France	Cow
Brie de Montereau	France	lle-de-France	Cow
Brie de Nangis	France	lle-de-France	Cow
Brie de Provins/Brie Le Provins	France	lle-de-France	Cow
Butte	France	lle-de-France	Cow
Caprice des Dieux	France	Champagne-Ardennes	Cow
Chanteraine	France	lle-de-France	Cow
Chèvre D'Amnois	France	Lyonnais	Cow
Coeur de Neufchâtel	France	Nommandy	Cow
Cooleeney	Ireland	Co Tipperary	Cow
Croupet	France	Ile de France	Cow
Delice de St-Cyr	France	lle-de-France	Cow
Drakensberg	South Africa		Cow
Dunbarra	Ireland	Co Dubin	Cow or goat
Emlett	England	Avon	Ewe
Fin-de-Siècle	France	Normandy	Cow
Finn	England	Hereford & Worcester	Cow
Fougerus	France	lle-de-France	Cow
Frinault	France	Orléannais	Cow
Fromage Monsieur	France	Normandy	Cow
Golden Cross	East Sussex	East Sussex	Goat
Grand Vatel	France	Burgundy	Cow
Hipima	New Zealand	Paraparaumu	Ewe

Kelston Park	England	Avon	Cow
Kervella Affiné	Australia	Western Australia	Goat
Kirima	New Zealand	Paraparaumu	Cow
Little Rydings	England	Avon	Ewe
Lucullus *see* Boursault	France	Ile-de-France	Cow
Mine-Gabhar	Ireland	Co Wexford	Goat
Mt Domet Double Cream	New Zealand	Oamaru	Cow
Olivet au Foin	France	Orléanais	Cow
Olivet Bleu	France	Orléanais	Cow
Ornelle Camembert	New Zealand	Auckland	Cow
Pencarreg	Wales	Dyfed	Cow
Pierre-Robert *see* Brillat Savarin			
Queso del Valle de Aran	Spain	Catalonia	Cow
Ragstone	England	Hereford & Worcester	Goat
Royal Tasman Camembert	New Zealand	Auckland	Cow
Ste-Maure	New Zealand	Wellington	Goat
Somerset Brie	England	Somerset	Cow
St-Albray	France	Aquitaine	Cow
St-Endellion	England	Cornwall	Cow
St-Francis	England	Shropshire	Cow
St-Tola	Ireland	Co Cork	Goat
Tomato & Basil Brie	New Zealand	Paraparaumu	Cow
Vermont Brie	US	Vermont	Cow
Vignotte or Les Vignottes	France	Champagne or Lorraine	Cow
Waimata Camembert	New Zealand	Gisbourne	Cow
Whitestone Blue Cliffs Brie	New Zealand	Oamaru	Cow
Whitestone Brie	New Zealand	Oamaru	Cow

Semi-soft cheeses

Above: A green casein label is applied to every Reblochon at birth – round for farmhouse, square for creamery.

Semi-soft cheeses can be divided into two distinct camps: washed-rind (or Trappist cheeses), from which most typical semi-soft descend, and washed-curd cheeses.

Washed-rind cheeses

Washed-rind cheese was born out of necessity. During the Dark Ages Trappist monks had to endure 100 fast days without meat each year. The monks set about making stronger, more meaty cheeses for their own consumption, without being constrained by the need for longevity or travel worthiness.

The moisture content of washed-rind cheese is similar to that of soft-white cheese, but more rennet helps achieve a firmer curd, the ripening rooms are more humid and the young cheeses are washed, rubbed or smeared with a mix of brine and bacteria linens. All this encourages a rapid growth of a bright orange to russet-red bacteria on the rind. These

bacteria attack the protein-rich, slightly grainy, moist interior, working from the outside in, creating a texture resembling *crème caramel*. The cheeses are ready after a few weeks, or just before the interior collapses into a torrent of pungent, runny mass.

Typical semi-soft cheeses

Unlike washed-rind cheeses, the curd for semi-soft cheeses is broken before being placed in moulds, which are often lined with muslin. Some are lightly pressed to release more whey. Once the moulded curds can hold their shape they are dipped into brine for preservation and to create a firm outer skin, before being placed in caves. Here moulds are encouraged to grow. These are often brushed or rubbed off so that a thin, leathery rind builds up, protecting the cheese.

Typical semi-soft cheeses are lower in moisture than washed-rind cheeses, so the fermentation process is slower, producing cheeses with a round, sweet-sour, full-bodied, rather than strong, flavour.

Washed-curd cheeses

Sometimes the curd and whey mix may be washed in water, preventing the bacteria from converting any remaining milk sugars into lactic acid. The result is a sweet cheese with a smooth, rubbery texture such as Edam or Colby. (*See also* pages 166–7).

1 *Serra da Estrela*
2 *Milleens*
3 *Raclette*
4 *Langres*
5 *Tetilla*
6 *St-Nectaire*
7 *Mont d'Or*

Epoisses de Bourgogne AOC (washed-rind)

France	Burgundy
Milk source	
Unpasteurised	✓
Maturing time	**30-45 days**
Average weight	**250g and 900g** **9oz and 2lb**
Vegetarian	✗
Shape	

Epoisses is made in a small area in the départements *of the Côte d'Or, the Yonne, and the Haute-Marne around the famous town of Dijon. This region is best-known for its superb Pinot Noir and Chardonnay wines, for which Epoisses makes an excellent partner.*

Not for the faint hearted, this is one of those cheeses that were, for a while, banned on public transport in France. I have cleared a railway carriage in England by simply placing one beneath my feet and feigning sleep. The warmth from the under-seat air-conditioning wafted the pervasive odour into the carriage and, rather than mention the unpleasant aroma, my fellow passengers simply left. Had I been travelling in northern France, I would more likely have been lynched if I had not shared it instantly.

The meaty, yeasty, farmyard aroma of Epoisses is encouraged by frequent washings of *marc* and the smearing of bacteria across the increasingly sticky, glistening rind. Meanwhile, within the innocent interior, the bacteria, oblivious to the external world, work to convert the grainy moist curd into a virtual river of sweet, savoury, smooth, voluptuous cheese.

Origin and history

The first recorded washed-rind cheese, Maroilles (*see* page 92), was created by the monks at the Maroilles Abbey in Thiérache in northern France around AD 960, after a lot of experimentation. Its popularity quickly spread.

The monks had a personal interest in improving the taste and variety of cheese. They were forbidden meat on fast days (of which there were over 100) and the prescribed diet of bread and cheese could have been decidedly monotonous for them.

The discovery, therefore, of a strong, meaty-flavoured style of cheese must have been a godsend to those whose appetites could not be sustained by bread and prayer alone. Some of these ancient cheeses, such as Cîteaux, Tamié and Mont des Cats, continue to be made in the abbeys after which they were named.

Running a dairy was not, however, without its problems, as comely dairy maids were a frequent distraction to the brothers. As a result, some abbots apparently ordered that only old and ill-favoured females were to be employed in the monastries!

Left: The young cheeses are dipped into brine, which is then smeared by hand to spread the bacteria across the surface.

The recipe

Epoisses is one of the last washed-rind cheeses that still uses lactic fermentation rather than rennet to coagulate the milk (although small amounts of rennet are used). Without rennet the coagulation process is much slower, taking a minimum of 16 hours to produce a very crumbly curd. This must then be carefully ladled into moulds so that it does not break up and lose too much whey.

Epoisses are left in a warm room (20°C/68°F), high in moisture and moulds, and turned three times in the first day to speed up the drainage. Once firm, they are turned out of their moulds, moved to a cooler room to be sprinkled with salt, and left to cool down for around 18 hours.

For the next four to six days the cheeses are placed in a drying room or *séchage,* where the correct level of moisture must be achieved for the final cheese to develop the ideal texture. Too much whey, and the yeasts will develop too fast. But if the atmosphere is too dry, the yeasts will not develop quickly enough.

Stacked floor to ceiling, each batch is easily identified by the gradual spread of the sticky orange moulds, from pale yellow-orange to deep tangerine on the more mature cheeses. A fine dusting of white flora or yeast also develops.

The balance of moisture is also vital to ensure that the internal bacteria have the perfect enviroment in which to work their magic, and that the exterior remains sticky. Each day the cheeses must be washed individually using a mix of brine – carotene is used to colour Langres but not Epoisses and bacteria linens. This is done by dunking the cheeses into baths of brine or rubbing the rind with a damp cloth or small soft brush to spread the moulds. Hence these cheeses are also referred to as 'smear-ripened'.

The last few washes contain Marc de Bourgogne, a powerful local brandy, giving the Epoisses its own unique flavour. After 30 days the cheeses are packed in small, round, wooden boxes (the wood comes from the nearby Jura) lined with paper leaves, in place of the more traditional fresh chestnut leaves, now banned by health regulations. The best Epoisses are made with the milk of two local cattle, the Pie-Noir and the Montbéliard, also used for Reblochon.

THE PERFECT CHEESE

Like many of France's wonderful cheeses, Epoisses is enjoyed by different people at distinctly different periods of their maturation.

Epoisses Frais (30 days) A mere shadow of its aged counterpart. Firm, moist and grainy, yet still creamy, with a fresh lemony acidity and mild, savoury, yeasty tang. The fine, pale orange rind is only lightly coated in yeast and bacteria linens.

Epoisses Affinée (40 days) Gradually the grainy interior, like Camembert, breaks down as the bacteria on the rind work from the outside in. The rind is brown, orange and very sticky. When the outer edges are near to collapsing, the inside is not far behind, and the pungent spicy aroma (some would say reminiscent of smelly old socks) is matched by the wickedly strong, strangely meaty, taste, and the yeasty tang has a salty edge on the finish.

Reblochon AOC (washed-rind)

France	Haute-Savoie
Milk source	
Unpasteurized	✓
Maturing time	2-4 weeks
Average weight	250g, 550g 9oz, 1lb 4oz
Vegetarian	✗
Shape	

The origin of Reblochon is as distinctively French as it is creative, innovative and clandestine. The cheese's history can be traced back to the 13th Century, when the farmers, whose cows grazed the summer Alpine pastures, indulged in their favourite pastime – tax evasion. The cheesemaker's rent was based on the yield of his herd so, on inspection day, the cows were only partially milked, to be remilked (re-blocher) when the steward had gone. The first milking produced richer, sweeter milk, which became Reblochon, discreetly kept for the farmers' own tables and not officially recognized until the time of the revolution of 1789. Today all the milk is used, but its name remains as a reminder of its dubious past. It is also an excellent benchmark for semi-soft cheese, against which they can all be measured.

The taste of Reblochon is of freshly picked, crunchy walnuts and a hint of the mountain flowers. Its supple, creamy texture flows over and caresses the palate like warm English custard. The farmhouse version (*fermier*) has a more intense, complex flavour and a farmyard aroma but do not be deterred.

Both farmhouse and factory versions come under the auspices of the AOC system, which defines the quality of various French products, including wine and cheese. Thus anyone wishing to make Reblochon must adhere to the AOC laws regarding the location, the raw materials and the recipe.

The location

Reblochon must be made and matured in the Haut-Savoie and northeastern parts of the Savoie, by individual farmers or commercial dairies (*fruitières*). A factory, however, can never reproduce the hint of resin from the wooden shelves, and the smell of the stone walls and woolly sheep, still used to keep the balance of warmth and humidity in the caves in winter. Nor can they emulate the mould and strange pigments which may grow on the rind, but then this is not everyone's idea of the perfect Reblochon.

I set out to find a small isolated producer recommended by the tourist board, situated in a mountain pass, Col de l'Aulp, above Lake Annecy in the heart of Reblochon country.

It transpired that Chalet d'Aulp was neither isolated nor 'inaccessible except to mountain goats and experienced trampers' – that was obviously tourist bunkum. I had, in fact, tramped unnecessarily in 30°C/86°F up a rough mountain track. I was greeted by tables of jolly people, drinking cool Apremont (a crisp local wine) and devouring Reblochon at the charming chalet, with its spectacular view down to Lake Annecy. Their cars were parked close by in the car park.

Top: Savoie's Montbéliard cow, with its complex alpine diet, contributes unique characteristics to Reblochon.

The raw materials

After annihilating a Reblochon and some wine, I was taken through the wooden milking parlour to the ripening room. The morning's cheeses, swaddled in their white cloths, were piled two high, gently pressing the curd. The simple cellars, dug into the mountainside, provided the perfect conditions for the cheeses.

I decided to climb a little higher and, once around the corner from the chalet, I was greeted by a mountain orchestra. Each cow had its own bell with a different tone, which echoed around the valleys and peaks of the Alps. Hundreds of feet above me, the animals were oblivious to the breathtaking views and the effect of their continuous concerto.

Shortly afterwards, a young shepherd called them for milking. They bounded down the steep valley walls, kicking up their heels and rotating their tails. Some had timidly approached me earlier, watching me through their impossibly long eyelashes and huge brown eyes, tossing their heads and munching elegantly on mouthfuls of wild flowers.

Reblochon must come from the milk of the Montbelairde, Abondance or Tarine cows, whose red and white coats make a rich contrast against their pastoral background. The milk must be fresh, whole and unpasteurized, to retain the taste of the cows' regulation mountain diet of grass, herbs and wild flowers in the summer and hay cut from the lowland meadows in the winter. They are never allowed silage or concentrates which can taint the milk.

The recipe

Reblochon is made in the morning and evening from whole raw milk, to which animal rennet is added. The curds are put into moulds and lightly pressed, using the weight of one cheese on top of another. The amount of rennet used must ensure coagulation occurs within 10 to 20 minutes, as the cheese should not undergo any fermentation in the vats. The rind is washed in brine frequently during maturation – which takes place in cool cellars, often carved into the hillside under the simple mountain chalets – and lasts a minimum of two weeks. A round, green casein plaque indicates the cheese is farmhouse made.

THE RIND AND THE CHEESE'S AROMA

The pinkish-yellow to pale, terracotta-red rind should be covered with a fine white mould or flora. It should be dry not damp, smooth not cracked or split, and it should feel supple (all Reblochon is packed with a little wooden disc on the base, and sometimes on top as well, so before you announce to anyone who cares to listen 'this Reblochon is too firm', either ask the assistant for help or gently squeeze the sides). Unfortunately, Reblochon is usually wrapped and so it is difficult to see and smell, but the slightly yeasty, fruity nose wafts out from under the paper sometimes.

The supple interior of Reblochon oozes from its rind, releasing the trapped aromas of the wild flowers and herbs of the Haut-Savoie mountain pastures. It is a piece of history, and a reflection of the unique geology of the region, the indigenous breed of cows and the people who make it.

Aisy Cendré

Popular in Burgundy, the young Aisy Cendré is washed in brine and occasionally local brandy. Once the yellow-orange mould has spread across the rind, the cheese is placed in a bed of ash for at least a month. In the wine regions, before refrigeration, some farmers used to store their cheese in wood-ash, preferably from the trimmings of the vines – to preserve them until they were needed for the workers during the grape harvest and into the winter. Aisy Cendré is slow to ripen and has a white, salty, slightly chalky centre surrounded by a softer, earthy-tasting outer layer with a distinct but not powerful tang.

France	Burgundy
Milk source	
Unpasteurized	✓
Maturing time	4-6 weeks
Average weight	200-250g 7-9oz
Vegetarian	✗
Shape	

Ardrahan (washed-rind)

The Burns are third-generation dairy farmers in West Cork, but Eugene was the first to start cheesemaking in the 1980s. Now, row upon row of her award-winning cheeses, with their corragated rinds encrusted with brown, ochre, grey and yellow moulds, fill the cellar, giving off a distinct, earthy aroma as they ripen. Meanwhile the firm, slightly chalky, deep yellow interior exudes its own wonderful complexity of flavours – the zesty acidity underscores a more buttery, savoury, meaty character, while the finish is fruity and reminiscent of young Gruyère. There is a certain magic hidden in Irish cheese which is indefinable. Perhaps the leprechauns sprinkle fairy dust on the grass!

Ireland	County Cork
Milk source	
Unpasteurized	✗
Maturing time	4-8 weeks
Average weight	400g, 1.6kg 14oz, 3½lb
Vegetarian	✗
Shape	

Baguette Laonnaise (washed-rind)

Created after the Second World War, this cheese is named 'Baguette' or 'Demi-Baguette' (250g/9oz) because it is roughly the same shape as the ubiquitous French bread, and 'Laonnaise' after the city of Laon. It is a milder, pasteurized version of Maroilles, the forefather of Trappist cheeses, and it has a glossy, ridged, orange-brown sticky rind and a supple dense interior dotted with tiny holes. Like all Trappist cheeses, it develops a strong pungent, spicy nose and taste and a finish reminiscent of the farmyard. In the wrong hands, or a cold fridge, the rind can dry out and the cheese will become bitter and unpleasant. Very similar but less commonly found are Baguette Avesnoise and Baguette de Thierache.

France	Ile-de-France/ Champagne
Milk source	
Unpasteurized	✗
Maturing time	3-4 months
Average weight	250 or 500g 9oz or 1lb 2oz
Vegetarian	✗
Shape	

Bel Paese

Bel Paese was created in 1906 by Egido Galbani to compete with the soft French cheeses, considered by the Italians of the day to be better than their own. The idea came from his frequent forays climbing the mountains around Lake Como and watching the mountain people make cheese. Less expensive than its French counterparts and with a luxurious feel, Bel Paese was the cornerstone for what is now the Galbani empire. This ivory-coloured cheese, with its delicately sweet flavour, is soft and yielding in the mouth and has won the hearts of thousands around the world. The label depicts a map of Itay and the face of a young priest whose book *Bel Paese* (beautiful land), inspired the name.

Italy	Lombardy
Milk source	
Unpasteurized	✗
Maturing time	1-3 months
Average weight	2.5kg/5½lb
Vegetarian	✗
Shape	⬭

Bethmale

Traditionally, the cheeses of the Pyrénées were almost exclusively made with ewe's milk, but over the last century many have been replaced with cow's milk versions. Bethmale, named after the town where it is made, was first recorded when King Louis VI passed through this spectacular and unspoilt region in the 12th Century. Beneath the leathery, orange-pink rind is a firm, open-textured cheese with a mild, slightly sweet flavour. After three to four months its more dense, supple interior is ready to release the flavours of the superb natural grazing, evocative of meadow flowers and the cellars or caves where it is ripened. Similar local cheeses include Erce, Ouset and Esbareich.

France	Midi-Pyrénées
Milk source	
Unpasteurized	✓
Maturing time	3-4 months
Average weight	5.5-7kg 12-15½lb
Vegetarian	✗
Shape	⬭

Bishop Kennedy (washed-rind)

Although it takes its name from Bishop Kennedy, founder of St-Andrew's University in the 15th Century, this cheese's history only began in the 1980s. Graeme Webster, wanting to create a washed-rind cheese with a distinct Scottish flair, experimented with a malt whisky wash. After much rubbing and washing, and no doubt the odd dram or two, this wonderful smooth, velvety almost runny cheese, with its spicy, pungent, yeasty tang, came to fruition. It takes six to eight weeks to achieve the optimum texture and distinctive orange-red sticky crust, which virtually hums when ripe, and is reminiscent of old socks or warm running shoes. I am sure Bishop Kennedy would be proud of his namesake.

Scotland	Perthshire
Milk source	
Unpasteurized	✗
Maturing time	8 weeks
Average weight	1.3kg/3lb
Vegetarian	✗
Shape	⬭

Boulette d'Avesnes

This unusual, colourful, hand-shaped cone, with its hotter than hell after-burn, has earned itself the dubious nickname 'the devil's suppository'. Doughy, moist and slightly crumbly, it is made by kneading and mashing together fresh curds, or under-ripe Maroilles, with parsley, tarragon, pepper and generous handfuls of fiery paprika. The resulting mix is like a vindaloo curry, yet still retains the creamy character of the cheese. Originally Boulette d'Avesnes was made almost exclusively in the home from buttermilk, but now production is in the big creameries, which use under-ripe or less than perfect Maroilles or Dauphine. Not for the faint-hearted, this cheese demands a goodly measure of a cool yeasty lager.

France	Pas-de-Calais
Milk source	
Unpasteurized	✗
Maturing time	3 months
Average weight	180g/6½oz
Vegetarian	✗
Shape	

Brick (washed-rind)

This is a Trappist-style cheese, similar to one first made in America in the early 1800s and introduced to New Zealand by Kapiti Cheese in 1994. New Zealand's first washed-rind cheese, it was an instant hit, receiving the Cheese Lovers' Trophy at the 1995 New Zealand Cheese Awards. Its thin, sticky, orange-brown rind has a marvellous pungent aroma, with overtones of yeast and roast meat, while the dense, velvety, pale yellow interior – characteristic of washed-rind cheeses – is sweet-savoury and almost smoky, finishing with a spicy tang. Despite some raised eyebrows, Brick has found its wicked way on to numerous cheeseboards and into the hearts of New Zealand's chefs.

New Zealand	Wellington
Milk source	
Unpasteurized	✗
Maturing time	1-2 months
Average weight	2kg/4½lb
Vegetarian	✓
Shape	

Brusselsekaas/Aettekees (washed-rind)

Brusselsekaas (Brussels Cheese) is found in cheese counters throughout Belgium, so I looked forward to my first taste with eager anticipation. The first hint of trouble came as I opened the small plastic pot and its obnoxious odour escaped. The innocuous, transparent rind and pale cream coloured interior closely resembled a fine slime over a soft blancmange, but the proof of the pudding was even worse than I imagined. The interior was scattered with tiny, clear, jelly-like chunks, marginally less salty but almost as crunchy as rock salt. It tasted like eating salty *fromage frais* in a farmyard. I have finally met my Waterloo: a cheese I truly cannot muster the courage to ever try again.

Belgium	
Milk source	
Unpasteurized	✗
Maturing time	3-4 months
Average weight	150g/5½oz
Vegetarian	✗
Shape	

Caciotta di Urbino DOC

Caciotta describes the many small, artisan cheeses made all over central
Italy and a few areas in the south. Made with cow's, goat's or ewe's milk,
some have smooth, firm, oiled rinds, while others have the basket-weave
imprint typical of Pecorino. The best are said to be Caciotta di Urbino
and Caciotta Toscana, while Umbrian Caciotta may be flavoured with
garlic (*agliato*), onion (*cipollato*) or truffle (*tartufato*). The cheese is at its
best when produced in spring, when grass is tender and wet from the
dew. The compact, friable, straw-coloured interior is sweet tasting, moist,
and with the aroma and taste of warm milk. This is a delicate cheese
with underlying flavours of green grass, nuts and wild flowers.

Italy	Tuscany and Umbria
Milk source	
Unpasteurized	✓
Maturing time	15-30 days
Average weight	1.2kg/2½lb
Vegetarian	✗
Shape	

Carré de l'Est (washed-rind)

There are two versions of this cheese: one with a soft white rind which
I find mild and lacklustre, and a washed-rind version which is an old
favourite. Washing the cheese frequently in brine seems to act as an
energizer for the local bacteria, creating a magnificent tangerine-orange,
sticky ridged rind. This gives way to a voluptuous, runny Brie-like interior
with a pungent smoky bacon aroma and full-bodied, spicy, barbecue taste.
Even the name sounds exotic, although in reality it simply translates as
'square' or 'paving stone of the East'. Occasionally washed in *eau-de-vie*
(sometimes *mirabelle*), each cheese is turned and washed by hand using a
small brush to spread the colourful bacteria over the whole cheese.

France	Champagne and Lorraine
Milk source	
Unpasteurized	✗
Maturing time	3-4 weeks
Average weight	200g/7oz
Vegetarian	✗
Shape	

Celtic Promise (washed-rind)

In 1998 there were 596 cheeses entered for the British Cheese Awards,
judged by 75 of Britain's finest cheese experts, food writers and chefs.
Gradually, over four hours, the cream of British cheeses rose to the top
and Celtic Promise was declared Supreme Champion. Made by John
Savage-Ontswedder (best known for his Dutch-style Gouda, Teifi), Celtic
Promise was developed under the guidance of the 'inventor' James
Aldridge, one of Britain's most talented cheesemakers. A smear-ripened
cheese with a smooth orange rind dusted with white mould, it is firmer
and more compact than Reblochon but has the pungent, farmyard aroma
and characteristic sweet-sour spicy character of washed-rind cheeses.

Wales	Dyfed
Milk source	
Unpasteurized	✓
Maturing time	8 weeks
Average weight	450g/1lb
Vegetarian	✓
Shape	

Chambertin (washed-rind)

The sound of the bacteria working their way through the fat and protein beneath the sticky brown-orange rind of Chambertin is almost palpable. Held in check by the thin wooden box in which it is sold, the interior gradually changes from a fine chalky consistency to a texture akin to *crème caramel*. In a similar way to Epoisses (page 78-9), Chambertin is regularly rubbed with a brine solution. However, after three weeks a large dose of Marc de Bourgogne (a local brandy) is added to the brine. As a result, the rind becomes even stickier and the aroma intensifies, becoming pungent and meaty with a whiff of alcohol, while the interior is spicy, vaguely sweet, with an aftertaste strangely reminiscent of smoky bacon.

France	Burgundy
Milk source	
Unpasteurized	✓
Maturing time	4 weeks
Average weight	250g/9oz
Vegetarian	✗
Shape	

Chaumes

When a group of producers in Jurançon came up with a new cheese in 1971, they cannot have foreseen its extraordinary success. The name comes from the local word for the high mountain pastures, while the recipe is based on the traditional Trappist-style cheeses. Less aggressive and more supple than Epoisses (page 78-9), it has a distinctive, deep tangerine-orange rind with a thin orange paper cover, and the bulging sides look ready to burst. Rich and creamy, its nutty, vaguely meaty taste and aroma are milder than you might suspect. It is a great starting point for those not yet ready to face the rigours of an Epoisses.

France	Savoie
Milk source	
Unpasteurized	✗
Maturing time	4 weeks
Average weight	2kg/4½lb
Vegetarian	✗
Shape	

Chevrotin des Aravis

Known locally as 'goat's Reblochon', this is a farmhouse cheese made only between March and October, when the Alpine and Sannen herds graze the high mountain pastures infusing the milk with a floral perfume. Goats are browsers, eating the taller, stalkier wild flowers and grasses ignored by the Montbéliard cows (whose milk goes into the better-known cow's milk cheese of the area, Reblochon). Chevrotin des Aravis is one of the few washed-rind goat's cheeses and is made in the same way as Reblochon, resembling its appearance and texture – smooth, melting, rich and sensuous. Chevrotin has a mild goat aroma and taste, nutty and quite savoury, and a wonderful complexity of character.

France	Rhône-Alpes
Milk source	
Unpasteurized	✓
Maturing time	3-6 weeks
Average weight	250-350g 9-12oz
Vegetarian	✗
Shape	

Chimay

Chimay, one of a number of excellent Trappist cheeses from Belgium, is named after the abbey where it is made. The attractive sticky, orange rind has a sweet-sour slightly, yeasty aroma, while the interior is rubbery to squishy and extremely nutty, with a savoury finish and with hints of smoked bacon. Definitely milder than the aroma would suggest. Some of the cheeses are washed in beer, also made by the abbey, which produces a deep yellow-orange rind that stinks of old socks and damp cellars and looks and feels like thin orange peel. Each mouthful melts on impact, releasing a sweet-sour taste like a mild cheese and onion quiche, with just a suggestion of hops and malt on the finish.

Belgium	Chimay
Milk source	
Unpasteurized	✗
Maturing time	4-6 weeks
Average weight	2kg/4½lb
Vegetarian	✗
Shape	⬭

Cîteaux (washed-rind)

The Cistercians at L'Abbaye de Notre Dame at Cîteaux in Burgundy – famous for their Clos de Vougeot wine – were the first to make this type of semi-soft cheese in the 11th Century. Today, variations can be found as far afield as Canada. Little has changed at the monastery and the monks still have their own herd of around 200 red and white Montbéliard cows. The cheese's soft, supple, full-bodied texture, similar to Reblochon, has an earthy, farmyard aroma which belies its sweet, fragrant, character, though there is a yeasty even meaty undertone on the finish. As a result of the quota system imposed by the EEC, production remains small and most is sold to visitors to the abbey or local shops.

France	Burgundy
Milk source	
Unpasteurized	✓
Maturing time	2 months
Average weight	700g/1½lb
Vegetarian	✗
Shape	⬭

Colby (washed-curd)

Like Edam, Colby is a washed-curd cheese, supple and springy, with a mild sweet buttery taste similar to that of a mild Cheddar. Named after the town in Wisconsin where it was invented in the late 1800s it was one of the first genuine American cheeses to be developed. Huge volumes are sold in supermarkets across the country packaged in sterile plastic packs, pre-grated, pre-sliced and pre-cut. The perfect functional fast food: no waste, no preparation cheese, ideal for sandwiches, hamburgers and school dinners. Consequently, generations of Americans have grown up believing this is a serious cheese – a belief that is being firmly shaken by a new generation of cheesemakers.

US	
Milk source	
Unpasteurized	✗
Maturing time	3-4 months
Average weight	250g/9oz
Vegetarian	✗
Shape	

Delicatus (washed-rind)

The Countess of Mar spends her time between the House of Lords and her recalcitrant herd of 20 goats. After two years of trial and error her friends persuaded her to 'go commercial' with her cheeses, and she now makes a range of small, attractive cheeses. Each bears a Latin name, because the Romans first brought goats to Britain and also her husband John is a Latin scholar. Delicatus, 'delicious' in Latin, is my favourite. Its orange-brown rind with patches of yellow and grey in the deep ridges contrasts with the very moist interior that feels like ice-cream in the mouth. Pleasantly goaty with a suggestion of hawthorn and almonds, the finish is intense but not strong.

England	Hereford
Milk source	
Unpasteurized	✓
Maturing time	3 months
Average weight	1kg/2¼lb
Vegetarian	✗
Shape	⬭

Durrus

Jeffa Gill is one of four cheesemakers in West Cork who have decided that the climate and grazing there lends itself to Trappist-style cheeses. Cheesemaking begins each day in a glistening copper cauldron, encased in a round wooden frame. After three hours, the fresh curds are ladled into moulds and gently pressed, imprinting the rind with a zipper pattern. After four weeks the rind is a mass of blue, grey and white moulds, the aroma is earthy and the texture is supple but firm. A multitude of flavours skip playfully across the palate tempting the tastebuds to name them – meadow flowers, a Cheddar-like tang and a nutty undertone of marzipan, tart apples and sea breezes.

Ireland	County Cork
Milk source	
Unpasteurized	✓
Maturing time	4-8 weeks
Average weight	1.3kg/3lb
Vegetarian	✗
Shape	⬭

Edam (washed-curd)

A washed-curd cheese, Edam is mild, almost bland, sweet and rubbery, and dates back to around the 12th Century. Part of the staple diet of the Dutch sailors, it was named after the port from which they sailed. In 1612 the harbour of Edam became a victim of land reclamation, but the cheese continued to be exported to the Baltic and the Mediterranean, and went with explorers to the New World. To protect the cheese during its long sea voyages, it was covered in cloth soaked in a mixture of wax and local herbs, then hung to dry over a vat of horse manure. The ammonia fumes gave the cloth a deep red colour. Fortunately, red wood from South America and then red paraffin wax replaced this rather dubious practice.

Holland	
Milk source	
Unpasteurized	✗
Maturing time	2-10 months
Average weight	1.5kg/3lb 5oz
Vegetarian	✗
Shape	

L'Edel de Cleron

Created in the 1980s, this is a commercially made, pasteurized version of one of France's greatest cheeses – Mont d'Or. Its warm, enveloping richness is attributed to the long curing period, rich milk and the belt of spruce bark that encircles it. The sweet, nutty, Brie-like interior is supple and almost runny, with hints of fresh vanilla and resin absorbed from the thin wooden band. Regular rubbings with brine result in a thick, pinkish-orange rind that is a little sticky and has a dusting of fine white powdery mould and a slightly sweet yet pungent aroma. Tourée de L'Aubier from Normandy is similar, but lacks the depth of flavour of the L'Edel de Cleron.

France	Franche-Comté
Milk source	
Unpasteurized	✓
Maturing time	4-6 weeks
Average weight	300g or 2kg 10½oz or 4½lb
Vegetarian	✗
Shape	

Elberta

'Jack of all cheeses and master of none' is certainly not true of the two intrepid cheesemakers responsible for the unique regional cheese, Elberta. Alyce Birchenough and Doug Wolbert's list of cheeses is awesome, and includes cottage cheese, Edam, Gouda, Jack and a blue. A semi-soft, washed-rind cheese, Elberta has a deep-sunshine yellow interior, characteristic of Guernsey milk. Supple, sweet and buttery, it melts in the mouth releasing a hint of meadow flowers and a savoury, onion tang. Alyce and Doug, who first made the cheese in 1986, use no pesticides, only natural fertilizers on the lush pastures and crops they produce for their herd of pure-bred Guernsey cows.

US	Alabama
Milk source	
Unpasteurized	✓
Maturing time	over 60 days
Average weight	3.6kg/8lb
Vegetarian	✗
Shape	

Fontina DOC

In the shadow of Mont Blanc are some of Europe's finest pastures. Their complexity and variety provide the cheesemaker with an exemplary milk that gives Fontina its unique character. Life, though, is not easy for the cheesemakers tucked away in their isolated chalets, or for the farmer. Some still take their milk by mule, twice a day, to the cheesemakers along the same paths used by Hannibal and his elephants. Luckily, government subsidies and the fierce pride of the Italians for this great cheese have kept Fontina alive. Its dense, smooth and slightly elastic, straw-coloured interior has a delicate nuttiness with a hint of wild honey, mushrooms and an earthy yet fresh acidity when melted.

Italy	Valle d'Aosta/ Piedmont
Milk source	
Unpasteurized	✓
Maturing time	3 months
Average weight	8-18kg 17½-39¾lb
Vegetarian	✗
Shape	

Gouda (washed-curd)

Sadly, it is only when you visit one of the superb cheese shops in Holland, where the shelves groan under the weight of aged cheeses, that you see and taste the best Goudas. Most sold in supermarkets are too young to have developed any depth of flavour. Supple, elastic, sometimes almost plastic and scattered with small holes, Gouda has a mild buttery taste characteristic of a washed-curd cheese with maybe a hint of things to come. Aged Gouda is as intense and complex as a mature Cheddar, with a savoury tang, hints of dark chocolate and a background of roasted nuts and caramelized onions. Some excellent Gouda is produced by Dutch immigrants in Wales, Ireland, New Zealand and America.

Holland	
Milk source	
Unpasteurized	✓ ✗
Maturing time	**2-24 months**
Average weight	**5-10kg** **11-22lb**
Vegetarian	✗
Shape	◯

Gubbeen

The wild coastline of West Cork is littered with ancient ruins, many of which are old monasteries and watch towers. One of these ruins still sits proudly at the end of the headland where Gubbeen is made. Based on an old recipe, this award-winning cheese has its own unique, wonderful, earthy sweetness. The local yeasts and moulds work enthusiastically alongside cheesemaker Jeffa Gill in the modern dairy to create the supple, dense creamy texture and undulating terracotta rind. Savoury, almost meaty, Gubbeen is rich and full-bodied with a finish reminiscent of roast onions – another great washed-rind cheese of West Cork. The smoked version is also worth trying, although it is less readily available.

Ireland	**County Cork**
Milk source	
Unpasteurized	✗
Maturing time	**4-8 weeks**
Average weight	**1.5kg/3lb 5oz**
Vegetarian	✓
Shape	⬭

Havarti

Cheese has been a cornerstone of the Danish economy since the Vikings first set out to pillage and trade with Europe and the Americas. They needed cheeses that would withstand the rigours of sea travel, and so concentrated on producing the hard, slow-ripening cheeses of Holland. In the mid 1800s, Hanne Nielsen, a woman with a mission, decided to create a range of unique Danish cheeses. Havarti, named after the farm where she first made the cheese, was her greatest success. Pale yellow-orange and slightly sticky, with a spongy texture and a full-bodied creamy taste, it becomes outspoken and pungent with age. It is also made with added cream or with caraway seeds.

Denmark	
Milk source	
Unpasteurized	✗
Maturing time	**1-3 months**
Average weight	**2-4.5kg** **4½-10lb**
Vegetarian	✗
Shape	

Herve (washed-rind)

Herve, named after the ancient town in northern Liège, dates back to the 7th Century when the first monasteries were established, and comes in various styles. Herve Doux, a double-cream version with a superb, voluptuous texture and a pervasive air, is my favourite. The exterior, too fine to be called a rind, is a very wet and sticky pale orange. Reeking of old socks, damp wood and forest leaves, the taste is licentious, yeasty and meaty, but neither harsh nor aggressive, while the finish is of charred roast meat. Herve is ideal served with the almost solid *sirop de pomme et poire*, whose concentration of fruit and bitter, burnt sugar bite lends a sweetness to the cheese. Both literally dissolve in the mouth.

Belgium	Liège
Milk source	
Unpasteurized	✗
Maturing time	2-3 months
Average weight	200g/7oz
Vegetarian	✗
Shape	

Jack or Monterey Jack

The original Jack cheese, although attributed to a Scotsman, David Jacks, can be traced back to the Spanish Franciscan monks who travelled from Mexico to California when it was still part of Mexico. They quickly set up farming units and introduced Quesco Blanco – a soft, delicate, Spanish-style cheese. David Jacks saw the potential of the cheese market, bought up land, and established his own brand called Jack's Cheese. Today producers wishing to distinguish their soft, moist, subtle-flavoured cheese dotted with holes, from the more bland, rubbery, easy-to-slice industrially made Jack, usually call their cheese 'Sonoma', 'Monterey' or 'California' Jack. Dry Jack, a mature version, can be found under Hard Cheeses.

US	California
Milk source	
Unpasteurized	✗
Maturing time	1-3 months
Average weight	various
Vegetarian	✗
Shape	

Langres AOC (washed-rind)

I first encountered Langres in a small restaurant in Champagne, where I was presented with a soft, creamy, bright orange cheese in a state of near collapse to go with my Bouzy Rouge, the red wine of the region. Unlike other washed-rind cheeses, Langres are not turned after each washing, so a crater forms in which the brine gathers and is gradually absorbed. This creates a smoother, richer consistency than Epoisses (pages 78-9). As the interior condenses into semi-liquid form, the rind (treated with annatto) becomes more vividly orange, very wrinkled and takes on a life and shape of its own. Pungent, with a smoky-bacon aroma and intense, meaty character, it was an excellent partner for my wine.

France	Haute-Marne
Milk source	
Unpasteurized	✓
Maturing time	6-12 weeks
Average weight	180g or 800g 6½oz or 1¾lb
Vegetarian	✗
Shape	

Limburger (washed-rind)

Although Limburger originated from the province of Limbourg, an area on the border of Holland and Belgium, it has become so popular in Germany (where the vast majority is now produced) that even some Belgians believe its origins are German. This is one of the smelliest cheeses in the world. Its aroma is unmistakable but, unlike many of the washed-rind cheeses, its rumbustious character carries through into the taste. Supple yet firm, the spicy, aromatic, almost meaty interior lacks the subtlety and depth of Epoisses (pages 78-9), and many are sold over-ripe, when they become vicious, runny and bitter. A milder version, introduced by German immigrants, is popular in the United States.

Germany	
Milk source	
Unpasteurized	✗
Maturing time	**6-12 weeks**
Average weight	**200g-600g**
	7oz-1lb 5oz
Vegetarian	✗
Shape	

Livarot AOC (washed-rind)

Known as 'the Colonel' because of the five stripes of sedge grass (or more likely orange plastic) that encircle the cheese, Livarot's origin is attributed to monks and it is named after the local market town. Today, fewer than a handful of artisan Livarot makers exist, so most is made in factories. However, the AOC regulations help ensure the cheese's authenticity. They state that the milk must come from a 20-kilometre/2½-mile radius around the village of Livarot; the curd must be kneaded by hand and only calf rennet may be used. Annatto is used to colour the rind. It then takes 8 to 12 weeks and 5 litres/9 pints of milk to produce the characteristic thick, supple texture, pungent earthiness and spicy finish of this superb cheese.

France	Pays d'Auge
Milk source	
Unpasteurized	✓
Maturing time	**2-3 months**
Average weight	**250g or 450g**
	9oz or 1lb
Vegetarian	✗
Shape	

Maroilles AOC (washed-rind)

The forefather of the Trappist cheeses, Maroilles was first made somewhere around the 10th Century at the Abbeye de Maroilles, founded by St-Humbert in 652. The cheese gained popularity among the aristocracy and other abbeys, and its production spread to nearby farms. Unlike most soft cheeses of the day, whose 'shelf life' could be measured in days, Maroilles could be ripened in humid cellars for months and provided a welcome break for the monks from their meagre diet. Placed on straw, its thick reddish-brown crust would prevent it from drying out. Maroilles is bouncy and porous, rather than supple and dense like most of its descendants, and it has a pungent, sweet, fermenting fruit aroma.

France	Flanders
Milk source	
Unpasteurized	✓
Maturing time	**3-4 months**
Average weight	**800g/1¾lb**
Vegetarian	✗
Shape	

Milleens (washed-rind)

Milleens is not just a cheese, but a living legend that embodies all the magic and majesty of the Irish countryside. The Beara Peninsula (the most westerly part of Ireland) conjures up images of windswept beaches and brightly painted stone cottages. But mostly it brings to mind two of my favourite cheesemakers – Veronica and Norman Steele. Milleens is soft and sensuous, pale yellow and dotted with tiny holes. It has the sweet-sour taste of Trappist cheese, and it fills the mouth with hints of sweet caramel, heather, sea breezes and wild yeast. Supreme Champion at the 1997 British Cheese Awards, it is more feisty and pungent than Reblochon, with layer upon layer of flavour waiting to be unfurled.

Ireland	West Cork
Milk source	
Unpasteurized	✓
Maturing time	4-10 weeks
Average weight	225g or 1.3kg 8oz or 3lb
Vegetarian	✗
Shape	

Mont d'Or/Vacherin du Haut-Doubs AOC

One of the world's treasures. Up until late summer, milk from the Pie Rouge de l'Est and Montbéliard cows is combined with other herds' milk to produce Comté (page 122). From the end of August, when the cows return to the valleys to a diet of sweet hay, the cheesemaker produces the smaller Mont d'Or. Enclosed in a band of spruce bark, the aroma of the soft, runny cheese is an addictive blend of chopped wood, farmyards and wild flowers, with a hint of fermentation and resin. Press the thick, uneven, pink-orange rind dusted with white, and watch the undulating movement go through the ripe cheese like a wave. Dollop it on your bread and feel your soul transported. Only available from September to March.

France	Franche-Comté
Milk source	
Unpasteurized	✓
Maturing time	2-4 months
Average weight	500g or 3kg 1lb 2oz or 6½lb
Vegetarian	✗
Shape	

Morbier

Dense, yet springy, with a fairly pungent yeasty aroma and a sweet, fruity taste, Morbier – like Mont d'Or – was originally made by farmers in the valleys during the winter months. The curd from the morning's milk would be hand squeezed and placed in wooden moulds. The cheese-maker would then brush the outside of his copper cauldron with his hand and run it over the surface of the wet curd. In the evening, a new batch of curd would be placed on top, and the two halves left overnight, pressed together with stones. Sadly, now the distinctive dusky layer of ash which covers Morbier is more likely to be food colouring. Typically, this cheese was melted by the fire and scraped on to crusty bread or hot potatoes.

France	Franche-Comté
Milk source	
Unpasteurized	✓
Maturing time	2-3 months
Average weight	11-20lb/5-9kg
Vegetarian	✗
Shape	

Munster AOC (washed-rind)

Do not be deterred by the smell, for this is a cheese of momentous character – supple, both sweet and savoury, almost yeasty, with an intense spicy, aromatic finish, just oozing charm from within the flesh-coloured rind. Despite reportedly being banned on public transport at the turn of the century, Munster has been capturing the hearts of cheese-lovers since the 7th Century, when the monastery of St-Grégoire was founded. Those from Alsace are called Munster (from the old word for monastery), while those from Lorraine are smaller and known as Géromé. Munster can be flavoured with handfuls of cumin, adding another dimension. Both are superb with the crisp and spicy or sweet and luscious Alsace wines.

France	Alsace
Milk source	
Unpasteurized	✓
Maturing time	5-12 weeks
Average weight	120g, 450g, 1.5kg/4¼oz, 1lb, 3¼lb
Vegetarian	✗
Shape	

Murol

A shadow of its mentor, St-Nectaire, this simple, uncomplicated cheese is nevertheless worth a mention. Easily recognized by the hole stamped out of the middle of its smooth, pinkish-red, leathery rind, Murol is a supple, creamy, almost velvety cheese with the sweetness of fresh milk and a delicate nutty taste and aroma. The inventor, local *affineur* Jules Bérioux, cannot have foreseen that the centre piece, known as Murolait, would become a popular addition to children's lunch boxes. Covered in red wax, the tiny cork-shaped cheese is not unlike the Laughing Cow – all it needs is a quick squeeze and the cheese pops out.

France	Auvergne
Milk source	
Unpasteurized	✓
Maturing time	6 weeks
Average weight	450g approx 1lb
Vegetarian	✗
Shape	

Nantais (washed-rind)

Also known as Curé de Nantais or Fromage de Curé, this cheese was a child of the French Revolution. In the early 1790s a young priest on the run found himself in Brittany, a region known for its butter but devoid of cheese. Wishing to secure a place in the community, he used the knowledge he had gleaned from the brothers of his order and taught the locals the art of cheesemaking. The result was a small, sticky, orange, washed-rind cheese, similar to Epoisses (pages 78-9), with a smelly, pungent, yeasty rind and voluptuous, creamy interior. Its rich, smoky-bacon taste and spicy finish makes it a natural partner for the fruity, dry local cider or a tangy Muscadet-de-Sèvre-et-Maine.

France	Bretagne
Milk source	
Unpasteurized	✗
Maturing time	1 month
Average weight	170g-200g 6-7lb
Vegetarian	✗
Shape	

Le Niolo, Niolin or Niulincu (washed-rind)

For centuries, Corsica has relied heavily on the half-wild herds of woolly sheep and demonic goats which graze on a feast of grasses, shrubs and herbs that cover its rugged hills and deep ravines. Le Niolo (or Niulincu, as it is called locally) is one of several ewe's milk cheeses formed in typically Corsican square basket moulds. Frequent washings and prolonged *affinage* results in a rough exterior covered in pungent red and yellow ferments against a pale beige-yellow background. This cheese is supple and moist, with some small holes, and is bursting with contrasting pungent flavours – burnt caramel and aromatic herbs. Stunning and vicious, it demands the companionship of a strong local red wine.

France	Corsica
Milk source	
Unpasteurized	✓
Maturing time	2 months
Average weight	500g 1lb 2oz
Vegetarian	✗
Shape	

Oka

Carrying on their ancient traditions, the Benedictine monks introduced Oka, named after a nearby village, when they established Quebec's first monastery in the late 1800s. Similar to the commercially made Trappist-style French cheese, Port-Salut, but more complex in flavour, Oka is the most popular Canadian cheese after Cheddar. Now made by Canada's largest dairy co-operative, it still retains some links with its past, as the cheese is matured in the cellars of the old monastery. Its fine, leathery, ochre-brown rind encloses the supple, rubbery interior, with its pleasantly pungent, sweet-savoury aroma that hints of smoky bacon and fried onions.

Canada	Montreal
Milk source	
Unpasteurized	✓
Maturing time	6 weeks
Average weight	500g-2kg 1lb 2oz-4½lb
Vegetarian	✗
Shape	

Orla

It was the isolation and unspoilt beauty of County Cork, combined with its rich grazing, that originally drew Oliver Jungwirth from Germany to the Manch Estate. In 1991 he returned and the owners agreed to rent him the land if he farmed organically. With 11 ewes and one Friesland ram, Oliver gradually built up the herd while experimenting with various cheeses. Since receiving the accolade of Best Semi-Soft Cheese in 1995 for Orla at the British Cheese Awards, he has not looked back. When young, it is definitely semi-soft, supple, and has a gentle flavour, but with ageing its texture more closely resembles Manchego. Orla becomes sharp and more salty, while retaining the earthy burnt caramel character of ewe's milk.

Ireland	County Cork
Milk source	
Unpasteurized	✓
Maturing time	1-3 months
Average weight	2kg/4½lb
Vegetarian	✓
Shape	

Polkolbin

Based in Malama, in the heart of the Hunter Valley (best known for its wines), the Hunter Valley Cheese Company produces several washed-rind and soft, white-rind cheeses under the guiding hand of cheesemaker Peter Curtis. Polkolbin, with its attractive orange, slightly wrinkled, sticky rind, and aroma of damp washing and the farmyard, is not unlike Pont-l'Evêque. Sharper, with a green, lingering spiciness that is almost meaty, Polkolbin has a natural synergy with the wines of the Hunter Valley. Wander over to the viewing window at the Hunter Valley Cheese Company, press a button, and for a few minutes you can look longingly into the maturing rooms.

Australia	Hunter Valley
Milk source	
Unpasteurized	✓
Maturing time	1 month
Average weight	250g/9oz
Vegetarian	✗
Shape	⬢

Pont-l'Evêque AOC (washed-rind)

The markets of Normandy are dominated by cheese stalls sagging under layer upon layer of squelchy Camembert, wrinkled Fromage de Chèvre, and France's best-known washed-rind cheeses – Livarot, Pavé d'Auge and the ridged, square-shaped Pont-l'Evêque. Competition is fierce, and every housewife has her own opinion as to which is the best *affineur* for each of the cheeses. Made in the heart of Pays d'Auge country, near the village of Pont-l'Evêque. This cheese's aroma is of damp washing, mouldy cellars and farmyards and the texture is springy and open, glistening due to the richness of the milk and dotted with small holes. The taste is savoury, piquant, with a trace of sweetness and a robust tang on the finish.

France	Normandy
Milk source	
Unpasteurized	✓
Maturing time	2-6 weeks
Average weight	350-400g 12-14oz
Vegetarian	✗
Shape	⬢

Port Nicholson

The prohibitive cost of importing European cheeses into New Zealand has forced producers to create alternatives to many of the traditional cheeses of Europe. Port Nicholson – named after the magnificent, sheltered harbour or 'safe haven' of New Zealand's capital city, Wellington – is based on the popular French Trappist-style cheese, Port-Salut (meaning 'safe haven'). Wax-coated, it is more supple and elastic than Reblochon, with the characteristic sweet-sour taste associated with semi-soft cheeses and an appealing hint of smoky bacon on the finish. Regrettably, the ban of raw-milk cheeses in New Zealand means Port Nicholson lacks the depth of its European cousins.

New Zealand	Wellington
Milk source	
Unpasteurized	✗
Maturing time	3 months
Average weight	1.8kg/4lb
Vegetarian	✓
Shape	⬭

Port-Salut

When the monks at Notre Dame du Port-du-Salut (safe haven) sold the trade name of their successful cheese to a large co-operative earlier this century, they could not have imagined how successful it would become internationally. Despite being made from pasteurized milk, the transition from *fermier* (farm) to *industriel* (factory) has left the cheese with enough of its original character to turn successive generations on to Trappist-type cheeses. Smooth and velvety in the mouth, it reminds me of a grown-up's version of Laughing Cow, although it has more depth of flavour. The pliable pale orange interior, coloured with beta carotene, has a smoky-bacon aroma, lightly acidic taste, and a pleasant sweet-sour balance.

France	Loire
Milk source	🐂
Unpasteurized	✗
Maturing time	1 month
Average weight	2kg/4½lb
Vegetarian	✗
Shape	⬭

Prästost

Most Swedish cheeses are semi-soft (apart from the strange sweet, fudge-like whey cheeses which were introduced by the Benedictine monks in the 9th Century). Prästost ('priest cheese') is a large wheel, pale yellow in colour, with rice-sized holes and is a rare exception. It is firmer than most Swedish cheeses and it has an unusual history. In the 16th Century, farmers paid their tithe to the local priest not in cheese, as elsewhere, but in milk. It was then the task of priest's wife to produce a cheese that would be sold at the local market – and this is how Prästost was invented. Now made only in factories, Prästost has a mellow to robust, sweet-sour character, with a fruity, gently aromatic zing on the finish.

Sweden	
Milk source	🐂
Unpasteurized	✗
Maturing time	2-3 months
Average weight	12-15kg 26½lb-33lb
Vegetarian	✗
Shape	⬭

Quartirolo Lombardo

Quartirolo Lombardo has been made by monks in Lombardy since the 11th Century. It takes its name from the ancient practice of thrice cutting the abundant grasses of the valleys. As the new grass sprouted for the fourth time (*erba quartirola*) the herdsmen would graze their cattle on the sweet shoots before moving the cows into the barns for winter. Although Quartirolo Lombardo cheeses are now made all year round, it is still worth seeking out. It is similar in appearance to a young Taleggio, and has a slightly crumbly, lumpy centre with a lemony fresh acidity and a delicate fragrance. After two months the cheese becomes dense, almost runny, and its fruity character is more savoury and distinctive.

Italy	Lombardy
Milk source	🐂
Unpasteurized	✓✗
Maturing time	10-45 days
Average weight	1-3kg/2¼-6½lb
Vegetarian	✗
Shape	⬜

Queso del Cebreiro or Cebrero

This oddly-shaped cheese from Galicia defies description – it looks like a cross between a squashed chef's hat and a huge mushroom with a thick stalk. But it is simple to make. The fresh curd is piled into cheesecloth, the corners are twisted and knotted, and then a narrow wooden hoop is slipped over the top. The hoop is not tall enough to enclose all the young curd which spills over the sides creating the mushroom effect. The pale, straw-coloured, crusty rind has a buttery aroma, while the interior is close-textured and granular but spreadable, with a fairly sharp rustic flavour, almost like yoghurt. This is the result of allowing the milk to sour rather than using rennet for coagulation.

Spain	Galicia
Milk source	
Unpasteurized	✗
Maturing time	3-4 days
Average weight	1 or 2kg 2¼ or 4½lb
Vegetarian	✗
Shape	

Raclette

Raclette, more than any other cheese, conjures up the joy of eating and demonstrates the profound influence that climate has on the types of cheese made. High in the Alps, cheese has been the staple diet for centuries. Traditionally, a half-wheel of Raclette would be propped up in front of the family fire, exposing the cut surface to the heat. Once the smooth interior had begun to blister, with the aid of a *racler* (scraper), the cheese would flow like lava into waiting bowls of steaming, boiled potatoes. Intensified by heat, the cheese oozes flavour – nutty, sweet and slightly fruity. The savoury farmyard rind becomes crunchy and proves irresistible, as any skier or climber will attest.

France	Savoie
Milk source	
Unpasteurized	✓
Maturing time	10-14 weeks
Average weight	6.5-8kg 14¼-17½lb
Vegetarian	✗
Shape	

Raschera DOC

The best Raschera are made in the alpine pastures and are labelled *'di alpessio'* and are square rather than round. The rind is thin and leathery, with a reddish or even yellow hue, and the texture is supple and elastic. The newly formed curd is bundled into cloth, placed in moulds, and pressed for 10 minutes, then turned out, milled and repressed for one to five days. Generally made with the sweet milk of the Piedmontese cow, Raschera has a pale ivory interior scattered with tiny holes which occasionally have a bluish tinge. Spring and summer cheeses are buttery, nutty, sweet and fresh, whereas winter produces a stronger, more solid cheese with a 'wet dog' aroma and a more aromatic, tart, salty finish.

Italy	Cuneo
Milk source	
Unpasteurized	✓
Maturing time	1-3 months
Average weight	7-10kg 15½-22lb
Vegetarian	✗
Shape	

St-Andrew's (washed-rind)

It seems the Vikings, or perhaps the wild, independent Scots, scared away the monks, for there is no record of any Trappist-style cheeses being made in Scotland until the early 1980s. Fascinated by the process, Graeme Webster of Howgate Cheese started cheesemaking in Dundee with the help of a young French cheesemaker. After establishing a market for their Scottish Camembert, they became more ambitious, and eventually St-Andrew's was born. Named after the patron saint of Scotland and the nearby home of golf, its distinctive deep-orange rind, supple, 'holey' texture and sweet-sour, slightly yeasty taste has found a ready market in Scotland and abroad.

Scotland	Perthshire
Milk source	🐄
Unpasteurized	✗
Maturing time	8-10 weeks
Average weight	2kg/5lb
Vegetarian	✓
Shape	⬭

St-Nectaire AOC

History is ingrained in the character of the people and the villages of the rugged Auvergne mountains, where the breezes carry the scent of thousands of wild flowers and native grasses from the valleys to the small mountain chalets. Here, cheese is still made following the tradition of centuries, and the ancestry of the cattle is as important as that of the people. The voluptuous cheese is cured on a bed of straw for eight weeks and seems to absorb some of its earthy, pastoral aromas. Like a large version of Reblochon, it is creamy, rich, and redolent of freshly cut grass, sweet hay, meadow flowers and wild herbs. An oval label indicates a *fermier* cheese, a square label an *industriel* cheese.

France	Auvergne
Milk source	🐄
Unpasteurized	✓
Maturing time	3-8 weeks
Average weight	1.5-1.8kg 3lb 5oz-4lb
Vegetarian	✗
Shape	⬭

San Simon

The vast chain of mountains which spread from the Atlantic to the Mediterranean coast have prevented many outsiders from reaching Galicia. As a consequence, the region's ancient culture and customs, including that of cheesemaking, have survived. This does not explain, however, why two of the best-known cheeses of the region – San Simon and Tetilla – bear a remarkable resemblance to breasts. Some more modest historians insist the cheeses were modelled on the mountains. The cheese has a supple, creamy, open consistency and rich buttery taste, with a slight acidity on the finish. Its attractive reddish brown, polished exterior, and slightly woody taste, are a result of gentle smoking.

Spain	Galicia
Milk source	
Unpasteurized	✗
Maturing time	2-4 weeks
Average weight	1kg/2¼lb
Vegetarian	✗
Shape	

La Serena (washed-rind)

Estremadura, 'the land of Extremes', provides winter pastures for the native Merino sheep. This breed has been long respected for its meat, wool and rich milk, which is in season from November until early May, when the infertile plain becomes a desolate land of scorched grass. 'Ladies Bed Straw', a wild flower, is used to coagulate the rich, creamy milk, adding a herbaceous quality to its lovely nutty acidity and distinct sheepy smell, ensuring the cheese develops a soft, almost spoonable, consistency. Yeasty and more pungent than Reblochon, La Serena is round, with a yellowish pink crust which bears the imprint of the plaited belt of *esparto* grass in which the cheese is contained while it drains.

Spain	**Estremadura**
Milk source	
Unpasteurized	✓
Maturing time	2-3 months
Average weight	1kg/2¼lb
Vegetarian	✓
Shape	

Serra da Estrela (washed-rind)

This cheese is rarely found outside of Portugal and it is still made by mountain shepherds who follow ancient traditions, using the native thistle to coagulate the milk and maturing the cheeses in caves. Beneath the fine, leathery, orange-brown rind, the cheese is soft and voluptuous. One mouthful reveals its magnificent, rich, perfumed intensity – a result of the superb grazing in the rocky wilderness. The sweet, slightly burnt-toffee character of the milk comes through on the finish, which is distinct but not as strong as you would expect. Sadly, the solitary lifestyle of the shepherds holds little appeal for the next generation, and like many of Europe's ancient cheeses, Serra da Estrela is threatened with extinction.

Portugal	**Beira**
Milk source	
Unpasteurized	✓
Maturing time	1-4 months
Average weight	1kg/2¼lb
Vegetarian	✗
Shape	

Stinking Bishop (washed-rind)

Not for the faint-hearted, this is a wonderfuly eccentric cheese created by an equally eccentric, quintessential English gentleman, Charles Martell. Unlike the traditional Double Gloucester, Charles's first cheese, Stinking Bishop, is aromatic, pungent, almost meaty, and oozes with flavour, while the velvety smooth interior is almost spoonable. Be careful not to discard the glistening pale orange-yellow rind, which will stick to the wrapper if you are not careful, as this is the best bit. This award-winning cheese is a recent invention, similar to Munster, but washed and rubbed with perry (an alcoholic drink made with a rare variety of pears called 'Stinking Bishop').

England	**Gloucestershire**
Milk source	
Unpasteurized	✗
Maturing time	6-8 weeks
Average weight	1.8kg/4lb
Vegetarian	✓
Shape	⬭

Taconic

Coming from a computer background, Jonathan White loves to
experiment, and has created cheeses of distinction and originality.
His latest creation, made in partnership with some fairly wild moulds,
is Taconic, an Iraquoi name given to the mountains between New York
and Massachusetts. The cheese starts life as a large brick but, once the
battle begins in earnest between bacteria, yeast and moulds, the thick
but expandable leathery rind can barely contain the supple, squidgey
interior. Flavoursome, rich and buttery, it has a fresh, green-grassy taste
and a lovely bitter sting on the finish. Jonathan's other cheeses include
Muscoot, Amawalk, Hudson and Wild Ripened Cheddar.

US	New York
Milk source	
Unpasteurized	✗
Maturing time	4 weeks
Average weight	3.2kg/7lb
Vegetarian	✗
Shape	

Taleggio DOC

When I first tasted Taleggio, named after a valley near Bergamo where it
originated, I found it dull, slightly salty, rubbery and grainy. Not until I
visited Lake Como years later did I discover the magic of this cheese –
aged in caves and made with milk from the cattle that graze the alpine
pastures. Beneath its rosy crust the curd had almost reached melting
point, exuding a gentle but insistent fragrant aroma and taste of sweet
hay – like eating a rich, cream of asparagus soup or broccoli sauce. So
why had I found it dull? Because sadly most cheeses are sold under-ripe
or over-the-top and eaten before they come to room temperature – killing
or hiding their true character.

Italy	Lombardy
Milk source	
Unpasteurized	✓✗
Maturing time	25-50 days
Average weight	2kg/4½lb
Vegetarian	✗
Shape	

Tamié (washed-rind)

Since the Middle Ages, the lives of the monks at the Abbaye de Tamié
have revolved around the principles of simplicity, solitude and
cheesemaking – their main source of income. The superb quality
milk, mainly from a very old breed of cows, 'La Tarine', comes from
just 20 farms in the area, one of which produces only 40 litres (70½
pints) a day. Similar to Reblochon, the rind of Tamié is a sticky pinkish-
orangey brown and the aroma is sweet, farmyardy and earthy. Tamié is
soft and supple and has a sweet herbaceous, vaguely nutty, flavour with
a rich fragrant tang. The cheese comes wrapped distinctively in blue
paper which is printed with the white cross of Malta.

France	Haute-Savoie
Milk source	
Unpasteurized	✓
Maturing time	1-2 months
Average weight	500g or 1.3kg 1lb 2oz or 3lb
Vegetarian	✗
Shape	

Teleme

The first time I tasted Teleme it had been ripened to perfection – its pale pinkish rind was by then mottled with numerous moulds and yeasts. It was literally bursting at the seams and, like a tidal wave, moved single-mindedly across the cheeseboard towards me. The taste conjured up conflicting images of meadow flowers and wild game, with a tart, sour-cream, yeasty finish. Its gooey texture is softer than Reblochon but firmer than Mont d'Or (page 93). The cheese was introduced by Greek immigrants, based on a goat's milk cheese, Telemes, and is only made by two companies. The one I tasted was made by the Peluso family, which has been making Tomales Bay Teleme for three generations.

US	California
Milk source	
Unpasteurized	✗
Maturing time	2-3 months
Average weight	5kg/11lb
Vegetarian	✓
Shape	

Tetilla DO

Galicia, the northwest corner of Spain, on the Atlantic coast, is steeped in history and has an abundance of rich, lush rolling hillsides which make ideal grazing for the Friesian and indigenous Gallega cows whose milk must be used in the making of Tetilla. Bearing a remarkable resemblance to a breast or a fig, Tetilla has a thin yellow exterior which is finely ridged but, unlike its taller cousin San Simon, it is not smoked. The cheese is creamy but rarely bland, and has a fresh, lemony tang with a hint of green grass and a supple consistency, rather like Monterey Jack or young Gouda. It is delicious when eaten with one of Spain's fruit 'cheeses', such as the local figs and walnuts pressed together with aniseed.

Spain	Galicia
Milk source	
Unpasteurized	✗
Maturing time	2-3 weeks
Average weight	750g-1.7kg 1lb 10oz-3¾lb
Vegetarian	✗
Shape	

Toma Piemontese DOC

Toma, the name used to describe a number of similar cheeses made in northwest Italy, is very like its French counterparts, the Tommes of Savoie. These are simple mountain cheeses, whose thin yellowish rinds appear to be stretched almost to bursting point, holding back the voluptuous, custard-like interiors. Impregnated with tiny holes, Toma simply melts in the mouth, revealing its gentle sweet-sour nature hinting at fresh cream, white wine and wild flowers with a distinctly nutty finish, getting tangier and spicier with age. A few cheesemakers, I am told, still filter the milk carefully through washed and boiled moss, ferns and nettles which impart their own wonderful perfume to the milk.

Italy	Piedmont
Milk source	
Unpasteurized	✓
Maturing time	a few days to 12 months plus
Average weight	2-4kg/4½-8¾lb
Vegetarian	✗
Shape	

Tomme de Savoie

I adore Tomme de Savoie, with its thick, furry, grey rind interspersed with yellow, white, red and orange blotches. Each mould contributes to the complexity of this ancient cheese. Beneath the rind awaits a medley of flavours that play across the tastebuds, fading in seconds to be replaced with others which defy you to name them – smoke, sweet flowers, herbs, fresh milk and walnuts. The best cheeses are labelled *lait cru* (raw milk). Traditionally, Tomme was made from the thick winter milk, while the cows were cosseted in their snug barns. In summer, when the cows grazed the mountain meadows, their milk was combined to produce one of France's most popular cheeses, Beaufort (*see* Hard Cheeses).

France	Savoie
Milk source	🐄
Unpasteurized	✓
Maturing time	6-12 weeks
Average weight	1.5-3kg 3lb 5oz-6½lb
Vegetarian	✗
Shape	⬭

Washed-rind

A former architect, Fred Leppin entered the mystical and frustrating world of cheese in the late 1980s. A one-day cheesemaking course provided the inspiration and the basics to start experimenting, which he did in the kitchen, driving his wife to distraction. Out of the frying pan and into a purpose-built factory on the farm, he found the concentrated flavour of the Red Shorthorn milk (*see* Allerdale page 116) combined with the drier climate resulted in a cheese of very different qualities to those of Europe. The meaty, pungent aroma and the soft, spring texture is similar to Epoisses (pages 78-9), but the flavour is less aggressive and seems to have absorbed the warm, vaguely minty aroma of the eucalyptus trees.

Australia	Victoria
Milk source	🐄
Unpasteurized	✗
Maturing time	2 months
Average weight	3kg/6½lb
Vegetarian	✗
Shape	⬭

Wigmore (washed-curd)

Anne Wigmore of Village Maid Cheese is a gifted cheesemaker producing masterpieces that find their way into the list of award winners at the British Cheese Awards each year. Combining tradition with technology, Anne brings out the subtleties and nuances of flavour in the raw milk. Smear ripened, the cheeses develop a pinkish-brown to grey-brown, uneven, wrinkled rind that has a yeasty, slightly sour aroma. Like Gouda, the curd is washed to remove excess whey, creating a low-acid cheese, but there the similarity between Wigmore and Gouda ends. Wigmore develops a voluptuous, smooth, supple consistency that is a taste sensation – wild flowers, burnt caramel, macadamia nuts and roast lamb.

England	Berkshire
Milk source	🐑
Unpasteurized	✓
Maturing time	6-10 weeks
Average weight	450g or 2kg 1lb or 4½lb
Vegetarian	✓
Shape	⬭

Semi-soft

Cheese name	Country of origin	Region	Milk source
Abbaye de la Coudre	France	Maine	Cow
Arthurs	England	Somerset	Ewe
Bagnes *see* Raclette	Switzerland	Valais	Cow
Beaumont	France	Savoie	Cow
Beauvoorde	Belguim	Flanders	Cow
Bergues	France	Pas de Calais	Cow
Bishop Gold	England	Somerset	Buffalo
Butterkäse	Germany	Various	Cow
Cantabria	Spain	Cantabria	DO Cow
Castlefarm Ballinlough	Ireland	Co Limerick	Goat
Chamberand	France	Dauphine	Cow
Chimay Vieux	Belgium	Chimay	Cow
Cloisters	England	Gloucestershire	Cow
Criffel	Scotland	Dumfries & Galloway	Cow
Crofton	England	Cumbria	Cow & goat
Croghan	Ireland	Co Wexford	Goat
Crowley	US	Vermont	Cow
Dauphin	France	Nord-Pas-de-Calais	Cow
Echourgnac	France	Perigord	Cow
Elsberg	New Zealand	Taranaki	Cow
Entrammes	France	Loire	Cow
Esrom	Denmark		Cow
Formai de Mut	Italy	Bergamo	Cow
Fromage à Raclette	Switzerland		Cow
Fromage Corse	France	Corsica	Ewe & goat
Géromé *see* Munster AOC	France	Alsace	Cow
Gräddost	Sweden		Cow
Grataron d'Areches	France	Savoie	Goat
Gris de Lille	France	Nord-Pas-de-Calais	Cow
Hansi	France	Alsace	Cow
Hushållsost	Sweden		Cow
Iambors	England	Somerset	Buffalo
Junas	England	Somerset	Buffalo
Lajta	Hungary		Cow
Le Fium'Orbo	France	Corsica	Ewe & goat
Loddiswell Avondale	England	Devon	Goat
Maasdam	Holland		Cow
Mamirolle	France	Franche-Comté	Cow
Maredsous	Belgium	Denee	Cow
Mont des Chats	France	Flanders	Cow
Mossholder Cheese	US	Wisconsin	Cow
Muenster	US	Wisconsin	Cow

Münster	Germany		Cow
Munster au Cumin	France	Alsace	Cow
Murolait	France	Auvergne	Cow
Muscoot	US	New York	Cow
Norsewood Goat	New Zealand	Rangiuru	Goat
Passendale	Belgium	Flanders	Cow
Pavé d'Auge/Moyaux	France	Normandy	Cow
Pierre qui Vire	France	Burgundy	Cow
Plateau de Herve	Belgium	Herve	Cow
Port-du-Salut	France	Loire	Cow
Postel	Belgium	Postel	Cow
Puant Macéré see Gris de Lille	France	Flanders	Cow
Remedou	Belgium	Liège	Cow
Ridder	Norway		Cow
Rollot	France	Picardie	Cow
Romadur/Romadurkäse	Germany		Cow
Romney Mature	Australia	Victoria	Ewe
Rubens	Belgium	Lo	Cow
Samsø	Denmark		Cow
Sonoma Jack	US	California	Cow
Soumaintrain	France	Burgundy	Cow
St-David's	Wales	Gwent	Cow
St-Paulin	France	Various	Cow
Stracchino	Italy	Lombardy	Cow
Tomme au Marc de Raisin	France	Savoie	Cow
Tomme de Chevret	Australia	New South Wales	Goat
Tortadel Casar	Spain	Badajoz	Ewe
Torville	England	Somerset	Cow
Tourrée de l'Aubier	France	Normandy	Cow
Trami d'Alsace	France	Alsace	Cow
Tronchon	Spain	Aragon	Ewe, cow or goat
Tutunmaa	Finland		Cow
Vacherin d'Abondance Fermier	France	Haute-Savoie	Cow
Vacherin des Bauges	France	Savoie	Cow
Vacherin Mont d'Or	Switzerland	Vaud	Cow
Vieux Lille	France	Flanders	Cow
Villalon or Pata de Mulo	Spain	Castile-León	Ewe
Waimana	New Zealand	Christchurch	Cow
Waterloo	England	Berkshire	Cow
Woodside Charleston	Australia	Adelaide	Cow

Hard cheeses

Above: Parmigiano Reggiano being moved to cool storage, where it will spend a minimum of 24 months.

Continental Europeans treat hard cheeses as 'table cheeses' and the cheese is placed on the table at most meals. Cheese may be the major part of the meal or eaten as a snack before, during or after the meal. English-speaking countries, however, seem to be obsessed with cooking with cheese rather than simply eating it, and often view it as dowdy and mundane. This is why the British eat significantly less cheese than the rest of Europe.

Modernization has not helped traditional British cheeses. The time and labour costs involved in producing them by hand are high compared with the cost of producing cheeses mechanically in blocks. Mechanically produced cheeses can stored in plastic to avoid weight loss and do not require turning as frequently. This significantly reduces the cheese's price as well as its texture and flavour.

Many of Europe's traditional hard cheeses are factory made, but the difference is not as marked.

They retain more or less the same shape, texture and taste; only the subtleties of taste are lost due to pasteurization, blending of milk from different farms or mechanized cutting of the curd. (*See* pages 15-17 to see how traditional Cheddar is made).

Some cheeses, such as Cheshire and Lancashire, are then lightly pressed, giving a moist, crumbly texture, while Cheddar is more firmly pressed to achieve a harder, more homogenous texture. European cheeses may be pressed or, in the case of Parmesan, placed in a brine bath for 21 days, where the action of the salt draws out the whey.

The more moisture that is removed, the longer the maturation period and the greater the intensity of flavour. This is because the fat and protein are broken down into their more simple form, releasing a complexity of flavours – the fat, protein, minerals and ashes gradually break down during the process of fermentation and ageing. Large cheeses tend to take months, or even years, to reach maturity.

As the cheeses age, their textures and tastes slowly change. Initially the curd is young, flexible, slightly acid or buttery sweet; with age, it becomes more intense, fruity, mouth-wateringly tangy, harder, drier and, in some cases such as Parmesan or Dry Jack, granular, as the cheese salts crystallize, giving the cheese a crunchy feel in the mouth.

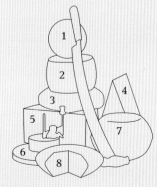

1 *Garrotxa*
2 *Pecorino*
3 *Mahon*
4 *Gabriel*
5 *Beaufort*
6 *Tête-de-Moine*
    (shaved on girolle*)*
7 *Berkswell*
8 *Ashdown Forresters*
(see Duddleswell*)*

Cheddar

England	Somerset
Milk source	
Unpasteurized	✓✗
Maturing time	4 months
Average weight	25.5kg/56lb
Vegetarian	✗
Shape	

The story of Cheddar can be traced right back to the Romans, who originally introduced hard cheeses to Britain. But it was not until the 16th Century that this cow's milk cheese, made in the Mendip Hills near Cheddar Gorge in the county of Somerset, became known as Cheddar.

Cheddar is the greatest of Britain's famous native cheeses, with its sweet, creamy, rich and complex scent and flavour. It can weigh as much as 41-54kg/90-120lb, and requires up to five years to reach maturity. Probably the biggest Cheddar ever made weighed 559kg/11 hundred-weight and measured 284cm/nine feet four inches in circumference and 51cm/20 inches high, and was presented to Queen Victoria in the late 18th Century.

English cheese, however, has not always been given good press. Ben Johnson's character Abel Drugger, a tobacconist in *The Alchemist* (1610), is accused of foul breath and having an exceptionally bad case of worms as a result of eating too much cheese. Shakespeare was also hard pushed to find a complimentary word for it and Mrs Beeton was dismissive in her *Book of Household Management* (1861): 'Cheese in its commonest shape is only fit for sedentary people, as an after dinner stimulant, and in very small quantity'.

By the early 1700s, the types of English cheeses that exist today were broadly established, and cheeses were either shipped from ports around Britain or transported by coach or barge up and down the country. Oddly, the advent of the railway proved to be a retrograde step for farmhouse cheeses in Britain. Suddenly liquid milk could be transported from farm to city, and the necessity of preserving milk by the labour-intensive process of converting it into cheese was no longer necessary. This coincided with the establishment of cheese factories and the large scale emigration from the farming community.

The factories provided a steady income for dairy farmers, many of whom turned their backs on cheesemaking forever, and by the end of the 19th Century a third of Cheddar consumed was imported from Canada, New Zealand, America and Australia. The First World War and the post-war economy were not conducive to small-scale cheesemaking, but it was the Second World War that had the most damaging effect on British farmhouse cheesemaking.

With labour and food in short supply, the British Ministry of Food was created to make the most of national resources. Regrettably, in their wisdom, they decided that all milk, should be transported to the factories and made into hard cheeses. In retrospect, this was an uneconomical use of fuel and milk as the

Left: When the pressed Cheddars are removed from the metal hoops, they are wrapped in cloth and sealed with lard.

British Cheddar has a reputation for its sweet, creamy, rich and complex scent and flavour.

Despite being copied the world over, cheese is never really Cheddar unless it comes from the green and verdant hills that are England, and more especially from Dorset, Devon and Somerset. For generations, Cheddar has been an integral part of the English diet, in sandwiches, simple snacks or as the solid dependable chunks proudly displayed on an oak sideboard or simple platter, embellished with Cox's Pippin apples, celery and the occasional oat cake.

To taste an unpasteurized, handmade, clothbound Cheddar is to taste a piece of England. The bite is like chocolate, firm and yielding; the aroma is fresh, nutty and slightly savoury; the flavours differ from farm to farm, but there is always the rich sweetness of the milk, a classic acid tang and a long lingering kaleidoscope of flavours normally only associated with a fine wine.

labour force (mainly women) was ready and able to make cheese on farms. Furthermore, transporting a shipment of cheese made more sense than transporting its much bulkier and more fragile equivalent in milk to a distant factory to make cheese.

Cheese finally came off the British ration books in 1954, but the revival of farmhouse cheeses would not take place until the late 1980s, despite efforts of the government to put things right. Of the 333 traditional Cheddar makers recorded in 1939, there were 57 remaining after the Second World War, and today there are just six. Using the same methods, they each produce Cheddars of distinction. Although the quality and texture of block Cheddars has improved enormously, big cheesemakers can never, like huge wine producers, match the individuality obtained by making cheese by hand and wrapping it in cloth.

The Cheddar flavour

The flavour of Cheddar is built up over months of silent activity. Tiny bacteria, enzymes and acids break down billions of molecules to create the flavours. Watching cows munching their way through the grasses of an English pasture, one can see why

THE FINEST CHEDDARS

Montgomery's (Somerset): An explosion of flavours with a superb richness, spicy green acidity, and real depth to the fruity finish. British Cheese Awards (BCA) 1996 and 1997 Best Cheddar.

Quicke's (Devon): Firm, chewy, buttery texture; tangy, nutty, complex aromas; a suggestion of green grass and fresh hay in the mouth. BCA Gold 1994-1995.

Keen's (Somerset): Full, complex flavour. Hints of liquorice, nutty, smooth and creamy, green fresh tang, melts in the mouth. BCA 1995 and 1997 Gold Medal.

Chewton (Somerset): An explosion of flavour – nutty, rounded, strong but not sharp or vicious, with a savoury cheese-and-onion tang and a hint of butter. BCA 1994 and 1995 Best Cheddar.

Green's (Somerset): Savoury cheese-and-onion; fragrant, tangy. BCA 1998 Best Cheddar.

Denhay (Dorset): A nutty, rich Cheddar with a strong savoury tang, the small truckle is particularly popular. BCA 1998 Gold Medal.

Parmigiano Reggiano

Italy

Milk source	
Unpasteurized	✓
Maturing time	**18-48 months**
Average weight	**24-40kg 50-83lb**
Vegetarian	✗
Shape	

The secret of the continuing success of Parmigiano Reggiano in a world obsessed with volume and modernization, is the determination of the Consortium to adhere to old methods, barely changed since the 12th Century. Even the cows' diet is controlled – no silage or turnips, only fresh grass, hay or alfalfa. The enforcement of these rules adds to the production cost, but the result is a cheese whose flavour and quality is guaranteed.

The aroma of Parmigiano Reggiano is sweet and fruity, the colour sandy yellow and the taste exquisite, filling the mouth with an explosion of delicate yet intense flavours, from fresh pineapple to caramelized onions. It is brittle and crumbly, with tiny crunchy crystals of calcium lactate.

As far back as the 1st Century, the Romans recognized that cheese, like wine, is influenced by the soil and climate. Even the smallest change in the cheesemaking process will influence the final outcome. Yet many people today believe this is a romantic notion of a few misguided food writers, or just marketing hype.

Parmigiano cheeses are made in 830 small dairies or *caselli,* which produce only 10 to 15 cheeses

per day, maintaining a close relationship between each batch of milk and its transformation into cheese. These dairies are within precisely defined areas of Parma, Reggio Emilia (from which it derives its name), Modena, Bologna and Mantua. Those produced elsewhere are called Grana (hard cheese) or Grana Lodigano (Lodi), Grana Piacentino (Piacenza) and the more common Grana Padano from the Po valley. Parmesan, a generic term, describes a multitude of cheeses made like Parmigiano, but in huge mechanized plants at the expense of the extraordinary flavour and character of authentic Parmigiano.

In Italy it is sold in rough, granite-like chunks chiselled from the magnificent shiny drums with the name emblazoned on the antique-looking rind.

The recipe

The evening milk is poured into copper cauldrons capable of holding 240 litres/100 gallons. The cream is skimmed off for Mascarpone and by morning the milk will have started to sour, providing a starter for the morning milk (to which it is added). Skimming off the cream reduces the fat content (about 32 per cent compared with Cheddar, made with full milk, at 35). A starter may be added to speed the development of lactic acid, and then the milk is gently heated until the acidity and temperature are ready for renneting.

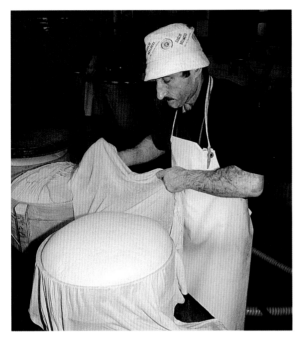

Above: The curd is placed in wooden moulds lined with cloth. Any creases and the cheese will be rejected by the grader.

Coagulation is quick (12 to 15 minutes), and after it the curd is cut up using a *spino* (a series of circular knives), which turns and breaks the curd into small, wheat-sized granules. The curd is then heated in the whey until it settles on the bottom of the cauldron.

Raising the mass requires two strong men and an even stronger piece of cloth, knotted and slung over a wooden rod. The curd is cut in two and hung for 24 hours to drain. The cheeses at this stage weigh about 40kg/88¼lb (they reduce over the next couple of years to between 30 and 35kg/66 and 77lb). The outside is lightly rubbed with salt, wrapped in fresh cloth and fitted into wooden moulds, not unlike small beer barrels, held together by a wooden toggle and rope. The cheeses are then lightly pressed over three days.

To prevent the cheeses from drying out over the next 18 to 48 months, they are floated in brine baths for around 21 days, then moved to storerooms, where they are constantly brushed, turned, checked and rechecked. After 12 months the cheeses are officially tested by an expert with a small hammer, a cheese iron that looks a little like a corkscrew, and a highly developed sense of smell and taste. The reverberations of the hammer reveal the level of quality and development the cheese has attained. Those that have developed internal splits or cracks will not ring true and will be relegated to grated Parmesan or Grana. The expert will also take a 'core' sample from each batch with his cheese iron. The aromas released after years inside the rock-hard rind are magical.

The words Parmigiano Reggiano are branded on the rind so that even a small piece can be easily identified. The final cheese, at least 18, and usually 24, months old, is higher in protein than any other cheese, yet it is low in cholesterol and saturated fats. It is also rich in calcium, phosphorous and vitamins and, because of the long maturation period, it is easily digestible. Never discard the rind – it adds flavour to any soup or casserole.

PARMIGIANO FACTS

Parmigiano will keep for months in a refrigerator, but the rough surface may grow some mould, so if you have bought a large chunk or use it rarely (an unthinkable possibility), grate it straight from the freezer. It will quickly defrost on a hot dish.

It is no coincidence that some of the finest hams come from areas renowned for their hard cheeses. The whey left over from Parmigiano, Manchego and several other European hard cheeses is not wasted, but fed to the local pigs. The result is sweet, luscious hams such as Parma, Serrano and Jambon de Bayonne.

It is quite common for small Parmigiano producers, unable to bear the cost of holding stock, either sell their cheeses to the Consortium or to their banks, who store the 'edible gold' as collateral.

Emmental

Switzerland	Central cantons
Milk source	
Unpasteurized	✓
Maturing time	4-18 months
Average weight	80-120kg 166-250lb
Vegetarian	✗
Shape	⬭

It is no coincidence that the Swiss landscape has retained its charm, with chalets, pine forests and small parcels of lush, green pastures. It is the result of Swiss agricultural policy to ensure farms are small and family owned. To achieve this, farmers receive subsidies towards keeping cattle, farming and summer grazing in the mountains. The result is that cheese is made in village dairies rather than factories. Meanwhile, to extract maximum benefit from the lowlands, cows are fed indoors, even in summer, so their hooves cannot trample the grass. Hence, the magnificent scenery, protection from erosion and avalanche, a healthy farming economy and superb cheeses, including Emmental – a deep sunshine-yellow cheese which, when squeezed, releases a sweet wine aroma and the perfume of a million meadow flowers.

Nor is it any coincidence that huge, hard cheeses are made in the alpine regions of Switzerland and neighbouring countries. The shepherds spend the summer in remote, mountain huts, and need to make cheeses that require months to mature. So for centuries they have pooled their milk to make the wheels of cheese which could be taken down the mountain with the cows before the first snowfall in autumn.

The average production of 80 cows is 1,000 litres/ 1220 gallons of milk per day, the amount required to make one 85kg/187lb Emmental. As the average herd is 10 to 15 cows, it takes the milk of six to eight farms

to make one cheese per day. Co-operatives normally involve 20 to 30 farmers and produce three to five cheeses daily. Some of these co-operatives date back to before the Swiss Confederation, and were the force behind the Swiss State as we know it today.

The recipe

Once the milk reaches 31°C/88°F the starter culture is added, followed by the rennet, which takes 40 minutes to curdle the milk. The cheesemaker runs the cutter or cheese harp – a wide rectangular frame with about 40 evenly spaced wires running end to end – through the milk, which now resembles yoghurt, chopping the curd into progressively small pieces or cheese grains.

The contents of the vat are stirred for 90 minutes, heated to around 52°C/126°F to harden the grains, then pumped into huge moulds, which have the same circumference as Emmental (81-89cm/32 to 35 inches) but are nearly three times the its final height. Much of the whey has already drained off before hydraulic presses force the excess whey through the moulds' fine metal sieves. The pressing takes around 20 hours.

Next the cheeses are immersed in brine baths for two days, where they absorb salt, discharge more

Left: Cows can sometimes be seen grazing Swiss pastures, but they are generally feed indoors, in barns.

featuring the country of origin, the name of the cheese and the alpenhorn-blower symbol common to all Swiss cheeses. The yellow-beige rind is also branded with a dairy identification number to ensure traceability.

With a similar rind to Gruyère, but smoother and more elastic, the aroma of Emmental is sweeter with hushed tones of fresh, cut hay and old cheese. Squeeze the deep sunshine yellow cheese to smell the sweet, wine aroma that continues on to the palate – very fruity with a mouth-tingling acidity. The perfume of a million meadow flowers is aroused like a breeze when the cheese is first cut. Gruyère, equal in quality to Emmental, is more dense, stronger and creamier. It is also nutty rather than fruity and has no holes.

Copied the world over, no cheese can equal the magnificent wheels that proudly carry the name of the country whose rich mountain pastures and rules of manufacture have protected their quality and character for centuries.

whey, and the rind begins to form. Once salted, the cheeses are stored at 10-14°C/50-57°F for between 10 and 14 days, then warmed to 18-20°C/64-68°F before spending between four and six weeks at 20-23°C/68-73°F. The rise in temperature is a signal to the tiny bacteria in the starter culture, previously dormant, to wake up, and a vigorous acid fermentation ensues. The almost feverish activity beneath the hard, smooth, leathery rind, produces bubbles of carbonic acid gas, creating the holes for which Emmental is famous and contributing to the subtle hint of nuts and fruity tang.

Now the cheese is moved to cooler storage, where it is cleaned, brushed and turned regularly for three and a half months before being graded. The grading is based on the number, size and distribution of the holes, and is done by tapping each cheese with a tiny hammer. The experts can tell from the resonance whether the cheese has smooth, round, evenly spread hazelnut-sized holes (considered to be the best), or clusters of oval, uneven holes, which will never achieve the depth and character of the very best. If you find an Emmental that has a tiny drop or 'tear' in the hole, it will be as near to perfect as possible.

At their peak (determined by the grader), the cheeses are cleaned and marked with a red pattern

'CHEESE' IN DIFFERENT LANGUAGES

Brindza	Romania
Cacio	Italy (old word for cheese)
Formaggio	Italy
Fromage	France
Jibneh	Jordan/Lebanon
Juusto	Finland
Kaas	Holland
Käse	Germany
Ost	Denmark, Norway, Sweden
Panir	India
Peynir	Turkey
Queijo	Portugal/Brazil
Queso	Spain/Mexico
Sajt	Hungary
Ser	Poland
Sir	Yugoslavia and Russia
Sirene	Bulgaria
Tiri	Greece

Manchego DOC

Spain	Castilla-La Mancha
Milk source	
Unpasteurized	✓
Maturing time	**min 60 days**
Average weight	**2.3-5kg/5-10lb**
Vegetarian	✗
Shape	

When I first travelled in Spain I was struck by the diversity of its sheep. Their shape, colour, size and wool varies from region to region. From Castile-León, with its high altitude, extremes of climate and the distinctive milk of the small, scruffy Churro and Castilian sheep, comes nearly 85 per cent of Spain's pure sheep's milk cheeses, including Queso Castellano and Queso Zamorano. The more lush mountain pastures of the Basque country are home to Lacha sheep, with their knotty dreadlocks and rich milk which produces Idiazábal cheese.

For a cheese to qualify for the famous DOC Manchego label, it must be made only from the thick, aromatic milk of the hardy La Mancha sheep, whose summer grazing is on the vast, barren plains of La Mancha.

The legend of Don Quixote first inspired me to visit La Mancha, the land of his heroic deeds as he protected the shepherds, his favourite cheese and their flock from marauding bandits. Baptised by the Arabs Al Mansha (land without water), La Mancha is the biggest region in Spain, with its mountains and vast, barren plains, scorched by temperatures of up to 50°C/122°F. In recent years the region has been been irrigated, and miles of verdant vineyards, olive groves,

high-yield crops and dilapidated windmills have replaced much of the indigenous shrubs, acorns, blackthorn, vetch and wild grasses.

Despite this, much of the natural, uncultivated land still exists and provides summer grazing for the hardy La Mancha sheep, whose milk gives Manchego its character. In autumn and winter their diet is supplemented by sweet autumn tendrils from the vines and the stubble from the crops and hay.

The modernization of Manchego

Known and highly respected since the time of the Romans, who probably introduced this style of cheesemaking, Manchego has changed little. However, to meet the growing demands of the local and export markets and to comply with EEC regulations, large, modern co-operatives have been set up. As the milk is transported over long distances, it must be pasteurized, but only a confirmed addict, such as Don Quixote, could distinguish the difference.

Most Manchego is now made in factories, but milking is still largely done by hand in stone barns or open corrals. The farm I visited made its own cheese. It had a flock of 2,000 sheep, divided into three groups so that about 600 sheep could be milked every day of the year. The ewe is lifted off her back feet, her milk-swollen udder overhangs the

Above: Herds of La Mancha sheep can be seen moving across the barren plains and foothills in search of grazing.

bucket that is attached to the shepherd's three-legged stool, and milking takes a few minutes. Some 700 sheep were caught and milked by four shepherds in one and a half hours when I was there – an awe-inspiring experience.

The cheese is made each morning and then stored in stone barns, sometimes dug into the sides of the limestone hills. Here a multitude of moulds and wild yeasts gather on the rind, aiding the ripening process and imparting their own character to the process.

To qualify for the famous DOC Manchego label, only the milk of the La Mancha sheep can be used. Each cheese must bear the classic zigzag markings along the sides and the 'flor' flower design on the top and bottom. Originally, these were made by encircling the fresh curd with a wide band of plaited *esparto* grass and placing the cheese on hand-carved wooden boards to drain. Regrettably, the wooden boards and the traditional plait are rapidly being replaced by round plastic moulds which have the distinctive patterns imprinted on the inside and on their base. They seem rather incongruous, hanging up to dry against the background of stone walls and rustic surroundings.

The texture of the ivory-coloured interior of the cheese must be firm and dry, yet rich and creamy, dotted with small irregular eyes. The depth and complexity depends on the ageing period, but there is a richness of brazil nuts and burnt caramel, the aroma of lanolin and roast lamb, while the cheese is salty on the finish. In those that reach a great age there is a peppery bite to the finish and, if cut in thin wedges and marinated in the strong aromatic local green olive oi –l *en aciete* – the flavour is intensified.

Manchego is sold at various stages of maturity, but usually not before 13 weeks, when it is described as *curado* (cured). At over three months it is referred to as *viejo* (aged). The distinctive rind gathers a multitude of moulds, and must be washed and scrubbed before being coated in wax. The colour of the wax apparently denotes a cheese's age, with black being the oldest and green the youngest. But I am not convinced that this is necessarily an accurate guide.

TRANSHUMANCE

Transhumance is the practice of shepherds taking their flocks away from their villages during the summer months, in search of better grazing lands. Each summer the shepherds would take their flock to the moutain pastures and live in small stone huts, where they would also make and store their cheese. Each week one would return to his family and another from the village would take his place. Then, at the end of the summer, they would return, bringing with them their cheeses.

Today, ownership and change of usage of the land makes transhumance increasingly difficult. Equally, young men of the villages no longer find the isolated beauty of the mountains or the plains of La Mancha appealing. The result is that many of the finest cheeses of Europe have disappeared or are under the threat of extinction. Some countries have tried to stem the tide, but sadly the consumer is more influenced by price than quality.

Abondance AOC

This cheese is still made from raw milk in chalets near the Swiss border in the Haute-Savoie, where no artificial fertilisers or herbicides have ever been used on the mass of wild flowers, herbs and grasses. Abondance cows provide the milk and contribute to the other great cheeses of the Savoie: Reblochon, Tomme de Savoie and Beaufort. Made from skimmed milk, Abondance is regularly washed, so the crust becomes golden brown while the pale interior is smooth, supple and finely grained. A yeasty aroma carries through onto the palate of this savoury yet fruity cheese. Like Raclette, Abondance can be cut in a half moon and placed in front of an open fire to melt like a hot avalanche over potatoes.

France	Haute-Savoie
Milk source	
Unpasteurized	✓
Maturing time	3-6 months
Average weight	7-15kg 15½-33lb
Vegetarian	✗
Shape	⬭

Airedale

Until the early 1980s the New Zealand cheese industry was dominated by huge co-operatives producing cheese, butter and milk powder, mainly for export. When the removal of all farming subsidies coincided with crippling droughts in North Otago, Bob Berry decided it was time for a change. An amateur wine buff, he realised the native grasses and limestone-rich pastures would impart unique qualities to milk, and suddenly cheesemaking seemed the solution. Whitestone was the first, a Brie-style cheese, but Airedale best reflects the style of the region. The reddy-brown rind conceals a slightly crumbly sun-yellow interior. Fruity and full-bodied, it has a cheese-and-onion aroma and savoury aftertaste.

New Zealand	Oamaru
Milk source	
Unpasteurized	✗
Maturing time	4 months
Average weight	2kg/4½lb
Vegetarian	✗
Shape	⬛

Allerdale

Like many of Britain's new generation of cheesemakers, Carole Fairburn was not satisfied with making just one cheese. Set in the heart of the hills and valleys of north Cumbria, Carole started with Cumberland – one of the few cheeses made solely from Shorthorn cow's milk (see also Washed Rind page 103). Its simple, rounded flavour is offset by the sweetness of the milk and the touch of exotic spices. Next came Allerdale – a personal favourite. After a few weeks it develops layers of character within its Cheshire-like texture: first the aromatic taste of goat's milk, then hawthorn and even peardrop and almonds. Too poetic? You will have to try it to find out, and while you are there try the smoked Cumberland.

England	Cumbria
Milk source	
Unpasteurized	✓
Maturing time	8-10 weeks
Average weight	500g, 1, 10kg 1lb 2oz, 2¼lb, 22lb
Vegetarian	✓
Shape	⬛

Appenzeller

Despite laws protecting the quality of their cheeses, the Swiss can do little about retailers' obsession with plastic wrap. Appenzeller is washed in spices, white wine and salt, and is accustomed to breathing crisp mountain air. It is too frequently strangled by plastic wrap, causing it to sweat which accentuates the otherwise subtle farmyard whiff and spicy aromas. Beneath the smooth, burnt-orange rind that hints at spicy fruit, is a dense, yet supple, interior scattered with peanut-sized holes. Buttery with fruity overtones, it matures to reveal complex flavours reminiscent of hot toast spread with *Marmite* (a popular British yeast extract). One of Switzerland's oldest cheeses, it dates back to the days of Charlemagne.

Switzerland	Appenzell and St-Gall
Milk source	
Unpasteurized	✓
Maturing time	3-4 months
Average weight	6-8kg 13¼-17½lb
Vegetarian	✗
Shape	

Ardi-Gasna

Several years and hundreds of cheeses after tasting Ardi-Gasna, I can smell it, taste it and see it on the kitchen table of the stone hut which was tucked into a hillside, surrounded by meadows knee-high in wild flowers and towering snow-capped peaks. Slightly greasy, Ardi-Gasna is coloured by the smoke it absorbs while hanging over the hearth to dry. Ripening continues in the attic and the cheeses are rubbed periodically with sheep fat to prevent surface moulds and dehydration. The rind is crusty, the texture is hard but rich in the mouth, and the flavour is clean and fresh, with a sweetness of mountain flowers and a nuttiness born of age. The finish has a touch of sharpness that increases as the cheese matures.

France	Aquitaine
Milk source	
Unpasteurized	✓
Maturing time	3-6 months
Average weight	3-5kg/6½-11lb
Vegetarian	✗
Shape	

Asiago DOC

The Asiago high plateau, renowned for centuries for its sheep, gradually gave way to the cow as the demand for and value of butter and cream increased. Described as one cheese with two different flavours, Asiago is in fact two very different cheeses. Asiago Pressato (fresh Asiago) uses full milk and is aged for 20 to 40 days, producing a springy, pale yellow interior, with a sweet undemanding flavour and fragrance. Allevo (matured Asiago) is the traditional style made with skimmed milk – slow maturation produces a fruity, slightly sharp cheese, with a compact, granular interior full of small holes – and the cheese can age for up to two years. Asiago is also made industrially in the US, though this often bears little resemblance to the original.

Italy	Vicenza and Trento
Milk source	
Unpasteurized	✓
Maturing time	1-12 months
Average weight	8-12kg 17½-26½lb
Vegetarian	✗
Shape	

Beaufort AOC

Beaufort has for centuries been made in remote mountain huts or co-operatives in the Savoie, surrounded by magnificent forests and a vast tapestry of alpine meadows. Far from the nearest markets, huge cheeses were created that would wait until the end of the summer before being taken down the mountain. Beaufort is a member of the Gruyère family, but has a higher fat content. It is irresistibly smooth, despite its hard texture, and the flavour is superbly fruity – reminiscent of mountain pastures with wild honey and nuts. Strictly controlled by AOC rules, the cheese is made only from the milk of the Abondance and Tarine herds. During winter months the milk may be used to make Tomme de Savoie.

France	Savoie
Milk source	
Unpasteurized	✓
Maturing time	5-18 months
Average weight	45kg/99¼lb
Vegetarian	✗
Shape	

Bergkäse

Each morning, in mountain chalets throughout the picturesque Tyrol, the cream is skimmed off the previous evening's milk to make sweet mountain butter. The rest is poured with the fresh morning's milk into a glistening copper cauldron. Three days later the large wheels are moved to the ripening rooms, where twice a week for six months they will be vigorously rubbed with a salty cloth, creating a firm, rich, golden-brown crust. Bergkase is similar in taste to Gruyère, but more supple and slightly sweeter, with a spicy finish and tiny holes. Each year, on the 8th September, you will find families at church, celebrating their return from the mountains and later selling the fruits of the summer pastures.

Austria	Tyrol and Vorarlberg
Milk source	
Unpasteurized	✓
Maturing time	6-18 months
Average weight	30kg/66lb
Vegetarian	✗
Shape	

Berkswell

Berkswell village takes its name from the Saxon chief, Bercul, who was baptised in the ancient local well. It was here, in 1989, that Stephen Fletcher and his mother set about creating a ewe's milk cheese. Using an old recipe for Caerphilly and the milk from their own East Friesland sheep, they created Berkswell. Five years later it won Best Modern British Cheese at the British Cheese Awards. Hard, almost granular, but more chewy and less oily than Manchego, it has a crusty, terracotta rind bearing the marks of the basket-weave moulds. Each morsel reveals more complex flavours – roasted nuts, caramelized onions and meadow flowers, with a prickly tang. Truly one of the great British cheeses.

England	West Midlands
Milk source	
Unpasteurized	✓
Maturing time	4-8 months
Average weight	3.2kg/7lb
Vegetarian	✓
Shape	

Bitto della Valtellina

This is an endangered cheese, made by only five producers in alpine pastures. The cheesemakers spend the traditional 84 days of the season in isolated huts. The cows and a few goats must be milked, the cheese made and the stock constantly moved to prevent over-grazing. The still-warm milk is poured into copper cauldrons and heated until it curdles. Once formed, the cheeses are dry salted every two to three days for around three weeks. Every mouthful is a reminder to the senses that the flocks graze on wild flowers, herbs and grasses, alive with the sound of bees, birds and running streams. Bitto is made in two styles, one eaten after one to six months, the other from one to three years.

Italy	Sondrio
Milk source	
Unpasteurized	✓
Maturing time	**1-6 months or 1-3 years**
Average weight	**7-8kg 15½-17½lb**
Vegetarian	✗
Shape	⬭

Bra DOC

The Piedmontese are fiercely protective of their cheeses, and consequently examples such as Bra virtually unknown in southern Italy, let alone elsewhere. DOC status has helped spread the word, but hasn't prevented the Piedmont breed of cow being replaced by the utilitarian Friesian. Young, soft Bra is mild and buttery – a shadow of its aged counterpart, with its polished oily rind; darker, orange-yellow interior, salty tang; texture similar to Cheddar, though not as creamy, and an intensity only achievable with raw milk and time. The few Bra cheeses still made in the mountains are stamped *di alpeggio*. Bra, like Stilton, is named after the place where it was originally sold, not where it is made.

Italy	Piedmont
Milk source	
Unpasteurized	✓
Maturing time	**45 days or 6 months**
Average weight	**8kg/17½lb**
Vegetarian	✗
Shape	⬭

Buffalo

Robert Palmer took a herd of buffalo from Bulgaria to England with the idea of making Mozzarella. He discovered, however, that his passion was for the beasts and not for cheesemaking and soon found a willing buyer for the excellent milk – Nick Hodgetts. Nick had already made a name for himself with a superb ewe's milk cheese, Malvern. When released in 1996, Buffalo won Best New or Experimental Cheese at the British Cheese Awards. The only hard buffalo milk cheese I have tasted, it has the distinct but subtle sweet, nutty milk and smooth feel of Mozzarella di Bufala. When pressed and aged, Buffalo becomes firm, yet supple and creamy, with a hint of almonds and a lemony zing on the finish.

England	Hereford and Worcester
Milk source	
Unpasteurized	✓
Maturing time	5-6 months
Average weight	2kg/4½lb
Vegetarian	✓
Shape	⬭

Bulk Farm Gouda

The Dutch were making cheese in North America as early as the 1600s, but to Walter Bulk it was unknown territory when, in 1982, he started cheesemaking after a visit to his native Holland for an apprenticeship. As with most Dutch cheeses, the curd for Bulk Farm Gouda is cut and 'washed' with hot water to keep the acidity down and produce a sweeter cheese. The curd is then gathered into a 270kg/600lb block, cut into 60 squares and transferred into moulds. The cheeses are brine-washed and waxed and matured for at least two months, to develop their firm but supple texture and delicious, rich, nutty flavour and fruity tang. Mainly sold through farmers' markets, mail-order and the farm's retail store.

US	California
Milk source	
Unpasteurized	✗
Maturing time	**2-12 months**
Average weight	**4-5kg/8¾-11lb**
Vegetarian	✗
Shape	

Caerphilly

Caerphilly, named after the town of Caerphilly and first made around 1830, is one of four British cheeses fondly referred to as the 'crumblies'. The others are Lancashire, Wensleydale and Cheshire. Weighing 1.8-2.2kg/4-5lb, the fresh curds are lightly pressed and soaked in brine, and within five days the small wheels of moist, crumbly cheese are ready to eat. Cheddarmakers in Somerset quickly recognised its advantages, compared with slow-ripening Cheddar, and when milk was abundant made Caerphilly. Since the 1980s, production has moved back to Wales, where five traditional makers now challenge Duckett's of Somerset, who for generations have produced a superb, fresh, lemony Caerphilly.

Wales	Caerphilly
Milk source	
Unpasteurized	✓✗
Maturing time	**5-60 days**
Average weight	**900g, 3.2kg 2lb, 7lb**
Vegetarian	✓
Shape	

Canestrato Pugliese DOC

This flavoursome Pecorino (the general term for pure ewe's milk cheese) is well known in Southern Italy due to the practice of transhumance (*see* Manchego, page 115). The sheep would be moved in spring from the plains of Foggia to the grazing of Abruzzo, returning the same way in winter. Today the flocks (Merinos or Apulian Gentile), are transported by lorries. The cheese is identified by the deep gold rind imprinted with the pattern of the hand-woven reed draining baskets or *canestrato*. After one to two months, the cheese has an aroma reminiscent of wet wool, lanolin and mould. The hard and grainy texture retains the rich, creaminess and burnt-caramel taste that is characteristic of ewe's milk cheeses.

Italy	Foggia and parts of Bari
Milk source	
Unpasteurized	✓
Maturing time	**up to 12 months**
Average weight	**7-14kg/15½-31lb**
Vegetarian	✗
Shape	

Cantal and Salers AOC

These cheeses have been made for at least 2,000 years, originally by putting the curd into a wooden cylinder called a *formage* (hence the origin of the French word for cheese, *fromage*). Today, AOC regulations dictate that Salers can only be made when the Salers cows graze the summer pastures; whereas Cantal is made all year round. Each cheese has a metal badge embedded in the rind, indicating the date, region and cheesemaker. When young (*jeune*), they are moist and springy, with a cheese-sauce tang not unlike creamy Lancashire. Over six months (*vieux*), they become more like mature Cheddar, with the intensity of raw onions, pineapple and fresh herbs. *Entre-deux* (between the two) are two to six months old.

France	Auvergne
Milk source	
Unpasteurized	✓
Maturing time	3-9 months
Average weight	35-45kg 77-99¼lb
Vegetarian	✗
Shape	

Castellano

The vast plateau of central Spain is paradise to the Castilian, Churra and Mancha sheep. Castellano is similar to Manchego, yet the breeds of sheep – mainly Churra and Castilian – the higher altitude and greater humidity profoundly influence both texture and taste. With tiny rice-sized holes, firm and dense texture (yet more moist than Manchego), Castellano has a delicate *crème-caramel* taste perfectly offset by fresh acidity and a hint of salt. Its pale yellowy beige rind bears the distinctive zigzag marks of the plaited grass hoops in which the fresh curds are drained while the top and base have distinctive markings from the carved wooden surface (identifying the cheesemaker) on which the cheese sits.

Spain	Castile-León
Milk source	
Unpasteurized	✓
Maturing time	2-3 months
Average weight	1-3kg/2¼-6½lb
Vegetarian	✗
Shape	

Cheshire

First recorded in the Domesday book, Cheshire has been made since time immemorial in the true British colours: red, white or blue. Traditionally, only cheeses made in the county of Cheshire had the right to be called Cheshire. The cheeses derive their peculiar qualities from the rich deposits of salt in the soil which impart a distinctive sea-breeze taste and slow-ripening quality. However, its fine, moist, yet flaky texture makes it susceptible to cracking or bluing, and sadly the market has demanded a more creamy, solid texture. Barely a handful of Cheshires are still made by those who respect and adhere to the old methods, retaining the typical fresh crumbly texture and zesty bite.

England	Cheshire
Milk source	
Unpasteurized	✓ ✗
Maturing time	2-9 months
Average weight	900g, 3.6kg, 20.5kg/2lb, 18lb, 45lb
Vegetarian	✗
Shape	

Comté or Gruyère de Comté AOC

Comté has been made in the Jura mountains for centuries using the milk of the indigenous Montbéliard or Pie Rouge de l'Est cows which graze on the summer pastures with their wild flowers, sweet young grasses and herbs. These magnificent, creamy to light orange-yellow cheeses, with holes no bigger than cherries, are exquisitely fruity, hinting at apricots, pears and fresh grass, while the long finish is more nutty, becoming spicy with age. Close textured, supple and slightly granular, Comté is sweeter than Beaufort and has a convex rather than concave rind. In winter months, the milk is used to make the equally delicious but very different Mont d'Or (*see* page 93).

France	Franche-Comté
Milk source	
Unpasteurized	✓
Maturing time	**3-6 months**
Average weight	**35-55kg** **77-121¼lb**
Vegetarian	✗
Shape	

Coolea

Helene and Dick Willems sold their restaurants and moved first to Provence and then Spain to escape the rat race of modern Holland. Finally, they settled for the remote hills of West Cork, and it was inevitable – with the excellent grazing at their feet – that they would turn to cheesemaking. The variety of herbage produces a richer, more nutty, Gouda than most I have tasted from Holland, although it does have the characteristic full fruity Gouda tang. Occasionally, some cheeses are matured for up to two years, when the fruity character is intensified and the colour deepens to an orange-yellow (in Holland, where hay substitutes grass, they tend to be paler) and the small holes glisten with moisture.

Ireland	County Cork
Milk source	
Unpasteurized	✓
Maturing time	**6-12 months plus**
Average weight	**900g, 5.4, 8.7kg** **2, 12, 20lb**
Vegetarian	✗
Shape	

Cotherstone

Cotherstone, originally a double-cream cheese, would have been sold in both white and blue-veined versions like many of the cheeses once made in almost every dale in the Pennines. Joan Cross, taught by her mother as a child, has been making Cotherstone for over 25 years. Still a cottage industry, the number of cheeses produced vary depending on the season, the size and the amount of space on the shelves. High in moisture, Cotherstone has a pale gold, barely formed rind, and a texture not unlike baked cheesecake. An exquisite subtlety of flavour conjures up images of green grass, wild heather, babbling brooks and ancient stone walls shrouded in mist.

England	County Durham
Milk source	
Unpasteurized	✓
Maturing time	**4-10 weeks**
Average weight	**900g or 3.6kg** **2 or 8lb**
Vegetarian	✗
Shape	

Cougar Gold

I have had an aversion to tinned cheese since my first introduction to Camembert. It had been made in Denmark and sent by sea to unwitting New Zealanders, and was claggy, bland, sweet and an insult to authentic Camembert de Normandie. I was therefore dubious when a Cougar Gold devotee heard of my experience and sent me a tin. Cougar Gold was first produced in 1948 by the Washington State University, and the tin has proved to be a successful marketing ploy. The cheese is creamy, smooth and rich with a mellow cheese-and-onion-sauce aroma and taste – I was pleasantly surprised, but not converted.

US	Washington
Milk source	🐄
Unpasteurized	✗
Maturing time	3-12 months
Average weight	900g/2lb
Vegetarian	✗
Shape	⬭

Derby

Derby was popular in London during the 18th Century, but in 1870 the barons of the industrial revolution saw the labour-intensive process of making Derby as their next conquest. In the following 20 years, this great British cheese was reduced to a mushy, bland Cheddar lookalike and sales plummeted. Today, most is made in factories and flavoured with sage. Derbys range from the sublime to the positively hideous, with their unnatural green, marbled appearance. The best Derby is softer than Cheddar, with an open texture and a more delicate curd that flakes rather than crumbles. It is deep honey in colour, with a melted-butter taste that mellows out, becoming more rounded with time.

England	Derbyshire
Milk source	🐄
Unpasteurized	✗
Maturing time	1-6 months
Average weight	4-13.6kg 9-30lb
Vegetarian	✗
Shape	⬭

Double Gloucester

The all but extinct Gloucester cows – once a familiar sight in the Vale of Berkeley – are a loss not just because their sweet fatty milk made superb cheese, but because of their striking beauty and long white horns tipped with black. Some 15 years ago, Charles Martell re-introduced the breed in order to make an authentic Double Gloucester, as close as possible to those popular in the 17th Century. As with the other excellent Double Gloucester made by Diana Smart, ripened evening milk is added to fresh morning milk, resulting in a large cheese with the texture of chocolate, a savoury cheese-and-onion tang, and a hint of smoke and refreshing citrus acidity. Annatto gives the light tangerine-orange colour.

England	Gloucestershire
Milk source	🐄
Unpasteurized	✓
Maturing time	4-6 months
Average weight	3.6-8kg 8-18lb
Vegetarian	✗
Shape	⬭

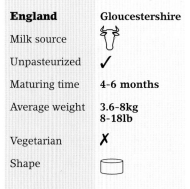

Dry Jack

Since 1931 the Vella family has been refining its recipe for Dry Jack, until today it stands among the best cheeses in the world. In the old ripening room, row upon shiny row await the day Ignacio Vella decides they have reached their peak; a rare few are kept for up to seven years, when they become brittle, like old Grana. The deep reddy brown rind is rubbed in cocoa and pepper and gleams like chocolate icing; it enshrines one of America's finest cheeses. Hard and deep yellow, with some crunchy crystallized calcium, it shatters rather than breaks when cut, releasing layer upon layer of flavour – sweet and fruity, sharp and mouthwatering, rich and full-bodied.

US	California
Milk source	
Unpasteurized	✓
Maturing time	**18-24 months**
Average weight	**3.6kg/8lb**
Vegetarian	✓
Shape	

Duddleswell

Ashdown Forest, the setting for Christopher Robin and Pooh Bear, is home to the Sussex High Weald Dairy, producers of Duddleswell. Like many modern British cheeses, Duddleswell is based on the original version of the cheese introduced to the Yorkshire Dales by the Normans, but it has been refined by Mark Hardy and his father Guy. This award-winning cheese is an elegant truckle with a hard, ridged, crust and a firm, almost flaky, interior which melts in the mouth, releasing its sweet, caramel flavour with a suggestion of brazil nuts and hay. Over 12 years the Hardys have also developed Slipcote (an old English fresh cheese), Ashdown (an organic, hard cow's milk cheese) and Halloumi.

England	East Sussex
Milk source	
Unpasteurized	✓
Maturing time	**10-12 weeks**
Average weight	**1.8kg/4lb**
Vegetarian	✗
Shape	

Dunlop

Forced to flee from Scotland to Ireland to escape the religious troubles in the time of King Charles II, Barbara Gilmour spent her time cheese-making. On her return she created Scotland's first hard cheese, Dunlop (named after the local village), using the rich milk of the native Ayrshire cattle. During the 18th and 19th Centuries the cheese industry flourished, but Dunlop was all but extinct by the early 1900s. It was revived by Anne Dorward in the late 1980s near Dunlop, and lately Wester Lawrenceton Farm has started making an organic version. Less dense than Cheddar, it is firm yet springy, almost chewy, and has a mild, buttery taste that retains the sweetness of fresh milk, with a gentle acidity to finish.

Scotland	Ayrshire
Milk source	
Unpasteurized	✓
Maturing time	**2-6 months**
Average weight	**1.6 and 4kg** **3½ and 9lb**
Vegetarian	✗
Shape	

Escarun

Guiseppe Occelli, not satisfied with the success of his small creamery in the foothills of Cuneo, set about reviving the old cheeses of the region before they could fade from memory. Among the handful he rescued from extinction was Escarun, not seen for 80 years and only made in spring and early summer. The crumbly, Cheshire-like texture melts in the mouth and is attributed to an unusual process – the curd is drained for five hours, reworked, then left in cloth bags for five days before being placed in moulds where it is left to age. When you cut through the pale beige-pink rind, the perfume of a million meadow flowers, trapped in the milk, is aroused like a gentle breeze.

Italy	Cuneo
Milk source	
Unpasteurized	✓
Maturing time	**9-12 months**
Average weight	**3kg/16½lb**
Vegetarian	✗
Shape	⬭

Etorki

Although Etorki is made in a purpose-built factory, the milk still comes from small flocks of mainly black- or red-faced Manech sheep, and the sound of their bells still echoes across the deep valleys – a reminder that in the Pyrénées at least, some things have remained unchanged for centuries. Similar to the traditional cheeses of the region, but more supple and close textured, Etorki is nevertheless an excellent cheese. Sold around the world, it has delighted customers new to ewe's milk with its burnt-caramel sweetness and creamy texture. Transhumance (*see* page 115) is still a way of life in the Pyrénées and many shepherds still make a small amount of cheese, with strange Basque names, for their own use.

France	Pyrénées
Milk source	
Unpasteurized	✗
Maturing time	**3-6 months**
Average weight	**4kg/8¾lb**
Vegetarian	✗
Shape	⬭

Fiore Sardo DOC

The people of Sardinia have been linked for nearly 2,000 years to the production of cheese from the native sheep whose habitat is the rocky hillsides, scattered with wild herbs, aromatic grasses and scrubby bushes. This flora gives the milk, and ultimately the cheese, its character. Fiore Sardo (the flower of Sardinia) is the basis for all other Pecorinos, and the sweetest. It is straw coloured, compact, hard, dry and grainy, with a wonderful summery aroma – wild flowers, warm earth, warm wool and the aroma of crushed herbs. The production differs from other Pecorinos as the curds are not cooked or heated in the whey. It is rich, with a caramel sweetness, a salty tang and a hint of fruit.

Italy	Sardinia
Milk source	⬭
Unpasteurized	✓
Maturing time	**3-6 months**
Average weight	**1.4-4kg/3-8¾lb**
Vegetarian	✗
Shape	⬭

Gabriel

Bill Hogan and Sean Ferry practice their alchemy, converting the verdant meadows into pure gold that takes the form of three great cheeses – Mizen, Desmond and Gabriel. Named after nearby mountain peaks, they are based on the great Swiss cheeses. Gabriel is a magnificent Gruyère type, full of flavour, with a strong fruity zing to the finish, and cured in an old stone barn near the coast, where the weather is wet but warm. This generates an ideal microclimate for the wild yeasts and bacteria that contribute to the complexity of the cheese. Desmond, similar to Gabriel, but smoother and sharper, resonates with flavour, while the enormous 45kg/100lb Mizen, not unlike Sbrinz, exudes strength, fruit and flavour.

Ireland	County Cork
Milk source	
Unpasteurized	✓
Maturing time	12 months plus
Average weight	6.8-27.2kg 15-60lb
Vegetarian	✗
Shape	⬭

Garrotxa

At a table shaded by vines and mimosa and spread with warm country bread, fresh walnuts and a carafe of local wine, I was gently nudged by one of the young goats to sample Garrotxa. Even in less idyllic surroundings, it remains one of my favourites. Garrotxa was created in the late 1980s by a group of disillusioned professionals, who have successfully applied their entrepreneurial skills to the art of cheesemaking. The rolling hills provide the raw materials for the Murciana and Granadina goats whose pure-white milk seems to absorb the scent of the mimosa and crunchy freshness of walnuts. Beneath the thick, grey, furry rind the cheese is compact, yet soft and springy, becoming smooth and velvety with age.

Spain	Catalonia
Milk source	
Unpasteurized	✓
Maturing time	1-2 months
Average weight	1kg/2¼lb
Vegetarian	✗
Shape	⬭

Gospel Green

Surrounded by woodlands, Gospel Green is a tiny hamlet and home to James and Cathy Lane. In the early 1980s they converted an old barn into a small dairy, the cheese and their two girls were born in quick succession. This small cloth-bound cheese has a slightly crumbly texture and fine leathery crust, and is impregnated with a multitude of fascinating moulds essential to the final flavour. Its character is as exuberant as its makers. Slightly softer and less dense than Cheddar, Gospel Green has tastes of the meadow flowers and lush green grass of the pastures. In late summer the milk is infused with the fruity scent of apples, as they are crushed in the old cider press outside the dairy.

England	Surrey
Milk source	
Unpasteurized	✓
Maturing time	2-3 months
Average weight	900g-3.2 2-7lb
Vegetarian	✓
Shape	

Gouda

Many of the magnificent 17th and 18th Century weighing houses are still standing, a testament to the important role cheese has played in the Dutch economy. The industry is highly mechanized, but some *boerenkaas* (farmers' cheese) is still made using raw milk. As property prices rose, many cheesemakers emigrated and they are now making superb farmhouse Gouda elsewhere. But Gouda still accounts for more than 60 per cent of Holland's cheese production. Smooth, yet supple when young, with a sweet fruity taste, it becomes firmer and more fruity with age. At 18 months, as the deep yellow interior becomes granular, Gouda is coated in a black wax, indicating a complexity of flavour that makes it irresistible.

Holland	
Milk source	
Unpasteurized	✗
Maturing time	2-24 months
Average weight	5-10kg 11-22lb
Vegetarian	✗
Shape	⬯

Grafton Village Cheddar

Entering the town of Grafton is like stepping back in time, with many old buildings lovingly restored. The Grafton Village Cheese Company, established in 1890, is one of the main attractions. Froma gallery visitors can watch the fascinating process of Cheddar making. By keeping to small-batch production and utilizing the old methods, Grafton produces excellent white (uncoloured) Cheddar, with the depth of flavour and character only possible when raw milk is used and the cheese aged for a long time. The rich pastures of the southern Vermont mountains also contribute to the intensity, producing milk with a high butterfat content. The company also makes an excellent Cheddar smoked over corn cobs.

US	Vermont
Milk source	
Unpasteurized	✓
Maturing time	6-24 months
Average weight	various
Vegetarian	✗
Shape	⬠

Grana Padano DOC

It is almost impossible to tell the difference between Grana Padano and Parmigiano Reggiano in a blind tasting, as they are both made in the same way and are subject to similar rigorous controls. The difference is mainly that the area where Grana Padano is made is bigger and the controls less stringent. Nevertheless, some Grana Padano is just as magnificent as a superb Reggiano – fresh, fruity and freezable. Those sold only as Grana, however, which simply means 'hard cheese', are definitely lesser mortals, having either been made outside the legally defined areas or not having achieved the standard of excellence required by the graders. They can be good, but they can also be disappointing.

Italy	North
Milk source	
Unpasteurized	✓
Maturing time	12-48 months
Average weight	40kg/88¼lb
Vegetarian	✗
Shape	⬭

Graviera

Through the centuries cheese has remained a staple part of the Greek diet, with cured or aged cheeses such as Graviera eaten with freshly made bread at practically every meal. Hence the Greeks consume more cheese per head than almost any other nation. Not unlike Gruyère, from which it is copied, Graviera is sweetish and fruity, with a firm yet supple texture, tiny holes and a rich, creamy feel. Those from Crete have a delicate fragrance of the wild pastures and the burnt-caramel taste of ewe's milk; while the Naxos Graviera, made in a small co-operative, is a lovely nutty cow's milk version. After Feta, Graviera is the most popular cheese in Greece.

Greece	Dodoni, Naxos and Crete
Milk source	
Unpasteurized	✓
Maturing time	3-9 months
Average weight	2-8kg 4¼-17½lb
Vegetarian	✗
Shape	

Grimbister

Grimbister Farm looks across the sea to the other islands of the Orkneys and down over the rolling flat meadows of strangely almost treeless, luscious-green pasturelands. Fed by the high rainfall and sea breezes, the soil provides rich pickings for the 14 friendly Friesian cows and wonderful milk for Hilda Seator, who has made cheese every day for 27 years. Similar to the Dale cheeses, Wensleydale or Cotherstone, Grimbister has been made for generations by the islanders using recipes handed down from mother to daughter. Grimbister has a mild, fresh and lemony taste, with a moist but crumbly texture and a hint of the sea on the finish.

Scotland	Orkney
Milk source	
Unpasteurized	✓
Maturing time	4-8 weeks
Average weight	1.8kg/4lb
Vegetarian	✓
Shape	

Gruyère

Copied the world over, none of the pretenders match the magnificent Gruyère wheels that proudly carry the name of the country whose rich mountain pastures and strict rules have protected their quality and character for centuries. Gruyère is denser than Emmental, but also stronger, less stringy and more creamy, making it better for *gratins*, soups and fondues. The combination for the ultimate fondue is as secret as Swiss banking, but Appenzeller gives strength of flavour, Emmental adds fruitiness and Gruyère gives a robust and nutty, yet creamy, quality. Slightly grainy, it has a complexity of flavours that are at first very fruity but soon reveal their more earthy nuttiness that lingers on the palate.

Switzerland	Gruyères
Milk source	
Unpasteurized	✓
Maturing time	4-10 months
Average weight	20-45kg 44-99¼lb
Vegetarian	✗
Shape	

Hawthorne Valley Cheese

Supple and flexible and dotted with holes, becoming firmer and more dense with age, Hawthorne Valley is based on Appenzeller, but has a sweet-savoury, mellow flavour. With age it divulges a more substantial character – almost meaty with hints of burnt toast and yeast on the finish. Hawthorne Valley Farm was created in the mid-1970s as an integrated living system and provides children from New York City with a hands-on experience of a real farm. It is a pioneer of biodynamic farming and has demonstrated that nature, and not chemicals, is best at controlling the environment. The cheese is sold at the farm, at the Union Square Farmers' market in New York City, or sent across the States by mail-order.

US	New York
Milk source	(cow)
Unpasteurized	✓
Maturing time	6-12 months
Average weight	5kg/11lb
Vegetarian	✗
Shape	(round)

Heidi Gruyère

Frank Marchand's magnificent Heidi Farmhouse, based on Swiss Gruyère, was judged Champion Cheese at the inaugural Australian Cheesemakers' Show in 1998. Frank, a Master Swiss cheesemaker, and his wife Elisabeth, started making cheese in 1985 in their new home in Exton, Tasmania. Using the milk from the family's 220-strong Friesian herd which graze on the local pastures, he created first Heidi Farmhouse, then other Swiss-style cheeses – each with their own Antipodean character. The milk is produced from sweet, fresh grass all year round, unlike in Europe where scarce grazing means cattle are kept inside during winter and fed hay. This cheese is firm yet supple, with pineapple nuttiness, and ages well.

Australia	Tasmania
Milk source	(cow)
Unpasteurized	✓
Maturing time	6-9 months
Average weight	30kg/66lb
Vegetarian	✗
Shape	(round)

Idiazábal DO

Cheesemaking and the herds of indigenous Laxta (or Lacha) sheep are integral to Basque culture and language and a few shepherds still practise transhumance (see page 115). Traditionally stored in the rafters of their simple mountain huts or txabolas, the cheese absorbed the sweet aromatic smoke from the open fires, creating a ruddy, ochre colour and delicious smoky taste. The co-operatives, down in the valleys, must use beech and hawthorn to smoke their cheese in order to carry the DO stamp. Compact and dry, but not crumbly, it feels pleasantly oily in the mouth, with the sweetness of the mountain pastures and wild meadow flowers and hints of caramel and roast lamb.

Spain	Basque and Navarra
Milk source	(sheep)
Unpasteurized	✓
Maturing time	2-4 months
Average weight	1-2kg/2¼-4½lb
Vegetarian	✗
Shape	(round)

Jarlsberg

Most of Norway is native forests and deep fjords and in the north, the tundra, it is still home to the Lapps. Less than one per cent of the tundra provides grazing land suitable for the comfort-loving cow. However, the almost continuous northern sunshine in the summer produces an abundance of rare and wonderful plants on which the cattle, whose milk produces Jarlsberg, feed. The cheese is based on an ancient recipe that was revived in the 1950s, and it has become very popular in Norway and abroad, particularly in America. It is golden yellow, similar to Emmental – but much sweeter, less nutty and lacking the depth – with holes of various sizes. A good everyday cheese and a cheaper alternative to Emmental.

Norway	
Milk source	
Unpasteurized	✗
Maturing time	**6 months**
Average weight	**10kg/22lb**
Vegetarian	✗
Shape	

Kefalotyri/Kefalotiri

The seemingly infertile islands and mountains of Greece, home to scraggy herds of almost feral goats and free-ranging sheep, produce the thickest, most aromatic milk, with the scent of the wild herbs, scrub and flowers concentrated in its richness. Made all over Greece since Byzantine times, Kefalotyri takes its name from the Greek hat *kefalo,* whose shape the cheese allegedly resembles. It is classified as a 'male cheese' since it is made with whole milk, not whey. It is firm but dry, with numerous irregular holes, and is white to pale yellow, depending on the mix of milk and the grazing. It has a freshness, with a distinct taste of ewe's milk and a slightly sharp finish, not unlike a very fruity, herbaceous olive oil.

Greece	
Milk source	
Unpasteurized	✓
Maturing time	**2-3 months**
Average weight	**6-8kg 13¼-17½lb**
Vegetarian	✗
Shape	

Lancashire

Until Mrs Kirkham's stunning Lancashire won Supreme Champion at the 1995 British Cheese Awards, traditional Lancashire was rarely found outside the county. Now only three Lancashire cheesemakers use the traditional method of combining the curd from three different days. The result is a mottled texture and a three-dimensional flavour, as the curds are all ripening at different rates within the cheese. 'Creamy' Lancashire is young, moist and like scrambled egg, with a cheese-and-chives savoury finish; while mature ('Tasty') Lancashire has an intense, burnt-onion and grilled-cheese flavour. 'Acid' Lancashire is a faster ripening, less crumbly cheese that has the bite, but lacks the depth, of a traditional Lancashire.

England	Lancashire
Milk source	
Unpasteurized	✓ ✗
Maturing time	**2-24 weeks**
Average weight	**18kg/39¾lb**
Vegetarian	✗
Shape	

Lincolnshire Poacher

It is no coincidence that Lincolnshire Poacher is the only cheese made in Lincolnshire, as the prevailing easterly winds blow unhindered off the nearby sea, drying out the fields in summer. Simon Jones, undaunted, called on cheese legend Dougal Campbell, and between them, the pedigree Holstein herds, and a tonic bottle of rennet, they created what would become Supreme Champion at the 1996 British Cheese Awards. Cheddar-like, Lincolnshire Poacher is compact and chewy, with a creamy, rich, nutty character that is sweet, yet balanced by a feisty acidity that has hints of green grass. The finish is bitter-sweet and long lasting.

England	Lincolnshire
Milk source	🐄
Unpasteurized	✓
Maturing time	8-18 months
Average weight	8 or 20kg 17½ or 44lb
Vegetarian	✗
Shape	⬭

Llangloffan Farmhouse

Once a senior musician in the Halle Orchestra, Leon Downey now shows equal skill in cheesemaking. With his wife and their herd of Brown Swiss cows, he has played the lead role in creating Llangloffan. A rough, pitted, millstone-shaped cheese, Llangloffan combines traditional techniques with poetic licence. Winner of the Dougal Campbell Memorial Trophy at the British Cheese Awards 1996 for Best Welsh Cheese, it is a hand-made Cheddar-like cheese with a rich yet dry, almost crumbly texture that dissolves in the mouth. Llangloffan is fruity and slightly grassy, with a hint of the fiery Welsh dragon on the finish. The farm is well worth a visit in summer.

Wales	Pembrokeshire
Milk source	🐄
Unpasteurized	✓
Maturing time	2-6 months
Average weight	5kg/11lb
Vegetarian	✓
Shape	⬭

Loch Arthur Farmhouse

The Loch Arthur Community was set up to care for and provide a meaningful and challenging way of life for those with learning difficulties. It is in a beautiful and secluded part of southern Scotland with the loch at the centre – an idyllic setting for its own herd of biodynamically reared Ayrshire cows. Under Barry Graham, the project continues to exceed expectations. Loch Arthur, a large clothbound cylinder, is firm and quite dry, yet melts in the mouth like hard chocolate, revealing a wonderful nutty character, overlaid by fresh green shoots and a strong 'fried-onion' tang on the finish. Less aggressive than mature Cheddar, it allows the fragrance and subtleties of the organic milk to come through.

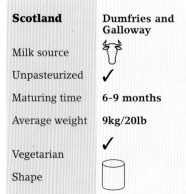

Scotland	Dumfries and Galloway
Milk source	🐄
Unpasteurized	✓
Maturing time	6-9 months
Average weight	9kg/20lb
Vegetarian	✓
Shape	⬭

Mahon DO

The Carthagians, Romans, Arabs, French and British have all invaded the tiny Mediterranean island of Menorca, each leaving an imprint of their culture on the language, landscape and local cheese. New breeds of sheep and then cows were introduced by the Romans and again in the 18th Century by the British, gradually changing Mahon's character. Today it is cushion-shaped and available at various stages of maturity, but is best when most mature. Hard and slightly granular, not unlike Parmesan, it has small irregular holes, a sharp bite with a salty tang, and should be eaten fresh. The ivory interior is offset against the bright orange rind, created by rubbing butter, paprika and oil into the rind after a month.

Spain	Menorca
Milk source	
Unpasteurized	✓
Maturing time	**10 days to 10 months**
Average weight	**1.5-3kg 3lb 5oz-6½lb**
Vegetarian	✗
Shape	

Malvern

Malvern Cheesewrights was established in 1998 within sight of the dramatic Malvern hills and on the river meadows, an area better known for the famous Battle of Worcester than its cheeses. Nick Hodgetts, however, set out to change history, and has developed an excellent range of cheeses, the best-known of which is Malvern, one of the first of a new generation of ewe's milk cheeses. Attention to detail and attractive packaging also gained Malvern a place on supermarket shelves. Its pale yellow interior is supple yet slightly dry, like Manchego, but feels rich and thick on the palate. There is a distinct sweetness of butterscotch with a hint of thyme and crushed nuts on the finish.

England	Hereford and Worcester
Milk source	
Unpasteurized	✓
Maturing time	**16 weeks**
Average weight	**1.3 and 2.25kg 3 and 5lb**
Vegetarian	✓
Shape	

Mimolette Française

The Romans originally built Holland's dykes and canals, which improved cattle and cereal crops. They also laid the foundations for Holland's economy, and as a consequence the simple fermented local cheese was replaced with pressed, long-lasting cheese. By the 17th Century, Mimolette had become so popular that Louis XIV banned imports of it, encouraging the French to make their own (where most is now made). These magnificent cheeses, coloured with annatto, look like giant oranges. Mimolette gradually changes from firm and slightly oily, with fruity aromas and a nutty flavour, to rock hard, granular and brittle. The colour and taste intensify to a sharp, mouth-watering fruit crescendo.

France	Flanders
Milk source	
Unpasteurized	✓
Maturing time	**6-12 months**
Average weight	**3-4.5kg 6½-10lb**
Vegetarian	✗
Shape	

Montasio DOC

This cheese was first made by the monks at the Monastry of Maggio, and dates back to the 13th Century. Today, most is made traditionally in small co-operatives. Even the same complex method as that devised a century ago is used to develop the special lactic culture. This, combined with the unique qualities of the milk (evening mixed with morning), the grazing and the microclimate of yeasts and moulds, produces a firm-bodied, pale yellow to straw-coloured cheese, with small holes. It is creamy, rich and fruity, with a hint of pineapple and tangy on the finish – not unlike a good medium Cheddar. As it matures the rind becomes hard, the interior granular and quite brittle, and the fruity taste intensifies.

Italy	**Friuli and Veneto**
Milk source	
Unpasteurized	✓
Maturing time	**3-18 months**
Average weight	**5-10kg/11-22lb**
Vegetarian	✗
Shape	

Ossau-Iraty-Brebis Pyrénées AOC

Patrick Rance likened the French AOC council's decision to combine the Basque Brebis with the equally wonderful Brebis of the Béarn under the banner Ossau-Iraty as 'lumping Chopin together with Tchaikovsky because both lived under Russian rule and both were composers'. The regions' cultures, heritages and cheeses deserve individual recognition. To conform to the AOC, the rennet and milk must come from the local Basco-Béarnaise and Manech breeds, who feed on local fodder and some cereals. Fermier, artisan, co-operative and industrial cheeses all come under this umbrella and include Matocq, Ardi-Gasna and Abbaye de Belloc. Those that do not conform are sold as Fromage de Brebis.

France	**Pyrénées**
Milk source	
Unpasteurized	✓
Maturing time	**2-3 months**
Average weight	**2-7kg/4½-15lb**
Vegetarian	✗
Shape	

Oszczpek (Olsztynski)

The history of Poland is turbulent and complex, its vast arable plains proving too great a temptation to the neighbouring countries. With its borders constantly threatened, even in the 20th Century, most crafts have become industrialized. Despite this, in the south, around Zakopane, some farmhouse cheese is still made. After kneading, the fresh curd is pressed into intricately carved elliptical wooden moulds, each a masterpiece of craftsmanship. Once drained, the curds would traditionally be stored in the eaves where the smoke from the fire would gradually be absorbed, coating the rind with a fine reddy-brown hue. Fine and crumbly in texture, Oszczpek has a sweet-sour, gently smoked yet fresh taste.

Poland	**Tatra Mountains**
Milk source	
Unpasteurized	✓
Maturing time	**1-4 weeks**
Average weight	**1kg/2¼lb**
Vegetarian	✗
Shape	

Pecorino Romano DOC

Hippocrates, Columella, Galen and Pliny the Elder each described the virtues of this great cheese, made in the countryside around Rome between November and late June. The recipe remains almost unchanged. As Rome and the demand for its cheeses grew, production moved in the early 19th Century to Sardinia, already known for its own smaller Pecorino. Pecorino Romano is white to pale yellow in colour and dotted with irregular small holes. As the cheese matures the straw-coloured rind becomes darker brown and its moist yet granular interior has a salty, rich fruity tang – sharp and robust. When grated over pasta this concentration of flavour, built up over months, is magnificently released.

Italy	Lazio and Sardinia
Milk source	
Unpasteurized	✓
Maturing time	**8-12 months**
Average weight	**22-33kg 48½-72¾lb**
Vegetarian	✗
Shape	

Pecorino Sardo DOC

Pecorino, the generic name for pure ewe's milk cheese, is usually used in conjunction with the name of the area where it is made. Pecorino Sardo, like most of Pecorino Romano, is made on the island of Sardinia, with its array of flowers, grasses, herbs and flora. Pecorino Sardo, smaller than the Romano, can only be made with the milk of the indigenous Sardinian sheep. Pecorino Sardo Dolce (1-2.3kg/2¼-5lb), aged between 20 and 60 days, is delicate, sweet, never tangy or sharp, with a firm but supple texture; Maturo (3-4kg/6½-8¾lb) is matured for up to 12 months, becoming hard, granular and dry, and developing a robust sharpness with a salty tang and a complexity of sweet, nutty, herbaceous flavours.

Italy	Sardinia
Milk source	
Unpasteurized	✓
Maturing time	**1-12 months**
Average weight	**3-4kg/6½-8¾lb**
Vegetarian	✗
Shape	

Pecorino Toscano DOC

Tuscany conjures up images of vineyards, medieval villages and cypress trees. Less visible, but just as important, are the herds of sheep that graze under the olive trees and on rocky hilltops, where the diversity of grazing produces the thick, luscious milk – the raw material for Pecorino. This cheese it embodies the history and spirit of Tuscany. The young cheese is supple, fruity and aromatic, but to taste the black-rinded Pecorino Toscano Crosta Nero in the full flush of its maturity is to taste heaven. Never has a cheese more justifiably been described as having the taste of walnuts, the real richness of burnt caramel or such complexity. Caciotta is the name for cheeses outside the DOC area.

Italy	Tuscany
Milk source	
Unpasteurized	✓
Maturing time	**1-3 months**
Average weight	**2.5kg/5½lb**
Vegetarian	✗
Shape	

Queso Anejo

When the Spanish invaded Mexico in 1591, they took with them pigs, chicken, cattle, cereals, olive oil and wine, but it would be many years before these were combined with the simple diet of the Mexican Indians to create the fascinating Mexican cuisine we now know. Cheesemaking was introduced by the Spanish monks, and cheese soon took its place among the most important ingredients in Mexican cuisine. Queso Anejo (aged cheese) is a white, rather dry, skimmed-milk cheese with a crumbly texture, somewhere between Feta and Parmesan, with a sharp, salty finish. Originally made with goat's milk, it is now more often made with cow's milk. Some is dusted with red chilli powder – Queso Enchilada.

Mexico	
Milk source	
Unpasteurized	✗
Maturing time	2-4 months
Average weight	5-10kg 11-22lb
Vegetarian	✗
Shape	⬭ ▱

Queso Ibores DO

The foothills of Extremadura are home to the indigenous Retinta and Verata goats with their distinctive dark coats. The scarce grazing and wild, sporadic nature of their habitat means their yield is low, but the milk is thick, floral and herbaceous. Since Roman times the cheese produced from this milk – Queso Ibores – has been immersed in olive oil then rubbed with freshly ground paprika, to deter the growth of unwanted moulds. The deep red rind, with its zigzag pattern, provides a wonderful contrast to the pure white interior. The distinct aroma of the paprika creates a subtle spicy tang, offset by the aromatic yet creamy nature of the goat's milk with its slightly sour finish. Hard to find but worth the effort.

Spain	Cácares
Milk source	
Unpasteurized	✓
Maturing time	2 months
Average weight	1-2kg/2¼-4½lb
Vegetarian	✗
Shape	⬭

Queso Majorero DO

The sunbaked island of Fuerteventura provides the native goat, the Cabra Canaria, with a veritable feast of prickly pear, thistles, cacti and straggly twiggy bushes which imbue the dense, flaky interior of Queso Majorero with the scent of wild thyme and almonds and a sharp, almost peppery finish of wild honey. The cheese has a tough amber-coloured rind which has distinctive geometric markings, top and bottom. Unfortunately, the tourist industry is rapidly expanding on this beautiful island and future generations of would-be cheesemakers are being tempted away from the isolated beauty of the villages and the traditional work of their forefathers, threatening Queso Majorero's existence.

Spain	Fuerteventura
Milk source	
Unpasteurized	✓
Maturing time	2-3 months
Average weight	5-7kg 11-15½lb
Vegetarian	✗
Shape	⬭

Red Leicester

Red Leicester is the sole survivor of a range of local cheeses once made in the region – Kingston cheese from Nottingham, the Lincolnshire (*see* page 131) and Suffolk cheeses and Blue Leicester have all disappeared. Red Leicester's familiar deep russet-red colour was originally created by adding beetroot and carrot juice to the milk, but since the turn of the century annatto has been used. Firm-bodied with a flaky feel, Red Leicester has a delicately sweet, medium-strong flavour, with a hint of green grass behind the more distinct butterscotch, nutty flavours. This was a favourite in Victorian times, but two World Wars and factory production has reduced farmhouse producers to fewer than a handful.

England	Leicestershire
Milk source	
Unpasteurized	✓
Maturing time	**6-9 months**
Average weight	**4-18kg/9-40lb**
Vegetarian	✗
Shape	

Ribblesdale Goat

High in the Pennines, close to the head of Yorkshire's bleakest and wettest Dales, lies Ashes Farm, above the river Ribble. With their backgrounds in fashion and engineering, Ian and Christine Hill may seem unlikely cheesemakers, but in Ribblesdale Goat they have created a cheese in sympathy with the region. Ribblesdale has a fresh, delicate flavour, in contrast to the pungency of some goat's cheeses, while its suppleness is not unlike Gouda. It is smooth and creamy with the spicy bite of chicory and a trace of misty hills and wild herbs on the finish. The sharp whiteness of the interior is enhanced by its pure-white wax coating. Ribblesdale is also made with cow's and buffalo's milk.

England	North Yorkshire
Milk source	
Unpasteurized	✓
Maturing time	**6-8 weeks**
Average weight	**1.8kg/4lb**
Vegetarian	✗
Shape	

Roncal DO

Since the 13th Century, the exact date in July when the flocks of Rasa and Lacha sheep start their ascent to the alpine pastures, and the date in September of their return to the Navarran valleys, have been officially regulated. In October, the sheep are moved to the winter pastures in the south of Navarra, where they remain until May. Roncal, Spain's first DO cheese, is made from December to July. The curd is shaped by hand, then pressed into flexible beechwood moulds. To extract the last drops of whey, the cheeses are punctured with wooden needles. Firm and slightly grainy, the richness of the milk imparts a 'sheepy' burnt-caramel sweetness, while the diverse pastures give a fresh herbaceous, slightly pungent tang.

Spain	Navarra
Milk source	
Unpasteurized	✓
Maturing time	**4 months**
Average weight	**2-3kg/4½-6½lb**
Vegetarian	✗
Shape	

São Jorge

Cheese has been made on São Jorge since the 15th Century, when a group of Flemish settlers made the nearby island of Faial their home. Their isolation from the mainland, the mild climate, rich volcanic soil and lush pastures, soon led to the development of a cheese similar to those of the settlers' native home. Long in flavour and slow to mature, the cheese quickly earned a reputation among the sailors of the day. Young, it is supple, rich and fruity, with a texture somewhere between Gouda and Cheddar. After six months or more it becomes crumbly and granular like Parmesan, with a strong suggestion of pineapple that is quickly overtaken by the hot, peppery mouth-puckering finish.

Portugal	Azores
Milk source	
Unpasteurized	✓
Maturing time	**3-6 months plus**
Average weight	**8-12kg 17½-26½lb**
Vegetarian	✗
Shape	

Sapsago

Fenugreek, a type of clover, was originally imported into Switzerland from Asia Minor by the crusaders in the 11th and 12th Centuries, and the local cheesemakers decided to incorporate it into this weird but wonderful cheese. The curd is fermented for three to five weeks then finely ground, mixed with herbs and pressed into flat-topped cones. The cheese is wrapped in tin foil and used for grating. Uniquely Swiss, Sapsago is pale lime green in colour. Hard, brittle and gritty, it dissolves like Parmesan when heated. Astringent, pungent, salty, sour and mouth-watering, with a farmyard undertone of warm cows, mixed with exotic, spicy notes. Not to be taken lightly. Also known as Schabziger.

Switzerland	
Milk source	
Unpasteurized	✓
Maturing time	**from 10 days**
Average weight	**150g/5½oz**
Vegetarian	✗
Shape	

Sbrinz

Around 500 litres/110 gallons of milk from the mainly Brown Swiss herds are needed to make a 40kg/88¼lb Sbrinz. Once formed, the young cheese is immersed in salt baths for 14 days (compare with Parmigiano, which is immersed for 21 days). It is no coincidence that Sbrinz and Parmigiano share similar traits, as the recipe for the former undoubtedly originates from the Romans. The Northern Italians appreciated its character as far back as the 17th Century and the cheeses were taken by mule, over the mountian passes, to be traded. Sbrinz has the same pineapple fruitiness and aroma as Parmigiano but is not as hard or as complex. The background flavour is of ground-nuts and the finish can be sharp and spicy.

Switzerland	Central
Milk source	
Unpasteurized	✓
Maturing time	**2-3 years**
Average weight	**40kg/88¼lb**
Vegetarian	✗
Shape	

Single Gloucester

Smaller than Double Gloucester and without the addition of annatto, Single Gloucester is made from a mixture of the semi-skimmed evening milk and the morning's whole milk, giving a lighter, more crumbly cheese. The leftover cream would originally have been turned into butter and the buttermilk used for making scones, quintessential for any English 'tea'. The result is a firm but moist cheese with a hint of vanilla and the freshness of creamy milk. More acid than Double Gloucester and smaller, it ripens more quickly and has a distinct but not overpowering savoury finish. Since 1997, Single Gloucester has become legally protected and can now only be produced in Gloucester or Gloucestershire.

England	Gloucestershire
Milk source	
Unpasteurized	✓
Maturing time	6-12 weeks
Average weight	3 or 5.5kg 7 or 12lb
Vegetarian	✗
Shape	⬭

Swaledale

To differentiate between the cheeses of the Yorkshire Dales, each one became known by specific a Dale name: Wensleydale, Coverdale, Nidderdale (no longer made) and Swaledale. In the 18th Century, most of these cheeses were sold either fresh (white) or ripe (blue), as the high-moisture and open-texture would easily blue if stored in the damp. By the 20th Century, Swaledale had disappeared until David Reed, in the early 1980s, revived it using ewe's milk. Soaked in brine, the cheese matures in humid cellars, growing its attractive grey-blue mould on the rind. Softer than Wensleydale and more moist, it has the freshness of the misty Dales and wild bracken, with the sweet caramel undertone of ewe's milk.

England	Swaledale
Milk source	
Unpasteurized	✓
Maturing time	1 month
Average weight	2.25kg/5lb
Vegetarian	✗
Shape	⬭

Teifi

After translating *The Complete Book of Self-Sufficiency* into Dutch, John and Patrice Savage-Ontswedder were invited by the Welsh author to experience life in Wales. Consequently, after Patrice spent a year working alongside one of Holland's finest makers of artisan Gouda, they moved to Glynhynod, 'Remarkable Valley'. Teifi combines the great traditions of Holland with rich Welsh milk, made sweet with local natural herbage. Similar to a Gouda in shape and texture, Teifi has a polished natural rind and a deep yellow interior. Firm, dense and fruity when young, it becomes hard, almost flaky with age and the flavour intensifies with a suggestion of bitter chocolate and young celery.

Wales	Dyfed
Milk source	
Unpasteurized	✓
Maturing time	2-9 months
Average weight	various
Vegetarian	✗
Shape	

Tête-de-Moine

It is unusual to see cows grazing in Swizerland. Against a backdrop of the Jura mountains graze the cows whose milk is used to produce Tête-de-Moine – first made by monks over 800 years ago. Strong, with a spicy, aromatic tang, its burnt-toast and yeasty full flavour is revealed when the cheese is scraped or peeled in thin ruffles or rosettes using a special machine called a *girolle*. One of the primary objectives of the country's agricultural ministry is to preserve the picture-postcard beauty of the countryside. With only 25 per cent of the land suitable for grazing, many cows live in barns, while farmers cut and gather the grass. Consequently, except in the inaccessible mountains, you will rarely see cows grazing.

Switzerland	**Bern**
Milk source	
Unpasteurized	✗
Maturing time	3 months
Average weight	750g/1lb 10oz
Vegetarian	✗
Shape	

Tillamook Cheddar

Founded in 1905, the Tillamook County Creamery is now owned by 160 dairymen who are responsible for nearly a third of all milk produced in Oregon. The plant operates 24 hours a day 365 days of the year to cope with this phenomenal volume, and the viewing gallery is well worth visiting. Every batch of milk is tested and heat-treated rather than pasteurized, and the farmers are paid on the quality and butterfat content of their milk. Made both coloured (with annatto) and white, Tillamook Cheddar is an excellent block Cheddar which is matured for a minimum of 60 days and packs a powerful, mouth-puckering punch with its sharp or extra-sharp flavour level.

US	**Oregon**
Milk source	
Unpasteurized	✗
Maturing time	3-12 months
Average weight	various
Vegetarian	✓
Shape	various

Toscana

Leaving behind a career as a pathologist, David Callahan his wife Cindy and son Liam moved to Northern California in search of the 'good life'. The hot summers and short availability of green pastures were ideal for sheep and they decided to raise lambs for the chefs of California. Like any traditional shepherd, Linda needed to utilize the excess milk after lambing, and with son Liam, she headed to Tuscany to work with artisan cheesemakers. The result is a unique and truly stunning cheese. Hard and flaky, it dissolves to reveal a complexity of flavours and aromas reminiscent of warm summers in the mountains – floral, aromatic, nutty and earthy, with an underlying sweetness of caramelized onions.

US	**California**
Milk source	
Unpasteurized	✗
Maturing time	3-4 months
Average weight	900g/2lb
Vegetarian	✓
Shape	

Vermont Shepherd

Some 10 years ago, when David and Cindy Major set about saving the family homestead, they didn't even know that you could milk sheep. The discovery of an old cheesemaking book at a local fair, a visit to the Pyrénées, and much trial and error has culminated in one of America's finest cheeses – Vermont Shepherd. Firm and dense rather than hard; buttery yellow, and shaped like a country loaf, it has the *crème-caramel* sweetness of ewe's milk, overlaid with a nutty herbaceousness attributed to the profundity of wild herbs and grasses. Using old cheesemaking methods David and Cindy have developed a modern artisan cheese. It is a mountain cheese worthy of comparison with any from Europe.

US	**Vermont**
Milk source	
Unpasteurized	✓
Maturing time	**over 3 months**
Average weight	**4.5kg/10lb**
Vegetarian	✓
Shape	

Wensleydale

Uniformity of feed, pasteurization and mechanization severely limit the texture and character of British cheeses, making this cheese virtually indistinguishable from the other great British cheeses, Caerphilly, Lancashire and Cheshire (collectively known as 'the Crumblies'). Fortunately in the early 1990s – when the last bastion of traditional Wensleydale, Hawes Creamery, was threatened with closure – the local community fought and won the battle for ownership. Firm yet supple, crumbly and moist, with a sweet wild-honey flavour balanced with a fresh acidity, Wensleydale's origins can be traced back to the Cistercian monks who travelled to Britain with William the Conqueror in the 11th Century.

England	**Yorkshire**
Milk source	
Unpasteurized	✗
Maturing time	**2-4 months**
Average weight	**4 or 20kg** **9 or 44lb**
Vegetarian	✗
Shape	

White Stilton

White Stilton is not, as has often been written, Blue Stilton that has failed to blue. In fact, it has been made for centuries by Stilton makers using the same recipe, but the blue penicillin mould is omitted. Consequently, the barely formed rind, with its aroma of yeast and fermenting fruit, is almost totally lacking in mould and the interior is a pale cream colour. At best it is an individual cheese, far removed from the consistency and flavour of the blue. With its crumbly texture and refreshing zesty acidity, it is not dissimilar to young Cheshire. However, it can quickly develop a bitter, sour taste and aroma if it is wrapped too tight and for too long and in the ubiquitous plastic wrap.

England	**Leicestershire**
Milk source	
Unpasteurized	✗
Maturing time	**6-8 weeks**
Average weight	**7.5kg/16½lb**
Vegetarian	✓
Shape	

Wild Ripened Cheddar

In 1994 Jonathan White, inspired by well-known New York restaurateur Charles Palmer, turned a hobby into a business. Jonathan's innate ability to marry tradition with modern technology enables him to harness nature's fickle helpers – wild bacteria and moulds – to create his unique cheese world. As it matures, Wild Ripened Cheddar attracts a multitude of moulds – mainly grey, with a few reds and yellows – to its straight, smooth surfaces. The result is not as firm-bodied as traditional Cheddar, but with its complex range of flavours – from the initial nutty, earthy sweetness to a savoury Cheddar tang, with just a hint of green grass on the finish – it is delicious.

US	New York
Milk source	
Unpasteurized	**Thermalized**
Maturing time	**6-12 months**
Average weight	**4.5kg/10lb**
Vegetarian	✓
Shape	

Yellow Branch Cheese

Yellow Branch Cheese is firm yet supple, high in butterfat (a characteristic of Jersey milk), and slides over the taste buds leaving a trail of flavours dominated by a savoury tang. Like many modern American cheeses, it is free from preservatives and artificial ingredients and, because herbicides and pesticides are not used, it is all but organic. Karen Mickler studied cheesemaking at university in Ontario and Wisconsin, then returned to the Smoky Mountains to create her own distinct style. She named the cheese after the river that runs through Yellow Branch Farm – the only farm in North Carolina making cow's milk cheese. Yellow Branch Cheese is also available with Jalapeno peppers.

USA	North Carolina
Milk source	
Unpasteurized	✓
Maturing time	**60 days**
Average weight	**8.25kg/18lb**
Vegetarian	✓
Shape	

Yerba Santa Shepherd's Cheese

For Jan and Chris Twohy, the northern corner of Scotts Valley, near Clear Lake – California's largest natural lake – is an idyllic place for goats, with its steep, hilly terrain covered with wild mountain grasses, brush, scrub, oak and mountain balm (Yerb Santa). The Twohys have no need for pesticides, artificial feed supplements or stabilizers. Demand continues for this very hard, dry, flaky cheese with its intensity and diversity of flavour. At first it has an almost minty freshness that tingles on the palate, then its more powerful aromatic fruity character of toffee, herbs and almonds steps in. A truly unforgettable cheese and easily as good as the hard artisan goat's cheeses of Spain.

US	California
Milk source	
Unpasteurized	✓
Maturing time	**9-12 months**
Average weight	**1.6kg/3.5lb**
Vegetarian	✗
Shape	

Hard

Cheese name	Country of origin	Region	Milk source
Acorn	Wales	Dyfed	Ewe
Allgäuer Emmentaler	Germany	Bavaria	Cow
Ardsallagh Goat's Cheese	Ireland	Co Cork	Goat
Ashdown Foresters	England	East Sussex	Cow
Basing	England	Kent	Goat
Belrose	New Zealand	Kerikeri	Cow
Bergkäse or Bavarian Bergkäse	Germany	Allgau	Cow
Bovemoor	England	Somerset	Goat
Cabot Vermont Cheddar	US	Vermont	Cow
Caerfai Caerfilly	Wales	Pembrokeshire	Cow
Caerphilly-Gorwydd	Wales	Dyfed	Cow
Cairnsmore	Scotland	Dumfries & Galloway	Ewe
Caithness	Scotland	Caithness	Cow
Campscott	England	Devon	Ewe
Capriano	US	Maine	Goat
Carrigaline	Ireland	Cork	Cow
Castelmagno DO	Italy	Cuneo	Cow with goat or ewe
Caws Cenarth *see* Caerphilly	Wales	Dyfed	Cow
Coquetdale	England	Northumberland	Cow
Cratloe Hills Gold	Ireland	Co Clare	Ewe
Cumberland Fammhouse	England	Cumbria	Cow
Curworthy	England	Devon	Cow
Desmond *see* Gabriel	Ireland	Co Cork	Cow
Doolin	Ireland	Co Waterford	Cow
Double Worcester	England	Hereford & Worcester	Cow
Drumkain	Scotland	Ayrshire	Cow
Drumleish	Scotland	Ayrshire	Cow
Egmont	New Zealand	Marlborough	Cow
Fifield	England	Oxfordshire	Goat
Fountains Gold	England	NorthYorkshire	Cow
Galtee More	South Africa	Natal	Cow
Gowrie	Scotland	Perthshire	Cow
Greveost or Greve	Sweden		Cow
Herrgårdsost	Sweden		Cow
Heydale Mellow	England	Lancashire	Ewe
Idaho Goatster	US	Idaho	Goat
Inverloch Cheese	Scotland	Argyll	Goat
Isle of Mull	Scotland	Isle of Mull	Cow
Languiole AOC	France	Laguiole	Cow
Laruns	France	Pyrénées	Ewe
Leafield	England	Oxfordshire	Ewe
Llanboidy	Wales	Dyfed	Cow

Lord of the Hundreds	England	East Sussex	Ewe
Mahoe Aged Gouda	New Zealand	Kerikeri	Cow
Matocq *see* Ossau-lraty AOC			
Menallack Fammhouse	England	Cornwall	Cow
Mercer Gouda	New Zealand	Hamilton	Cow
Meyer Vintage Gouda	New Zealand	Hamilton	Cow
Mull of Kintryre	Scotland	Ayrshire	Cow
Nanny's Goat Cheese	England	Somerset	Goat
Northumberland	England	Northumberland	Cow
Old Plawhatch Cheese	England	West Sussex	Cow
Oschyepka	Slovakia	Carpathian Mountains	Cow & ewe
Pen y Bont	Wales	Dyfed	Goat
Penbryn Cheese	Wales	Dyfed	Cow
Plymouth Cheese	US	Vermont	Cow
Podhalanski	Poland		Cow & ewe
Pyengana Cheddar	Australia	Tasmania	Cow
Queso Enchilado *see* Queso Anejo			
Ragusano DOC	Italy	Sicily	Cow
Royalp-Tilsiter	Switzerland	St-Gall	Cow
Saanen	Switzerland	Fribourg	Cow
Seriously Strong Cheddar	Scotland	Dumfries & Galloway	Cow
Shelburne Cheddar	US	Vermont	Cow
Sierra de Zuheros	Spain	Andalusia	Goat
Spenwood	England	Berkshire	Ewe
St-Claire	Australia	Tasmania	Cow
Stamp Collection 'Troy'	England	East Sussex	Ewe
Stitchill	Scotland	Roxburghshire	Cow
Sussex Grana	England	East Sussex	Cow
Sveciaost	Sweden		Cow
Tagon	England	Devon	Cow
Tala	England	Cornwall	Ewe
Ticklemore Goat	England	Devon	Goat
Tyn Grug	Wales	Dyfed	Cow
Vacherin Fribourgeoise *see* Fribourgeoise			
Wieninger's Goat Cheese	US	New York	Goat
Womerton Goat	England	Shropshire	Goat
Woolsery	England	Devon	Goat
Zamorano DO	Spain	Castile-León	Ewe

Blue cheeses

Above: The ageing process of Stilton is closely observed: the blue mould should spread evenly, right out to the rind.

The creation of these often maligned cheeses was inspired by a combination of Mother Nature, chance and man's entrepreneurial spirit. Originally, cheesemakers stored cheeses in natural caves, stone cellars or barns, with near constant temperature and humidity providing a breeding ground for wild moulds and yeasts. These wild characters would lurk about looking for somewhere sweet and tasty to settle, and found the moist curd their perfect canvas.

The recipe
A starter culture is added to the milk and, as the acidity rises, a blue penicillin mould is sprinkled in, followed by rennet. The coagulated curd is then cut into large chunks, the whey drained off, and the sloppy curd piled into tall, open-ended hoops or moulds. These have small holes in the sides, allowing more whey to escape. The top is covered with a round, fitted disk (or follower), and the bottom sits on another follower or a close-weave mat.

Blue cheeses are never pressed, as it is essential the curd remains loosely packed, leaving space for the blue mould to grow and spread. Instead, the young

cheeses are frequently turned, allowing the weight of the curd to force out excess whey. After about two weeks the cheese is removed from the moulds and the sides are scraped smooth to cover over any cracks before being rubbed with salt. The cheeses are then returned to the humid cellars, where the bacteria go about their business, breaking down the lumpy curds of fat and protein into a smooth, creamy texture.

The *Penicillium roqueforti,* or glaucum mould, which gives blue cheese its wonderful colour, will not turn blue unless it is exposed to air. This is generally done by piercing the cheese with rods, letting the air into the still young, slightly crumbly cheese, and the blue grows along the tunnels and into the nooks and crannies between the curd, producing the shattered porcelain look that typifies European blues.

Brie-style blue cheeses
The first examples of the milder, Brie-style blue cheeses were created in the 1950s and have proved popular. High in moisture and compact in texture, the mould is prevented from spreading, so the blue must be inoculated or injected into the young cheese. This results in pockets, not streaks, of blue. Sometimes, if the white mould has already developed on the rind, it will be pushed into the interior during inoculation and white mould will form around the blue.

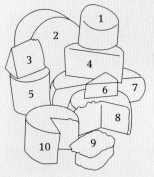

1 *Fourme d'Ambert*
2 *Shropshire Blue*
3 *Beenleigh Blue*
4 *Maytag Blue*
5 *Kikorangi*
6 *Cambozola*
7 *Bleu de Gex*
8 *Valdeon*
9 *Dolcelatte Torta*
10 *Cashel Blue*

Stilton

England	Derbyshire Leicestershire Nottinghamshire
Milk source	🐂
Unpasteurized	✗
Maturing time	**9-14 weeks**
Average weight	**7.7kg/17lb**
Vegetarian	✗ ✓
Shape	⬭

Doubtless the creation of Britain's most famous blue cheese, Stilton, was a gradual process, involving many years of trial and error. But it seems that Lady Beaumont of Quenby Hall in Leicester was responsible for recording the 'recipe' for this cheese. This recipe was followed by her housekeeper, whose daughter, Mrs Francis Paulet, put Stilton on the map in around 1740, when she started supplying it to the Bell Inn at Stilton, which was a day's journey from London by coach. Owned by her kinsman, Cooper Thornhill, the Bell Inn was the main stopping-off point for many of the coaches travelling along the Great North Road. Cooper sold the cheese to his customers and travellers, among whom was the writer Daniel Defoe.

In 1772 Defoe wrote 'it is called our English Parmesan and brought to the table with the mites so thick around it that they bring a spoon for you to eat the mites with, as you do the cheese'. Cooper Thornhill was undoubtedly responsible for establishing Stilton as a recognised industry. He sent stage coaches laden with Stilton to his contacts in London, selling more than 1,000 cheeses every week. However, the advent of the railway in the 1840s dealt a cruel blow to the village of Stilton. Trade virtually stopped overnight when the mail and passengers started to travel by train.

Initially made on small farms, the time-consuming, cantankerous nature of Stilton lead an Edwardian Stilton maker to say '...with the exception they make no noise, (Stilton) are more trouble than babies'. This, no doubt, influenced other makers to join forces and produce the first factory-made Stilton in 1875. Production continued to increase in the 19th Century and eventually there was hardly a village in the areas of Lincolnshire and Nottinghamshire that did not have a farm making Stilton.

A cheese noted for its character and individuality, Stilton attracted world attention in October 1878, when its makers constructed a tower of more than 3,000 cheeses at the Islington Dairy Show. The Stilton Makers' Association, which formed in 1910, registered Stilton as a trade mark,

Left: Hygiene is now strictly observed in commercial creameries, such as here at Stilton-makers, Long Clawson.

weeks the cheese is pierced with stainless steel needles (they could be plastic or wooden, but steel is easier to clean), allowing air into it. The blue grows along the paths left by these needles and between the 'chunks' of curd which have not yet combined together. This creates the classic shattered porcelain effect.

How to eat Stilton

'Digging' the Stilton was a good idea when the cheese was to be devoured by many guests in one or two sittings. However, when gouged it will quickly develop unwanted mould and the fresh, clean sparkle of life will soon be lost from the cheese.

The pouring of port into the heart of a Stilton was originally done to kill the maggots that gathered at the bottom of traditional Stilton bells. With modern refrigeration there is no longer a necessity to spoil the Stilton or waste the port.

stating that it could only be produced in three counties: Derbyshire, Leicestershire and Nottinghamshire. This decision ultimately saved it from mediocrity or even extinction, the fate of most of Britain's other fine territorial cheeses. Today the same rules and recipe apply and Stilton is only made by seven creameries.

Despite the fact that the milk has had to be pasteurized since January 1990, it still embodies much of the subtlety of the magnificent grazing. Consequently, Stilton is at its peak three months after the flowering of the meadows in April/May, and again three months after the end of summer when the September showers produced fresh, sweet, new grass among the stubble of the cut hay, which may explain the tradition of Stilton at Christmas.

The recipe

Some 77.25 litres/17 gallons of milk need three months of loving care and attention to develop into a mature 7.7kg/17lb Stilton full of character and potential. The milk is warmed and cooled, cut and stirred, sprinkled with *Penicillium roqueforti* (the blue mould), coagulated into curds and whey, and eventually put into moulds and left to drain. After two

CHOOSING AND SERVING STILTON

A Stilton should have straight sides – if the base is wider than the top, the cheese has not been turned and it will be dry on top and soggy and bitter nearer the base. The rind should be dry and rough and the pierced holes quite visible, but the cheese must not be split or cracked. The rind is edible, but gritty and sharp and best left to the mice.

The interior should be creamy in texture and a straw-yellow colour, not brown and dull around the edges. It should have evenly spread, jagged blue lines, radiating erratically from the centre to the outside. Don't buy a piece if it has been strangled in clingfilm, or you will find it sweaty and rather salty.

The traditional marriage of port and Stilton is often not as harmonious as one would expect. The sweet richness of port can overpower Stilton and the aromatic, alluring tang of Stilton can annihilate all but the most elegant of ports. A well-balanced sweet wine such as Monbazillac can make a better partner.

Roquefort AOC

France	Rouergue
Milk source	
Unpasteurized	✓✗
Maturing time	**12-14 weeks**
Average weight	**2.5-2.9kg** **5½-6½lb**
Vegetarian	✗
Shape	

Folklore has it that Roquefort was created some 2,000 years ago, by a careless, love-struck shepherd. Distracted by his young love from tending his sheep, he abandoned his lunch (bread and a piece of cheese) in the cave in which he had been sheltering from the elements. A few days later, the shepherd remembered the cheese and found that it had developed a greenish mould that spread through the centre.

Ever since then, shepherds have been maturing their cheeses in the deep limestone caves of Combalou, where the blue moulds that exist naturally are encouraged to grow by the presence of some local rye bread, which is left beside the cheeses.

One maker still 'grows' his own moulds. Each year, when the new moon appears in early September, he bakes 400 loaves of rye bread and stores them in the caves of Combalou. After nearly three months, the bread is desiccated and covered in spores of four or five strains of blue mould. The bread is forced through a sieve to separate the crumbs from the mould, which

is then added to the young curd to create the spicy, sharp taste and characteristic blue of Roquefort.

Rouergue, with its often harsh climate of hot, dry summers and cold winters, and its rugged rocky geography, has for centuries been home to a local breed of hardy, indigenous sheep. Eating a tenth the amount of dry matter required by cows, these sheep can give up to 8 litres/14 pints of milk per day, despite the lean pickings of scrub, tussock grasses and wild herbs. However, flavour and richness, not volume, are the measures of this milk's quality.

To ensure the milking season is as long as possible without upsetting the natural cycle of the animals, the rams are put among the first ewes in November and their introduction is staggered over the next four to six weeks. The first lambs are born around 1st April, and milk is then available for the next five to six months. By November the milk has dried up and the cycle begins again.

The recipe

The cheesemakers sprinkle the blue moulds into the milk and, once the milk has separated into its curds and whey, the curd is cut and ladled into open-ended moulds. These are left to drain until the cheese is firm enough to be rubbed with salt and the process of ripening begins.

Above: Thousands of Roquefort fill the caves of Combalou,
where they are carefully nurtured to perfection.

First to appear are the white moulds on the outside of the cheese, and these are gradually invaded by the indigenous bluish green moulds prevalent in the caves.

Unlike other blues, Roquefort is not pierced. This is because the texture is more open than that of other blues and the air, necessary for the mould to go blue, is trapped between the curd. Little by little the moulds sneak into the cheese through the fissures, cracks and crevices of the rind, filling up the spaces and drawing nourishment from the lactic acid. In nature's competent and creative hands, complex biochemical reactions occur between the activity of the moulds, yeasts and bacteria on the fats, proteins and minerals of the milk, radically changing the texture and viscosity of the cheese and giving off an invisible cloud of pungent aromatic aromas.

Meanwhile, armies of colourful yeasts march across the rind, attacking the protein and adding a harsh whiff to the cheese. It is hard to believe that such furious activity takes place silently.

As the cheeses ripen, their place is taken by younger cheeses, ensuring the complexity of the microclimate is maintained. This is no place for chemical cleaners, stainless steel shelves and power hoses. Nothing must disturb the delicate balance that has for centuries produced one of the world's finest cheeses and inspired poets and politicians, chefs and cheese-lovers alike. Only those who are ignorant of the process would compare other ewe's milk cheeses with Roquefort.

The phenomenal success of this cheese in America was partly a result of a comment made by the surrealist painter Salvador Dali. When asked what he thought of New York, he replied 'New York is a gothic Roquefort'. This was an unknown metaphor to many Americans, but it appealed to their curiosity and love of all things European, and the fame of, and desire for, Roquefort quickly spread.

BUYING ROQUEFORT

The biggest producer, whose cheeses are sold around the world, is Roquefort Société. The smaller producers, sold mainly in France, have their own distinctive, individual character. Roquefort Carles, Papillon and Gabriel Coulet have always been my favourites because of the sweet, burnt-caramel flavour of the ewe's milk, with its hint of cut grass still coming through despite the spicy strings of metallic blue and the strong salty finish.

When a Roquefort is fully aged, the mould has fanned out to the edges of the buttery mass and the flavour is spicy, strong and mouth-watering. Sadly, much Roquefort is consumed too young, when there is barely a hint of blue, the texture is crumbly rather than cohesive and the bite has no backbone to it.

Roquefort, like many French cheeses, is protected by AOC regulations, and the fate of each cheese is in the hands of the cheesemonger.

Gorgonzola

Italy	Lombardy and Piedmont
Milk source	🐄
Unpasteurized	✓
Maturing time	3-6 months
Average weight	6-12kg 13¼-26½lb
Vegetarian	✗
Shape	⬭

As with so many of the great cheeses of Europe, the origin of Gorgonzola is shrouded in mystery. Only folk legends remain to explain how this distinctive cheese became one of the very first blues.

Some say the cheese was discovered inadvertently by an innkeeper of Gorgonzola. He had purchased several young cheeses from cattle herders as they passed through the village on their way back from the mountain pastures to the winter lowlands. After a few weeks of being stored in his damp cellars, the cheeses turned 'blue'. Conscious of his profit margin, the innkeeper decided to dish them up to some passing customers. Far from protesting, the customers demanded more.

Another story about the origin of Gorgonzola has it that, as with Roquefort, the cheese was created by a careless youth. Distracted by his young love, he left a bundle of curd hanging on a hook in the damp cellar to drain overnight. The next day, hoping to disguise his mistake, he added the curd to the morning batch. Weeks later he found the cheese had a greenish

mould through the centre. Fear and curiosity tempted him to try it and the rest, as they say, is history.

Now, under strict regulations, Gorgonzola is made by some 80 producers in Lomdardy and Piedmont in the north of Italy. A few small artisan producers still use unpasteurized milk and follow the traditional 'shepherd's' method. Rennet is added to the evening milk and the curd is hung up to dry until the next morning. During this time, the precious blue spores endemic to the area invade or inoculate the curd. The following day the morning milk is coagulated and then alternating layers of evening and morning curd are gently scooped into large, cloth-lined moulds.

Once firm, the cheese is removed from the moulds, rubbed and rolled in salt, then encased in a wide belt made of fine wooden slats, and left to mature. Blueing is achieved by piercing the cheese, traditionally with hard-wood nails, but today with stainless steel. The result is a strong, piquant taste and creamy consistency.

The modernization of Gorgonzola

Most Gorgonzola is made in large factories using pasteurized milk, and the blue-green penicillin mould is added to the milk before the rennet. At about four weeks the cheeses are pierced with thick needles to encourage the spread of the blue-green mould. First one flat side is pierced half way through then, a few

Above: The ripeness is constantly checked while the cheeses sit on shelves, wrapped in close-fitting wooden belts.

days later, the cheese is turned and the other flat surface is pierced. Air is thus allowed into the interior, and the mould to which Gorgonzola owes its character can develop and spread. This process is done in a place called 'purgatory', where the cheese is kept at around 22°C/72°F with up to 95 per cent humidity.

Traditionally, the cheeses were ripened in the natural caves (*casere*) at Valsassina and Lodi, which provided ideal conditions for natural mould formations. Today, however, Gorgonzolas are ripened in controlled purpose-built store rooms to ensure they attain the consistency and quality demanded by today's market.

As with Roquefort, when Gorgonzola is ready for sale it is wrapped in tin foil. This is not only to stop the cheese from losing too much weight by evaporation, but also to prevent it from breaking or cracking. Furthermore, it enables the consumer to identify the prestigious mark of the consortium which controls the quality of Italy's most famous blue.

Enjoying Gorgonzola

The crust of Gorgonzola is hard, compact, rough and reddish in colour, while the interior is white or pale yellow streaked with green-blue. Those cheeses that pass the rigid grading of the Gorgonzola consortium are stamped with the letters 'CG'.

Gorgonzola has its own greenish-blue microscopic mould, *Penicillium glaucum,* that imparts a sharp, spicy flavour. This provides a contrast to the delicate, rich, creamy interior that melts on the tongue, releasing a complexity of flavours. The cheese is creamier and sweeter than Stilton, but similar in strength. If sold under-ripe, however, the interior can be blotchy, the texture too firm and crumbly, and the cheese is likely to have an unappealing bitter green taste. Around the edges it can be slightly greyish, but should never be brown, as this would indicate excess drying and poor handling. Sensibly, Italian producers recommend you buy Gorgonzola in small amounts, as it is a live food still undergoing maturation.

Blue cheeses come into their own crumbled into a salad of leaves, sundried tomatoes, olives and flageolet beans, sprinkled with a slightly sweet vinaigrette.

BUYING AND SERVING BLUE CHEESES

Blue cheeses are normally wrapped in tin foil to prevent them from drying out, so the moisture pumped out by the bacteria during fermentation gathers on the rind. Scrape this off before serving. If a traditional blue develops too much white mould (an indication of poor handling), it is normally accompanied by a bitter, damp, mouldy cellar smell. Your nose will tell you this is not good, and the cheese should be returned to the supplier.

Blue cheeses are often accused of being salty, yet no more salt is used in their production than in the making of hard cheeses. The problem lies with the retailer. If cut surfaces are wrapped in plastic wrap for long periods, the soft whey will be drawn to the surface and deliver a powerful punch to the next unwitting customer. To avoid this, when you buy a piece of blue, just before serving, pat the cut surface with a piece of damp paper to absorb the salt.

Beenleigh Blue

Robin Congdon is a master of his art and, with his partner Sari Cooper, he has created a family of magnificent blue cheeses. Beenleigh Blue is my favourite – moist yet crumbly, with a white interior streaked with greeny blue. Its flavour is steely blue, with the burnt-caramel sweetness that is characteristic of fine ewe's milk, and it only releases its spiciness as it melts on the palate. Beenleigh Blue shows how the essence of organic grazing can be evoked in the hands of a great cheesemaker to produce an exquisite complexity of aromas and tastes. It is available from September to February, whereas Harbourne Blue (goat) and Devon Blue (cow) are available all year round and are equally magnificent.

England	Devon
Milk source	
Unpasteurized	✓
Maturing time	6 months
Average weight	2.7kg/6lb
Vegetarian	✓
Shape	

Bergère Bleue

The Pyrénées are renowned for their artisan ewe's milk cheeses. It was here, amidst the deep valleys, towering peaks, abundant wild flowers and woolly sheep, that Jane North fell in love with, and stayed to learn about, cheesemaking. Returning home to the US, she and husband Karl built their farm at Freetown and embarked on their new career. Bergère Bleue, though similar to Roquefort, has its own three-dimensional personality, with an aroma of lanolin and yeast. This organic cheese melts like butter, releasing trapped flavours of burnt caramel laced with a spicy piquancy from the blue-green streaks of *Penicillium roqueforti* that penetrate the pale lemon yellow, moist, slightly crumbly cheese.

US	New York
Milk source	
Unpasteurized	✗
Maturing time	6-8 weeks
Average weight	1.3kg/3lb
Vegetarian	✗
Shape	

Bleu d'Auvergne AOC

The Auvergne is a landscape dotted with waterfalls, lakes, springs and Renaissance towns with names that read like a page from a cheese book – Cantal, Gaperon and Salers, to name but a few. Bleu d'Auvergne, along with St-Nectaire, is the best-known Auvergne cheese outside France. With its reddish-orange crusty rind and firm, supple, yet moist creamy interior, it has a sharp, clean taste. The evenly spread small pockets and broken threads of blue-grey mould hint at herbs and melted butter. As the interior of the maturing cheese starts to collapse, the flavour intensifies to a spicy tang. Some farmhouse examples, using raw milk, still exist, but are rarely found outside the Auvergne.

France	Auvergne
Milk source	
Unpasteurized	✓
Maturing time	1-2 months
Average weight	2.5kg/5½lb
Vegetarian	✗
Shape	

Bleu de Gex or Bleu du Haut-Jura AOC

Bleu du Haut-Jura, which encompasses Bleu de Gex and Bleu de Septmoncel, is made exclusively from raw milk from Montbéliarde cows. Unlike Stilton, the blue spores are not sprinkled into the milk (although this is starting to happen), but they exist naturally in the ripening cellars and, allegedly, in local plants eaten by the cows. The fine streaks of blue are encouraged by pricking and re-pricking the cheese through the rough, pock-marked, crusty rind, created by lining the moulds with the jute sacks in which the salt is delivered. The cheese is made in large flat wheels and has a supple, less creamy feel, and mild taste with a hint of mushrooms, tarragon and fresh milk.

France	Franche-Comté
Milk source	
Unpasteurized	✓
Maturing time	2-3 months
Average weight	7.5-9kg 16½-20lb
Vegetarian	✗
Shape	⬭

Bleu des Causses AOC

A region of great natural beauty, the Causses is a rock-strewn plateau studded with ancient ruins and fortified towns. Beneath are limestone caves with vents (*fleurines*) allowing air currents to circulate around the cheeses, spreading the natural moulds and yeasts that influence the final texture and taste. Bleu des Causses is more moist and crumbly than other French blues, melting in the mouth to release its pungent aromatic flavours. Fresh and spicy, it is a great alternative to Roquefort – the area's most famous cheese – and not as salty. A proportion used to be made with ewe's milk, although AOC rules now state that it must be made with cow's milk to differentiate it from Roquefort.

France	Rouergue
Milk source	
Unpasteurized	✓
Maturing time	3-6 months
Average weight	2.3-3.5kg 5-7¾lb
Vegetarian	✗
Shape	⬭

Blue Vinny

Local historians caused Mike Davis problems with the local authorities in 1982 when he decided to revive Blue Vinny (old English for 'veining'). They were convinced the blue was obtained by dragging mouldy old horse harnesses through the milk or leaving mouldy boots beside the vats. In fact, the mould existed in many old caves and cellars as well as on old leather. Today the bluing is not left to chance – spores are added to the semi-skimmed milk. The blue gradually invades the young, moist, open-textured curd, creating a mass of uneven, spidery blue-grey streaks. The cheese is hard, almost brittle, in texture and has a herbaceous freshness like cut grass with a sharp, piquant finish.

England	Dorset
Milk source	
Unpasteurized	✓
Maturing time	3-5 months
Average weight	6-7kg 13¼-15lb
Vegetarian	✓
Shape	⬭

Bresse Bleu (Brie-style)

Bresse Bleu started life during the Second World War as an alternative to strong blue. However, air – required to turn blue moulds blue – cannot penetrate the cheese's moist, dense, creamy texture. Consequently, the blue must be injected directly into the young cheese, rather than being introduced through the traditional method of pricking the cheese. Injection produces pockets rather than streaks of blue-grey mould. Sometimes the white penicillin mould on the rind is also carried into the cheese, appearing as patches of fluffy white mould around the blue. These small individual cheeses which are slightly spicy, with a rich, buttery feel, travel well and are now copied the world over.

France	Rhône-Alpes
Milk source	
Unpasteurized	✗
Maturing time	2-4 weeks
Average weight	125-500g 4½oz-1lb 2oz
Vegetarian	✗
Shape	⬭

Cabrales DO

Picos de Europa – the limestone peaks of Northern Spain – are a warren of caves, ideal for ripening Cabrales. For centuries, the locals have raised livestock on the rich, virtually inaccessible mountain pastures, and made cheese. Purely artisan, Cabrales is made with cow's, goat's or ewe's milk in varying proportions, depending on the season. The best cheese, produced in late spring, uses cow's milk for acidity, goat's milk for piquancy and ewe's milk for sweetness and a buttery texture. The cheese is compact yet open-textured, with a sticky orange-yellow rind. The blue moulds work their way into the cheese through the cavities, forming the irregular streaks of blue that give Cabrales its piquant, outspoken character.

Spain	Asturias
Milk source	
Unpasteurized	✓
Maturing time	2-3 months
Average weight	2-4kg/4¼-8¾lb
Vegetarian	✗
Shape	⬭

Caillote de Brebis

Sold in small, attractive terracotta pots with a rustic paper 'lid', Caillote de Brebis is a delicacy appreciated only by those who revel in the powerful, almost insolent, nature of a strong blue. This complex beast packs a mean but satisfying punch, though not as vicious as the local *fromages forts*. It retains the distinct, spicy bite of Roquefort and is rich and creamy, yet light and sharp. Through this intensity the sweet, burnt-caramel character of the exceptional local ewe's milk can still be distinguished. An ideal gift for the true addict, as it will keep almost indefinitely. Caillote de Brebis is at its most distinguished on crusty, toasted walnut bread, or grilled and served with an equally forceful local wine.

France	Rouergue
Milk source	
Unpasteurized	✓
Maturing time	Min 60 days
Average weight	150g/5½oz
Vegetarian	✗
Shape	

Cambozola (Brie-style)

Cambozola is a modern success story and, although creameries around the world have tried to emulate it since its creation in the 1970s, few have achieved the consistency of quality and texture to which Cambozola owes its success. This cheese is, as its name and style implies, an amalgamation of Camembert and Gorgonzola. Cream is added to the milk, giving its smooth, creamy texture and its subtle, spicy, slightly sweet-sour taste. It is designed to appeal to those who otherwise find blue cheese a little too ferocious and spicy, and its sales continue to grow. Similar cheeses are Bavarian Blue, Blue Brie, and the now extinct English cheese, Lymeswold.

Germany	
Milk source	
Unpasteurized	✗
Maturing time	1-2 months
Average weight	2kg/4½lb
Vegetarian	✗
Shape	

Cashel Blue

Cashel Blue, made by Jane and Louis Grubb, was one of the first Irish cheeses I encountered when I opened my shop, Jeroboams, in London in 1986. The cheese's habit of collapsing when at its peak of perfection merely adds authenticity according to my mainly French clientele. At six weeks, Cashel Blue is firm and crumbly, with a hint of tarragon and crisp white wine; gradually it mellows and becomes creamier. However, it takes at least 12 weeks to really come into its own. Too strong for some, but sheer perfection for others, Cashel Blue is frequently served at one of Ireland's best-known country house hotels, Ballymaloe House, near Cork.

Ireland	County Tipperary
Milk source	
Unpasteurized	✓
Maturing time	8-14 weeks
Average weight	1.3kg/3lb
Vegetarian	✓
Shape	

Danish Blue/Danablu

Despite its enormous milk production and the preponderance of lush meadows, Denmark produces few original cheeses. Most are highly efficient copies of the great cheeses of Europe, bearing Danish names. After the Second World War, with rationing and food shortages, the Danes decided to create a mass-production blue to fill the gap left by Stilton, Gorgonzola and Roquefort. The result was a sharp, salty, robust blue with a creamy consistency and wide appeal. Its shiny, creamy white interior is a mass of blue-black streaks and splodges, while the rind is almost free of mould. Its major appeal is its up-front, direct character and consistency of quality, but to me it lacks finesse.

Denmark	
Milk source	
Unpasteurized	✗
Maturing time	2-3 months
Average weight	3kg/6½lb
Vegetarian	✗
Shape	

Dietrich's Pur Chèvre Bleu

One of a handful of cheesemakers in Illinois, Tom Dietrich is in the ranks of America's modern farmstead cheesemakers. His passion for cheese is matched by his fascination with the animals whose milk is used to make it. Allowing nature to show the way, he has created three very individual cheeses. Dietrich's Pur Chèvre Bleu, like Roquefort, is moist yet crumbly and the pure white of the goat's milk contrasts dramatically with the deep blue-black streaks that impart a powerful spicy punch without overpowering the aromatic herbaceous taste of the milk. Fleur du Praire is like Crottin, while Fleur de Nuit is an attractive ash-covered variation. Each has real character, with a generous dose of wild moulds.

US	Illinois
Milk source	
Unpasteurized	✗
Maturing time	4-6 weeks
Average weight	1.8kg/4lb
Vegetarian	✗
Shape	

Dolcelatte

Almost as well known outside Italy as Gorgonzola, Dolcelatte means 'sweet milk' in Italian and has a luscious, sweet feel and taste, melting in the mouth like ice-cream. It was created in 1967 by Galbani, a famous Italian cheese company, for those who prefer softer, milder tones than those offered by the more robust and spicy traditional blues. Made only in factories, it may also be labelled Gorgonzola Dolce if it uses a vegetarian rennet. The thick, cream interior contains grey and blue splotches of mould and is encased in a thick orange rind, dusted with blue and white moulds. It is superb with served with warm crusty bread.

Italy	Lombardy
Milk source	
Unpasteurized	✓
Maturing time	2-3 months
Average weight	6kg/13¼lb
Vegetarian	✗
Shape	

Dolcelatte Torta

If you think Dolcelatte is wickedly rich, think again. Dolcelatte Torta consists of thick layers of rich Mascarpone cream alternating with soft, sweet Dolcelatte, making an irresistible combination. The cream mellows the blue and the feel in the mouth is indescribably soft and velvety. Pile it on to thick fresh bread, stir it into your favourite pasta, or savour it in solitude with a Madeira or a sweet Italian pudding wine to help cut through the higher-than-average fat content (75 per cent). Its huge success in Italy and abroad has lead to the creation of other *tortas* – some good, some almost inedible. The best example has layers of pesto alternating with Mascarpone.

Italy	
Milk source	
Unpasteurized	✗
Maturing time	1-2 months
Average weight	2.5kg/5½lb
Vegetarian	✗
Shape	

Fourme d'Ambert AOC

Fourme is the old French word for cheese, while Ambert is a town in the mountainous Auvergne region, where cheesemaking is still, for many, a way of life. Fourme d'Ambert is at its most charming when the creamy interior has caused its magnificent colourful crust to develop thick, uneven wrinkles, creating a rather jaunty lopsided look. Orange and slightly sticky, the rind is dusted with fine white and grey moulds, overlaid with patches of red, blue and yellow. All this chaos provides a frame for the creamy white interior and its numerous erratic patches and streaks of blue. This cheese is dense like Stilton, but more supple and nutty in flavour – not too rich, with a wonderful savoury tang to finish.

France	Auvergne
Milk source	
Unpasteurized	✗
Maturing time	2 months
Average weight	2kg/4½lb
Vegetarian	✗
Shape	⬭

Gammelost

Gammelost is as fearsome as the Vikings who reputedly enjoyed it on their long sea voyages. It is a strong-flavoured, hard, almost brittle cheese when aged, made with milk from the goats who graze beside the spectacular 200km-/124-mile-long Sognefjorden. The name means 'old cheese' and stems from the fact that the rind grows a green-brown mould and looks old before its time. To encourage the moulds and protect the cheese from unwanted creatures or bacteria, the young Gammelost was (and some still are) wrapped in gin-soaked straw and juniper berries. These contribute to the extremely robust, sharp, aromatic flavour and erratic bluing. Best after dinner with local gin or Aquavit.

Norway	
Milk source	
Unpasteurized	✗
Maturing time	1 month
Average weight	3kg/6½lb
Vegetarian	✗
Shape	⬭

Gippsland Blue

Gippsland Blue, probably the first genuine Australian farmhouse cheese, was the result of a joint venture started in 1982 by two local farming families. It is sharp, yet sweet and buttery with a spicy lingering blue-cheese tang and, according to cheesemaker Laurie Jensen, it has a mind of its own: 'once its on its way, you have little control over the maturing process'. The pink-orange rind, dusted with a microclimate of yeasts and moulds, thickens and wrinkles, while the chunky veins spread unevenly through the dense, rich interior. Still one of Australia's finest and best-known blues, Gippsland Blue is now part of a range of cheeses from this enterprising team.

Australia	Tarago River
Milk source	
Unpasteurized	✗
Maturing time	8-10 weeks
Average weight	5kg/11lb
Vegetarian	✗
Shape	⬭

Kikorangi

The company Kapiti Cheese has used Maori names to give its cheeses a New Zealand identity. A spoken rather than written language, Maori echoes with the richness of the land and its people. Kikorangi, Maori for 'dark' or 'strong blue', lives up to its name. The slightly moist, cream-coloured rind, dusted with furry grey or blotchy blue moulds, hides a rich golden curd with pockets and streaks of blue that give the cheese its strong piquant spicy taste. Vibrant but not vicious, it makes the tastebuds hum, while its almost buttery texture glides across the palate like a canoe through the calm waters of one of New Zealand's magnificent lakes.

New Zealand	Wellington
Milk source	
Unpasteurized	✗
Maturing time	2 months
Average weight	2kg/4½lb
Vegetarian	✗
Shape	

Lanark Blue

Lanark Blue hit the headlines in December 1994 as a 'killer cheese', when local environmental officers decided that this raw-milk cheese had dangerously high levels of Listeria. Subsequent tests proved this was erroneous, but it nearly cost Humphrey Errington his farm and his sanity before the courts finally ruled in his favour. He will not be the last cheesemaker to battle against bureaucracy, ignorance and a paranoid fear of raw milk. The sheep graze on heather-covered hills and wild natural pastures that give the milk its herbaceous, aromatic character and richness – a contrast to the spicy blue-grey streak in this firm yet moist Scottish blue. A slightly sweet, Roquefort-style cheese.

Scotland	Lanarkshire
Milk source	
Unpasteurized	✓
Maturing time	6-12 weeks
Average weight	2.7-3.6kg 6-8lb
Vegetarian	✓
Shape	

Maytag Blue

When E H Maytag, son of the inventor of the washing machine, died, his family was unsure what to do with his prize-winning herd of Fresian-Holstein cattle. Fortunately, Iowa State University was ready to test its new blue-cheese process. The experimental cheeses were given to the washing machine salesmen to take home. Word quickly spread and the mail-order business was born. In cellars built into the side of a hill, the mould, yeasts, temperature and humidity are influenced by nature rather than technology, allowing the cheese to ripen slowly over six months. The result is a smooth, creamy blue with streaks of spicy, blue-grey mould scattered through it. The finish is hot, with a delicious bite.

US	Iowa
Milk source	
Unpasteurized	✓
Maturing time	5-6 months
Average weight	1.8kg/4lb
Vegetarian	✓
Shape	

Meredith Blue

Ballarat, Victoria, is where Julie Cameron makes Australia's first ewe's milk cheese. The region has a character, climate and geography that bears no resemblance to the sparse grazing and rocky land of Roquefort, with which Julie's cheese is erroneously compared. Meredith Blue is a cheese in its own right, with its brown-orange knobbly rind that gathers a multitude of blue, green, grey and white moulds; its rich, satisfying flavour hinting at wild mushrooms and burnt caramel; and its soft and silky ivory-coloured curd. While the cheese is always good, it is subject to the inconsistency of nature and the difficulty in persuading sheep to mate out of season, and so it is sometimes in short supply.

Australia	Victoria
Milk source	
Unpasteurized	✗
Maturing time	2 months
Average weight	1.5kg/3lb 5oz
Vegetarian	✗
Shape	⬭

Milawa Blue

Pioneers of modern Australian cheeses, David and Anne Brown's cheesemaking began to take serious shape when they stumbled across an old butter factory in the dairy country of Milawa, north of Melbourne. Their first cheese, Milawa Blue, was born with the help of Richard Thomas, stepfather to numerous Australian cheeses. Similar to Gorgonzola, it is soft with wide, unevenly spaced chunky streaks of crusty blue that invade the rich buttery interior. Milawa Blue has a lovely, nutty, vegetal taste with undertones of bitter chocolate and a rugged, wrinkled, crusty rind with various shadings of mould. It is a particular favourite with the excellent sweet wines from nearby Brown Brothers.

Australia	Victoria
Milk source	🐂
Unpasteurized	✗
Maturing time	8-12weeks
Average weight	6kg/13¼lb
Vegetarian	✗
Shape	⬭

Mrs Bell's Blue

In 1987, looking for a way to help her farmer husband Nigel diversify, Judy Bell discovered sheep had been milked in Yorkshire since around the 8th Century. Not wishing to be too ambitious, her first cheese was Olde Yorke, a delicious, wax-coated Feta-style cheese. Six years later she decided to produce a blue cheese, the first in the area since 1960, when the local creamery had stopped production of all blues. First came Yorkshire Blue, a cow's milk cheese, and more recently Mrs Bell's Blue. Nutty, with an underlying sweetness, yet with a distinct but gentle aromatic tang, it has a complexity and richness of texture that has met with universal approval.

England	Yorkshire
Milk source	
Unpasteurized	✗
Maturing time	8-10 weeks
Average weight	3.25kg/7lb
Vegetarian	✓
Shape	⬭

New Zealand Blue Vein

The New Zealand Rennet Company was founded in 1916, alleviating the need for cheesemakers to make their own rennet. As the cost of shipping cheeses all the way from Europe became prohibitive, the company turned to cheesemaking. In 1951 it produced Blue Vein, New Zealand's first, and for many years only, blue cheese. To many New Zealanders, including my father, it is still the best, as 'it's a man's cheese'. Sold only in wedges, it is moist and crumbly with a sharp acidity and a mass of gritty grey-blue streaks. Without it, *Edmond's Cook Book* and the recipes from Alison Holst, New Zealand's answer to Delia Smith, would seem incomplete.

New Zealand	Taranaki
Milk source	🐂
Unpasteurized	✗
Maturing time	**6-8 weeks**
Average weight	**3.25kg/7lb**
Vegetarian	✗
Shape	⬭

Oxford Blue

Oxford Blue, generally associated with a sporting achievement at the famous university, was born in 1993 when Robert Pouget, an irascible French baron, decided to add cheese to this famous city's list of accolades. After 10 years of selling cheese from all over the world in the Oxford Covered Market, he decide to create the Oxford Don of the cheese world and set about producing a more French-style English blue as an alternative to Stilton. Luscious, moist and creamy, it is aromatic and spicy with a hint of dark chocolate and white wine and a distinct but not vicious blue tang. It has a wet, sticky rind rather than the drier, rough Stilton crust.

England	Oxfordshire
Milk source	🐂
Unpasteurized	✓
Maturing time	**14-16 weeks**
Average weight	**2.25kg/5lb**
Vegetarian	✗
Shape	⬭

Shropshire Blue

First made in Inverness earlier this century, Shropshire Blue was later introduced to the Stilton makers, who have taken it to their hearts. It comes from the same clover, and the same milk from the black-and-white cows that are responsible for Stilton. The difference is the addition to the milk of annatto, creating a distinct orange colour contrasting with the royal blue of the mould. The cheese maintains its wonderful blue taste, yet there is an underlying hint of rich, buttery, burnt caramel, lifting Shropshire Blue onto a pedestal, like nutmeg lifts spinach. This English beauty is sadly underrated and certainly deserves a place on an English cheeseboard.

England	Derbyshire Leicestershire Nottinghamshire
Milk source	🐂
Unpasteurized	✗
Maturing time	**10-12 weeks**
Average weight	**7.5kg/16½lb**
Vegetarian	✓
Shape	⬭

St-Agur

Since the late 1980s many of the small creameries and co-operatives
of France have been bought out and the market is now dominated by
a handful of huge conglomerates producing mainly lacklustre cheese
destined for the international market. St-Agur is very much the
exception, and demonstrates that big can still be beautiful. Made in the
Auvergne, where blue cheeses have been made for centuries, its unique
hexagonal shape catches the consumer's eye in supermarkets around the
world, and its taste and texture do not disappoint. Moist and creamy, the
spicy, evenly spread patches of blue leave a tingle on the palate, and its
shape makes it easy for cutting.

France	Auvergne
Milk source	🐄
Unpasteurized	✗
Maturing time	2 months
Average weight	2kg/4½lb
Vegetarian	✗
Shape	⬡

Valdeon DO

The Picos de Europa, the Peaks of Europe, are aptly named, towering
over the wooded foothills and tiny villages, providing a safe haven for the
millions of tiny blue spores that lurk in the limestone caves. Farmhouse
blue-cheese makers use a blend of cow's milk with either goat's or sheep's
milk depending on the season. Valdeon is creamy and moist with blue-
green veins similar to those in Stilton, but with a more pungent aroma, a
salty bite and a clean piquant finish. Wrapped in plane-tree leaves, it
gives a cheeseboard a rustic yet elegant look. The cheese is eaten locally
with wild honey and fruity wines. Valdeon is more commonly known by
the brand name Picos de Europa. *(See also* Cabrales.)

Spain	Picos de Europa
Milk source	🐄
Unpasteurized	✗
Maturing time	2-3 months
Average weight	3kg/6½lb
Vegetarian	✗
Shape	⬭

Waimata Farmhouse Blue

Vivacious and intriguing, former fruit grower, Carole Thorpe is a force
to be reckoned with. She is a relative newcomer to the cheese world and
has taken the market by storm. Each year at the New Zealand Cheese
Awards, Carole and her husband Rick produce yet another stunning
cheese. Determined to survive the crash in 1992 of the Kiwi fruit market,
Carole set about creating cheeses that were unique, rather than emulating
those of Europe. Already aware of the importance of the soil and climate
in the wine industry, she started experimenting. Today Waimata Blue, one
of only a handful of genuine New Zealand farmhouse blues, is joined by
an increasing number of diverse and excellent cheeses.

New Zealand	Gisbourne
Milk source	🐄
Unpasteurized	✗
Maturing time	6-9 weeks
Average weight	2.5kg/5½lb
Vegetarian	✗
Shape	

Blue

Cheese name	Country of origin	Region	Milk source
Aaran Blue	Scotland	Isle of Arran	Cow
Abbey Blue Brie	Ireland	Co Laois	Cow
Adelost	Sweden		Cow
Ascaig Blue	Scotland	Ross & Cromarty	Goat
Bass Strait Blue	Australia	Tasmania	Cow
Berkshire Blue	US	New York	Goat
Bleu de Corse	France	Corsica	Ewe
Bleu de Costaros	France	Auvergne	Cow
Bleu de Langeac	France	Auvergne	Cow
Bleu de Lacqueuille	France	Auvergne	Cow
Bleu de Loudes	France	Auvergne	Cow
Bleu de Montagne	New Zealand	Taranaki	Cow
Bleu de Sassenage AOC	France	Rhône-Alpes	Cow
Bleu de Septmoncel	France	Franche-Comté	Cow
Bleu de Termignon	France	Rhône-Alpes	Cow
Bleu de Thiezac	France	Auvergne	Cow
Bleu du Quercy	France	Midi-Pyrénées	Cow
Bleu du Queyras	France	Dauphine	Cow and some goat
Blue Castello or Bla Castello	Denmark		Cow
Blue Cheddar	England	Derbyshire	Cow
Blue Cheshire	England	Nottinghamshire	Cow
Blue Rathgore	Northern Ireland	Antrim	Goat
Blue Supreme	New Zealand	Taranaki	Cow
Blue Wensleydale	England	North Yorkshire	Cow
Brendon Blue	England	Somerset	Goat
Brodick Blue	Scotland	Isle of Arran	Ewe
Buxton Blue	England	Derbyshire	Cow
Cambridge Blue	England	Leicestershire	Cow
Captain's Bay Blue	New Zealand	Taranaki	Cow
Chetwynd Blue	Ireland	Cork	Cow
Clemson Blue	US	South Carolina	Cow
Coleford Blue	Ewe	Somerset	Ewe

Coro Blue	New Zealand	Coromandel	Cow
Crozier Blue	Ireland	Co Tipperary	Ewe
Devon Blue	England	Devon	Cow
Dorset Blue Vinny	England	Dorset	Cow
Dovedale	England	Derbyshire	Cow
Dunsyre Blue	Scotland	Lanarkshire	Cow
Evansdale Blue	New Zealand	Dunedin	Ewe
Exmoor Jersey Blue	England	Somerset	Cow
Fairview Estate Blue Brie	South Africa	Stellenbosch	Cow
Fourme de Montbrisso	France	Loire	Cow
Galloway Blue	Scotland	Dumfries & Galloway	Goat
Granston Blue	Wales	Dyfed	Cow
Harbourne Blue	England	Devon	Goat
Jubilee Blue	New Zealand	Taranaki	Cow
Kahurangi	New Zealand	Paraparauma	Cow
Kapiti Island Blue	New Zealand	Paraparauma	Cow
King Island Blue	Australia	Tasmania	Cow
Madelva	Spain	Asturias	Cow
Melton Intrigue	England	Leicestershire	Cow
Mycella	Denmark		Cow
Pas de Bleu	Belgium	Liège	Cow
Picon DO *see* Picos de Europa	Spain	Cantabria	Cow
Picos de Europa DO	Spain	León	Cow
Quantock Blue	England	Somerset	Ewe
Rogue River Blue	US	Oregon	Cow
Rosetta	South Africa	Mooi River	Cow
Shades of Blue	New Zealand	Taranaki	Cow
Somerset Blue	England	Somerset	Cow
Strathdon Blue	Scotland	Grampian	Cow
Timboon Blue Brie	Australia	Victoria	Cow
Waimata Blue Brie	New Zealand	Gisbourne	Cow
Windsor Blue	New Zealand	Oamaru	Cow
Yorkshire Blue	England	North Yorkshire	Cow

Speciality cheeses

Above: The overlapping leaves of fresh, sterile nettles must be placed by hand on each individual Cornish Yarg.

Double Gloucester with Cream Cheese, Dill and Smoked Salmon, or Cheddar with Lime Pickle are just two examples.

Equally, there are many speciality cheeses that appeal to cheese-lovers looking for the unusual. However, my preference, with the odd exception, lies in cheeses that allow the subtleties of the milk and unique qualities of the grazing to come to the fore. Nevertheless, speciality cheeses comprise a rapidly growing area of the market and offer an alternative to people who like dessert rather than cheese, or who are not sure they like cheese.

The recipe for speciality cheeses

There are two distinct methods of production. The traditional method is to add the fresh or dried herbs or spices to the freshly formed curd so they can mature together. However, most of the factory versions are made by taking semi-cured cheeses, breaking them up, blending in the flavourings, then re-pressing the new cheese into various shapes to mature for a few weeks. Typical additives include fruits, nuts, herbs, spices, wine, fish, other cheeses and even ham. Cheeses with fruits, such as White Stilton with Apricots and Wensleydale with Cranberries, can be quite sweet and are appropriate for desserts.

P eople have always been fascinated by the complexity of flavours possible when herbs, spices and nuts are combined with simple everyday foods. Cheese is no exception. The Romans added fresh herbs to many of their cheeses and, since the 16th Century, the Dutch have added the exotic spices they brought back from the East Indies.

However, until 10 years ago the number of hard or semi-soft cheeses with added ingredients, known as 'speciality' or 'flavoured' cheeses, could be counted on two hands. Now there are over 100. Most have as their base a familiar cheese such as Pecorino or Cheddar, to which a subtle sprinkling of herbs, spices or nuts is added, resulting in cheeses such as Pecorino with Truffles or Lancashire with Chives.

However, some speciality cheeses were no doubt created as the result of a think-tank of young advertising account executives, and show not a modicum of respect towards tradition or convention.

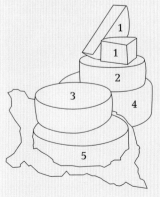

1 *Hereford Hop*
2 *Devon Garland*
3 *Tiskey Meadow*
     (see *Devon Garland*)
4 *Gouda with cloves*
     (see *Leiden*)
5 *Cornish Yarg*

Leiden or Leidsekaas

Holland	Leiden
Milk source	🐄
Unpasteurised	✗
Maturing time	3-6 months
Average weight	3-10kg 6½-22lb
Vegetarian	✗
Shape	⬭

During the 17th Century, the Dutch East Indies Company was founded, marking the beginning of the spice trade between Indonesia and Europe. The Dutch, whose cheeses were already well known internationally and ideal for sea voyages, experimented with adding exotic spices to their cheeses, particularly cumin, caraway, peppercorns and cloves (as in Gouda with Cloves).

Leiden, which includes cumin, salt and sometimes carraway seeds, was one of the first speciality cheeses to be created, and it is still popular today. However, Leiden is made with semi-skimmed milk and it should not be confused with Gouda with Cumin, which is sold younger than Leiden and is somewhat smoother and more creamy.

Not only a classic example of a speciality cheese, Leiden is also a washed-curd cheese, a technique used in the manufacture of most Dutch cheeses. Once the milk has formed a semi-solid mass, the curds are cut, releasing the yellow-green whey, and the mixture is stirred, encouraging more whey to leave the curd. Some of the whey is then drained off and replaced with warm water, the mixture is

stirred, and then some of the diluted whey is again drained off and replaced with more water.

The water removes the lactose and other solubles from the curd, and some is re-absorbed into the curd. The result is a lower level of acidity in the curd than in other cheeses, because the activity of the lactic bacteria is reduced by removing any remaining lactose. Well-known examples of washed curd cheeses include Edam, Colby, Gouda, Cottage Cheese (washed in cold water) and Havarti.

Hot water is also used to form the curds in *pasta filata* (or stretched-curd) cheeses. However, it is added after the curd has formed, so these cheeses are not regarded as washed-curd cheeses.

The recipe

To create Leiden, the liquid is then drained off and the curds, a sprinkling of cumin, salt and sometimes caraway seeds, are evenly distributed into moulds lined with cloth and pressed. The custom of treading the cumin into the curd by feet rather than by hand has, needless to say, been replaced by machine.

After a few days in the press the cheeses are soaked in brine baths and, to identify the cheese as genuine Leiden, the rind is imprinted with the city of Leiden's emblem – the famous crossed keys. However,

Above: Row upon row of cheeses are matured on wooden shelves, where they will be checked and turned regularly.

this procedure is imitated by the Norwegians on their Nokkelost. To further distinguish a Leiden, the rind is rubbed with annatto to obtain a shiny red-orange colour, or it is 'painted' with red plastic. Of all the Dutch cheeses, Boeren Leidse (farmhouse Leiden), made by only a few cheesemakers by the Rhine river, is one of the most sought-after by the Dutch *Kaaskoppen* or 'cheese heads'.

Leiden is similar in texture to Gouda, but it is made with semi-skimmed milk, so it feels slightly drier. The distinctive, spicy, aromatic flavour of the cumin provides an excellent contrast for the creamy, nutty character of the cheese.

History of cheesemaking in Holland

Pots and vessels discovered in Holland indicate cheese was made there in the 2nd Century BC. But the Romans taught the Dutch the art of cheesemaking. The Romans were also responsible for the systems of dykes that drained the land known as the polders, creating huge flat meadow lands ideal for dairy cows,

and thus laying the foundations for the famous cheeses of Holland: Edam, Gouda and their derivatives, of which Leiden or Leidse is the best-known.

For centuries, cheesemaking in Holland was done mainly by women. But at the turn of the 20th Century, cheesemaking moved to the creameries. Today the Netherlands produce about 630 million kg/620,536 tons of cheese annually, of which 80 per cent is exported.

Many European countries have adopted the Dutch style of cheesemaking, most notably Sweden. In the 19th Century, Dutch immigrants in America and Australia started making farmhouse versions of their native land's cheeses, retaining the old methods, although regulations prevent most from using raw milk.

You still see many old weigh-houses, where the cheeses were brought to be weighed and the quality checked. However, today they are mainly tourist attractions and the best cheeses are sold at weekly farmers' markets at Bodegraven and Woerden.

FAT AND CHEESE

Fat content is usually expressed as the percentage of fat in dry matter, rather than in the cheese as a whole. These figures, more appropriately, represent the latter.

Type of cheese			Average % fat
Fresh		Feta	20.2
Range	1-26%	Cream cheese	47.4
		Mozzarella	21.7
Natural rind		Crottin	24.0
Range	22-26%		
Soft, white-rind		Camembert	24.5
Range	20-26%	Double-cream Bries	47.0
Semi-soft		Epoisses	24.5
Range	24-30%	Edam	25.4
		Gouda	31.0
Hard		Cheddar	34.5
Range	28-34%	Parmesan	29.5
Blue		Blue Brie-type	38.0
Range	29-33%	Dolcelatte	36.0
		Stilton	35.5
Speciality		Same as for the base cheese.	

Casciotta al Tartufo

The scent of truffles transports me to a 14th-Century farmhouse kitchen in Tuscany. I can smell it, taste it and feel the warmth of the open fire and the hospitality of my hosts. On a scrubbed wooden table were freshly dug spring onions, fat broad beans bursting from their skins, finely sliced pink Parma ham and warm, yeasty bread. Filling the room with its intense, earthy, nutty, sensuous aroma was a generous hunk of Casciotta al Tartufo. Slivers of precious Umbrian black truffle are added to the curd and, as it matures, the essence of the truffle is absorbed by the fat globules. This results in a compact, friable, moist cheese and concentrates the flavour of the truffle to heavenly heights.

Italy	Tuscany, Umbria
Milk source	
Unpasteurized	✓✗
Maturing time	3-6 months
Average weight	2-3kg/4½-6½lb
Vegetarian	✗
Shape	

Conciato alle Noci

Volpetti is the quintessential Italian deli and is also renowned as an *affineur*. To make Conciato alle Noci, the best young Pecorino, preferably those made in May to June, are rubbed with oil every day for six weeks or so. In August they are washed with vinegar, covered with ash and sealed in old wine barrels with alternating layers of walnut-tree leaves. After 90 days and 90 nights, the now flaky cheese has absorbed the sweet, nutty vegetal taste of the leaves and the sweet yeasty character of old wine. Tangy, creamy and very nutty, it has a hint of fermenting apples yet still retains the sweetness of the ewe's milk. Don't be deterred by the purple, wine stained, blotchy rind – the taste is stunning.

Italy	Umbria
Milk source	
Unpasteurized	✓
Maturing time	3-5 months
Average weight	2kg/4½lb
Vegetarian	✗
Shape	

Cornish Yarg

The recipe for Cornish Yarg is relatively new, having been invented and handed on to the Horrells in 1983 by Alan Gray. When he was trying to find an appropriate name, a lateral-thinking friend suggested that Gray spelt backwards sounded very Cornish, and the name stuck. The fine, barely formed, rind is wrapped in overlapping silvery green nettles, providing an unusual and attractive contrast to the white interior and imparting a slightly vegetal taste to the cheese. Moist but crumbly, it is not dissimilar to Caerphilly and has a lovely freshness. As it matures the nettles attract a pale grey mould, the interior softens and the flavour is reminiscent of meadow flowers and creamed spinach.

England	Cornwall
Milk source	
Unpasteurized	✓
Maturing time	10-15 weeks
Average weight	900g or 2.7kg 2 or 6lb
Vegetarian	✗
Shape	

Devon Garland

This is an old West-Country recipe, rediscovered by Hilary Charnley in the 1970s. Before retiring, Hilary passed on her wisdom and experience to Jeremy Frankpitt of Peverstone Cheese, who has continued to make this handsome crusty wheel. The 'garland', or layer of spring onions, thyme and oregano, is sprinkled over the fresh curd, covered with more curd, then lightly pressed, before being aged for up to eight weeks. The moist, loosely packed curd, similar to Caerphilly, is lemony fresh and absorbs and concentrates the natural oils of the herbs, resulting in a fresh, clean, savoury taste. Another of their cheeses, Tisky Meadow, contains a blend of sun-dried tomatoes and basil.

England	Devon
Milk source	
Unpasteurized	✓
Maturing time	6-8 weeks
Average weight	3.6kg/8lb
Vegetarian	✓
Shape	

Hereford Hop

In 1988 Charles Martell, a cheesemaker already renowned for his traditional Double and Single Gloucester, discovered a recipe for Hereford Hop in the local archives. Fascinated and curious, he began to experiment. The best results were obtained by lightly toasting the hops, which he pressed into the rind, creating a crunchy texture and a yeasty aroma. The hoppy taste was further emphasised when they were absorbed into the surface. The Caerphilly-like interior, with its mellow, yellow, sweet, buttery taste, provided an excellent contrast to the hops. Not recommended for cooking, but ideal with a glass of beer or cider. It is now also made by Malvern Cheesewrights.

England	Gloucestershire
Milk source	
Unpasteurized	✓
Maturing time	1-3 months
Average weight	2kg/4½lb
Vegetarian	✗
Shape	

Oak Smoked Cheddar

Many of the mountain cheeses of Spain, Italy and France were stored in the rafters of the small mountain huts where they were made, and would gradually absorb the sweet smoke from the open fire. However, smoking Cheddar is a recent trend. Usually Cheddar is stored in large cellars or curing rooms and its cloth wrapping and size would prevent any smoke from penetrating the rind. In the last 15 years, though, block or traditional Cheddar makers have found a ready market for their cheese when smoked over oak chips. The result is delicious. Some, unfortunately, are simply brushed with 'liquid smoke' and the taste and texture of the cheese is both synthetic and most unpleasant, but it sells well.

England	
Milk source	
Unpasteurized	✓ ✗
Maturing time	2-18 months
Average weight	various
Vegetarian	✓ ✗
Shape	

Sage Derby

The custom of adding sage to the delicate, local cheese in Derby was devised in the 17th Century when it was believed that the herb was beneficial to health. However, the method used then is very different to that of today, when most Sage Derby is reconstituted cheese blended with green vegetable dye and dried, colourless sage. Traditionally, pulped sage leaves were blended with spinach juice and stirred into the curd. This coloured curd would be placed in moulds in layers with contrasting plain Derby, resulting in an attractive layered effect when cut. Lovers of sage can still enjoy the combination of creamy, moist Derby with the distinctive savoury taste of sage, despite the strange marbled appearance.

England	Yorkshire
Milk source	
Unpasteurized	✗
Maturing time	1-3 months
Average weight	4-13.6kg 9-30lb
Vegetarian	✓
Shape	

Sally Jackson Cheeses

One cannot not blame the Jacksons for exchanging the over-heated offices and pavements of Washington for the warmth of the cheesemaking room and sense of nature and purpose that envelops you in the Okanogan Valley Highlands. But when you visit them you realise that a cheesemaker's life is hard, particularly if, like the Jacksons, you also milk your own flock. Almost impossible to categorize, but somewhere between a natural rind, hard or speciality cheese, their ewe's milk cheese is wrapped in brandy-soaked chestnut leaves that impart a vegetal, earthy, vaguely alcoholic subtlety to the firm, yet melt-in-the-mouth texture.

US	Washington State
Milk source	
Unpasteurized	✓
Maturing time	various
Average weight	375g/13oz
Vegetarian	✗
Shape	

Staffordshire Organic

David Deauville has been making Staffordshire Organic since 1984, and it is still one of only a handful of organic hard cheeses in the UK, (although the movement is growing rapidly). Smooth and creamy, yet firm and moist, it is worth seeking out particularly if you find one with wild garlic, as opposed to the usual herb and chive version. To most farmers wild garlic is a noxious weed whose aroma taints the milk, but not to the Deauvilles. They harvest it in spring, mince it up and freeze it, adding it in small quantities to the fresh curd. The result is a cheese with a symphony of flavours – young radicchio, fried onions, cheese and onion sauce and a delicious, sharp, mouth-watering tang.

England	Staffordshire
Milk source	
Unpasteurized	✓
Maturing time	2-12 months
Average weight	1.5, 10 or 20kg/3lb 5oz, 22 or 44lb
Vegetarian	✓
Shape	

Cheese name	Country of origin	Region	Milk source	**Speciality**
Applemint Swaledale	England	North Yorkshire	Cow	
Aukai	New Zealand	Paraparauma	Cow	
Cotswold	England	Leicestershire	Cow	
Crème Café	England	North Yorkshire	Ewe	
Danegate Gold	England	East Sussex	Ewe	
Double Gloucester with Chives	England	Somerset	Cow	
Duddleswell Smoked	England	East Sussex	Ewe	
Fonti Farm Cheese	Australia	Western Australia	Cow	
Formaio Embriago Trevigiano	Italy	Treviso	Cow	
Friese Nagelkaas	Holland		Cow	
Gouda with Cloves	New Zealand	Hamilton	Cow	
Hatherton	England	Cheshire	Cow	
Hunting Pink	England	Devon	Cow	
Karikaas Leiden	New Zealand	Christchurch	Cow	
Karikaas with Red & Black Pepper	New Zealand	Christchurch	Cow	
Knockanore Smoked	Ireland	County Waterford	Cow	
Kominjnekaas	Holland		Cow	
Kruidenkaas or Herb Cheese	Holland		Cow	
Lemon Grove	England	Leicestershire	Cow	
Llanboidy with Laverbread	Wales	Dyfed	Cow	
Loch Arthur with Caraway	Scotland	Dumfries & Galloway	Cow	
Montachio	New Zealand	Paraparauma	Cow	
Nokkelost	Norway		Cow	
Old Peculiar Swaledale	England	North Yorkshire	Cow	
Orange Grove	England	Leicestershire	Cow	
Piacintinu de Enna	Italy	Sicily	Ewe	
Pineapple Grove	England	Leicestershire	Cow	
Queso Curado	Spain	Canary lslands	Goat & ewe	
Queso Palmero	Spain	Canary Islands	Goat	
Red Leicester and Pecans	England	Shropshire	Cow	
Smoked Ardrahan	Ireland	County Cork	Cow	
Tiskey Meadow	England	Devon	Cow	
Walnut Cheese	New Zealand	Christchurch	Cow	
Warwickshire Truckle	England	West Midlands	Cow	
Wensleydale with Cranberries	England	North Yorkshire	Cow	
Wensleydale with Stem Ginger	England	North Yorkshire	Cow	
White Stilton with Apricots	England	Leicestershire	Cow	
White Stilton with Lemon	England	Leicestershire	Cow	
Worcester Sauce Cheese	England	Hereford & Worcester	Cow	
Y Fenni	Wales	Gwent	Cow	

Selecting and serving cheeses

Above: Charming signs, such as this one in Gevrey-Chambertin in Burgundy, France, can be seen outside many small cheesemakers tempting passers-by to stop.

Whether you are in the local supermarket, your favourite cheese shop or a market in Greece, the problems are always the same: how do you choose a cheese? What will it taste like? And is it ripe? Assuming you know which of the seven types your chosen cheese is, you can determine its texture, taste and strength of flavour. For the rind is as expressive as the face of a young girl caught wearing her mother's makeup – her secret is obvious.

However, the history, regulations and geographical position of a country will significantly affect the cheeses on sale. In America you cannot buy raw-milk cheese under 60 days old, so soft cheeses will – almost without exception – be pasteurized. New Zealand and Australia prohibit the sale of raw-milk cheese, including great traditional cheeses such as Cheddar, Roquefort and Parmigiano. Consequently, in many cases the native people have created their own. Some are good, some almost unrecognizable.

Cheesemongers who are proud of their cheeses will usually let you taste a selection, tell you what is in season, what is ripe and what is local, and recommend their favourite cheeses. If you cannot taste cheeses before buying, it is best to stick to hard cheeses or go elsewhere.

Once home, keep cheese wrapped in its original paper in a cool cellar or larder. If, like most of us, you are not blessed with a larder, store cheese in a sealed plastic box in the fridge. Placing a damp cloth over cheese to keep it moist was, in its day, an excellent technique, but that was when the butler was available to ensure the cloth remained damp. If you do not keep the cloth damp, as it dries, it draws the moisture from around it, making the cheese dry out twice as fast as it would without the cloth.

Plastic wrap, on the other hand, is a modern convenience, seen as a panacea to prevent strong aromas from escaping or being absorbed, to keep out unwanted bugs and to prevent food from drying out. However, if you embalm the cheese, it will sweat and the gasses given off during fermentation will be absorbed into the cheese, giving it a bitter, ammonia-sour aroma and sweaty, salty taste. Wax paper or unwrinkled aluminium foil is best.

The French serve cheese before pudding, simply because they finish the red wine from the main course with the cheese. Then they have blue cheese followed by dessert with the sweeter pudding wine. They would never dream of going from red wine to sweet wine and back again.

Experience and experimentation will help you fine tune your sensitivity to the nuances of cheese. Wherever you are, I leave it to you to decide which cheeses appeal, which shout 'pick me' and which wine to serve. Just remember the pleasure of discovering what the French have always known, that 'one lives to eat, not eats to live'.

Left: Whether you are in a market in France or an emporium of cheese in Italy, Britain or America, you will find this book an invaluable guide as it enables you to judge a cheese by its cover. The best shops, however, will insist you taste the cheeses before you buy.

Assembling the perfect cheeseboard

Modern distribution has brought with it many problems for the environment, but it has also enabled producers in isolated areas to reach a larger market and us, the consumers, to enjoy a wealth of unique handcrafted and commercially made cheeses. Consequently, creating the perfect cheeseboard, using a combination of modern and traditional cheeses, is a pleasure.

Use the following guidelines, and nobody will doubt your prowess as a cheese-lover.

1) Vary the texture by choosing cheeses from the different categories.
2) Avoid biscuits – their crunchy texture detracts from the cheese. Instead serve rustic breads.
3) A good array of colour is important and can be achieved by choosing cheeses from the different categories. Colour should not come from grapes, apples, twirly tomatoes, sculptured carrots or celery.
4) Offer a choice of mild and strong cheeses. The categories of cheese appear in this book roughly in order of strength (from mild to strong) although, as with all rules, there are exceptions and reasons for breaking them.
5) One superb cheese is better than several pieces of cheese that end up as shrivelled morsels in the bottom of your fridge.
6) Variety is the spice of life, so have at least one goat's or ewe's milk cheese or one that is new, outrageous or unfamiliar to you. Be courageous.
7) Try to have a selection of shapes to enhance the board. If you cannot avoid using wedges, present them in different ways – stand some upright, some on their side, and cut one or two into different shapes.
8) For decoration, emphasize the seasonal nature of cheese by using local flora – brambles, wild flowers, leaves, fresh herbs and even a bunch of dried grasses tied with raffia.
9) Serving butter with cheese is an English habit – originally done because most cheeses were hard and dry. Butter was introduced to soften the feel and reduce the punch of the often strong, sharp, aged cheeses. It is now rarely needed.
10) If all the cheeses are around the same size or weight, you will have less wastage.
11) It's good to support your local cheesemakers by serving cheeses from your region.
12) If you want your cheeseboard to reflect the mood or style of your menu, or you wish to serve cheeses that complement a particular wine, then introduce a theme – all blues, all goat's, all British, etc.
13) Don't let accompaniments like pickles or chutneys overpower your cheese. Use lightly spiced home-made fruit chutneys. Try a slice of sweet-sour Spanish *membrillo*, a fruit 'cheese' made of concentrated quince jelly, with hard ewe's milk cheeses such as Manchego, or broad beans and spring onions with a sharp, nutty Pecorino. Alternatively,
dried fruit and nuts can provide appropriate contrasts without overpowering the cheeses.
14) Take cheese out of the fridge and leave it at room temperature for an hour or more if it is large or thick.

What to serve cheese on

Wooden boards Gnarled pieces of wood, collected from beaches make inexpensive, elegant or rustic cheeseboards – but if necessary, make sure they are cleaned up thoroughly first. Their imperfections, unusual patterns, holes and cracks emphasise the natural, pastoral nature of cheese.

Marble platters Marble boards, with their distinctive patterns and colours, have been used since the Middle Ages as a means of keeping cheeses cool. However, cheese should not be stored on marble as it prevents the cheese from breathing.

Straw mats and wicker trays These allow the cheese to breathe and lend a rustic appeal to the presentation.

Platters Use any flat surface as a platter – just cover it with a crisp, white linen napkin and use vine or chestnut leaves for contrast.

The diversity of cheese is endless and it is at its best when served simply with a bottle of wine and crusty bread. There is little wastage with cheese. and even less preparation, so it makes a wonderful lunch, a salacious snack, an ideal *apéritif* or a sensational end to a wonderful dinner. The possibilities are only limited by your imagination, budget and cheese merchant.

Cooking with cheese

Cheese is generally eaten for its own inherent character. You rarely buy a wine with the sole purpose of converting it into a casserole, soup or sauce; instead you buy it for the pleasure of the wine itself. The same should apply to cheese. A selection of ripe, luscious cheeses served with country breads, fresh or dried fruits and a bottle or two of wine is already a banquet.

It is the preoccupation with recipes and cooking with cheese that has prevented the development of a cheese culture in English-speaking countries. That is not to say cheese is not good to cook with. On the contrary, it is the most versatile ingredient in my kitchen. Without it, many traditional dishes – such as the ubiquitous cheese on toast with a thousand variations around the world, vegetable gratin, moussaka, cheese straws, caesar salad, fondue, pizza and innumerable pasta dishes or salads – would have faded into insignificance.

You don't need a recipe to convert those tasty little morsels in the bottom of the fridge into a culinary wonder. Simply grate, chop or melt them into sauces, over fresh pasta or on toast, and enjoy your own creation. Here are a few suggestions and basic rules for cooking with cheese:

Fresh

Subtle, even bland in flavour, fresh cheeses are at home in sweet or savoury dishes. But their high moisture content means that most will disintegrate when heated, so they are best in cold dishes or stirred into hot pasta or sauces at the last minute. Stretched curd and whey cheeses are exceptions, giving texture rather than taste to many European dishes. Pickled cheeses, such as Feta, are firmer and can be grilled or served as part of a salad.

Natural rind

These cheeses are ideal for eating simply with country breads and a glass of crisp white wine. They are delicious in Chèvre Salade (*see* page 48). They grill superbly and the

small cheeses are excellent baked whole when their aromatic character takes on a more nutty flavour.

Soft, white-rind

Soft, white-rind cheeses can be grilled or baked, but they refuse to integrate into sauces. Remove the rind as it can impart a bitter flavour and affect the texture of your dish. To me, deep-frying Camembert is like deep-frying butter, and serving it with gooseberry conserve, an insult.

Semi-soft

The more elastic and rubbery a semi-soft cheese is, the better it is when grilled – the tension holds the slice together, so it doesn't slide off the edge of your grilled fish, burger or steak. Semi-soft cheeses do not

melt well in sauces, although the less elastic variety will, with some elbow grease, blend. Cut the rind off when cooking, as it may be gritty, tough or overpower your other ingredients when heated. The pungent, soft washed-rind cheeses melt superbly, but the aroma and taste become even more pervasive – use sparingly.

Hard

These are the most versatile cheeses to cook with: grate, grill, slice or bake them. If they are supple-textured like Emmental, they will be stringy when cooked. Harder, crumbly or brittle cheeses (eg aged Cheddar, Lancashire, Parmigiano, Pecorino) will completely melt in with other ingredients, contributing a superb savoury taste but not distracting from the texture of casseroles, soups, sauces, muffins or pastries. When grilled, hard cheeses tend to run, so put them on a surface that they can melt into, such as over bread or vegetables, or they will slip over the edge, forming a delicious but ill-placed gooey mass in the bottom of your barbecue or grill. Hard cheese and pastry make wonderful companions, and are combined in innumerable dishes.

Blue

Outspoken in flavour, most blues will overpower all but the most robust of ingredients. Consequently they are best when they are the *raison d'être* of a dish. Try crumbling into salads and use a vinaigrette laced with honey. White wine, cream or butter will soften the more pungent aspects of blue cheese. The Brie-style blues, such as Cambozola, behave like soft, white-rind cheeses and their sweet, spiciness is often replaced with the old socks and damp washing characteristics when cooked.

Speciality

Use cheeses flavoured with savoury ingredients as you would the original cheese, but ensure they do not go into combat with other ingredients. Keep the dish simple. Pasta, baked potatoes, vegetables or toast can provide an excellent background for cheeses such as Double Gloucester with Chives, Smoked Cheddar or Gouda with Cumin. Speciality cheeses that incorporate fruits, such as Wensleydale with Cranberries or Stilton with Apricots, are best thought of as puddings and served simply with a sweet wine. Cooking rarely enhances their characters.

Wine with cheese

Strange chemistry occurs when you match wines with food. Certain combinations, such as asparagus and Beaujolais, are distinctly unpleasant. Equally, Champagne and smoked salmon – a favourite combination for celebration across the world – in my opinion behave like spoilt brats together. The Champagne steals the sweetness and delicate feel of the salmon, while the salmon makes the Champagne develop a smarmy attitude, leaving both without charm or elegance (although rosé Champagne can be excellent).

Cheese and wine can provide disreputable or distinguished matches. When the complex blends of acids and fats meet, as with any blind date, hidden flaws may be revealed, subtle characteristics released, or rough edges smoothed away. New and unique sensations of tastes and textures may be created or the personalities of both the cheese and wine annihilated.

Unfortunately, many of the classic matches, such as Cheddar and Bordeaux and Stilton and port, are based on historical or political alliances rather than gastronomic suitability. Equally biased are some wine-lovers, who eulogize over matches where the wine is carried to new heights, while the cheese is forced to absorb the wine's harsh edges and imperfections at the expense of its own distinct character.

The following suggestions are based on tried-and-tested recommendations from those who love both cheese and wine and who want to bring out the best in both. Use them as starting points and do not be afraid to experiment.

Cheese matches

Fresh These cheeses are mild, with varying degrees of acidity. They respond well to fresh, light, crisp white wines or fruity rosés. Red wines are too heavy, unless the cheese is part of a more savoury or spicy dish, such as pizza, when a more demonstrative partner is required.

Natural rind Nutty, sharp, creamy and aromatic, with overtones of hawthorn and tarragon, these cheeses prefer dry, white wines with some acidity, such as Sauvignon Blanc. The fruity acidity encourages the cheese to open up, giving some cheeses a marvellous ice-cream feel in the mouth. Aged cheeses are more intense in flavour and need a heavier wine such as the young, fruity reds of the Loire or wines from the gentle-natured Merlot grape.

Soft, white-rind Young, slightly sharp, salty Neufchâtel-style varieties prefer sweet, late-harvest wines, while the rich, double-cream cheeses need a fruitier wine with a good acidity, such as rosé, ripe New World whites or Champagne, to cut through the extra fats. More meaty Bries prefer a full-bodied, oaked white (white burgundy or Bordeaux) or smooth red, such as Pinot Noir; heavier reds are too tannic.

Semi-soft Generally, the sweet-savoury character and elastic texture of these cheeses marries well with oaked Chardonnay or soft, fruity reds such as Merlot. With firmer, more distinctly flavoured cheeses, try Chianti, Rioja or even young, juicy Cabernet Sauvignon (especially from Chile). The meaty, pungent washed-rind style demands the complex but mellow character of full-bodied Pinot Noir (especially from New Zealand, California and Oregon), Cabernet-Merlot blends, the spicy wines of Alsace, or even fruity ciders or hoppy beers.

Hard Because they range from mild, smooth and buttery to mouth-puckeringly tangy, almost any wine can be a potential match. However, the stronger and darker the cheese, the bigger and darker the wine you'll need. White wine loses itself to a strong, mature cheese – the cheese's butterfat coats the palate, blocking the wine's flavour. Fortified wines, such as fino sherry, vintage port, Marsala or old Madeira, can be truly magnificent with the very old, very brittle cheeses.

Blue Their salty tang and old-socks aroma holds a strong affinity with sweet, luscious dessert wines, such as Southern French or Spanish Muscat, late-harvest Gewürztraminer, Monbazillac and New World late-harvest or botrytized wines, creating a marvellous marriage of opposites. The right match will also emphasize the hidden sweetness of the milk, particularly with Roquefort. With red, the salt often emphasizes the wine's astringency (its tannin and acidity), although red wines can work well with softer, creamy blues; Pinot Noir tends to work best.

Speciality It is impossible to give a general recommendation for these

GENERAL COMMENTS

If all this is too much to
  remember, here is a summary:

Acid likes acid.
Fruit likes fruit.
Weight needs weight or a
  complete contrast.
Sweetness kills acidity.
Combining cheese and wine is
  about taste as well as texture.
The whiter and fresher the
  cheese, the whiter and crisper
  the wine; the darker and
  stronger the cheese, the darker
  and heavier the wine.

cheeses as the ingredients vary from sweet fruit to robust garlic. However, those with a savoury taste can handle most chunky reds. The dessert-style cheeses with apricots, orange, etc are best treated as desserts and served with sweet wines (*see* blue cheeses) or perhaps even a Spanish cava or tawny port.

Wine matches

Sauvignon Blanc With its fresh acidity and grassy, herbaceous character this wine is the perfect match for many of the fresh and young natural rind cheeses, particularly those made from goat's milk.

Chardonnay When lighter and more citrussy, these wines make excellent soul-mates for cheeses with character but not too

much tang or bite. A fatter, oaked Chardonnay needs a cheese with more depth, more guts and more spice.

Pinot Noir (and to a lesser extent Merlot) These are generally marvellous partners for most cheeses. Their juicy soft fruit, supple tannins, aromatic qualities and earthiness embrace most cheeses, in particular aged goat's cheeses, mature soft white and the sweeter, buttery semi-soft types. Ewe's milk cheese brings out the best in Pinot Noir.

Aged Cabernet Sauvignon needs rich, creamy, full-bodied, but not strong, aged cheeses, such as Comté, Double Gloucester and firm ewe's milk cheeses. The tannin cuts through the butterfat, allowing the wine's deeper flavours to emerge. Younger, more robust and tannic wines welcome stronger, more assertive hard cheeses.

Unfortunately, rich red wines with ripe, sweet fruit from hot climates such as the finest, intense examples of **Australian Shiraz, California Zinfandels** and hefty **Southern Italian** wines, rarely favour cheese, producing sickly, floral aromas. They are best drunk with sweet, mild firm cheeses such as Edam, young Tommes and Caerphilly.

Fortified wines These have a rich sweetness and powerful presence that is a superb foil for extra-strong hard cheeses.

Other milk products

Milk not only provides nourishment for young mammals until they are able to fend for themselves – it has also been turned into numerous delicious and nutritious products. These can be divided into four main categories: butter, cream, fermented milk and cheese. Each category possesses its own unique culinary behavioural patterns, depending on the moisture content, fat content and the thickening method used. Here is a guide to how each of those categories can be broken down.

Butter

(85% fat) Although there are many different types of butter, home-made butter is still the best – and it is easy to make. Simply skim off the cream that rises to the surface of the milk, leaving behind the skimmed or semi-skimmed milk (or buy double cream). Beat the cream until it forms a solid mass, pour off the liquid or buttermilk, press the butter flat using two butter pats or flat wooden spoons, and keep rinsing it under cold, running water as you press, until all the liquid comes out clear. The result is sweet, nutty and delicious butter.

Cream

Unfortunately there is no consistency in the names used to describe the different styles of creams available. However, using the fat content as a guide you should be able to select the best cream for your recipe.

Half cream (12% fat) For pouring only, ideal with coffee, pancakes, fresh fruit, etc.

Single cream (18% fat) This will not whip, but adds texture and character to soups and casseroles, and is ideal for pouring.

Whipping cream (35% fat) Thick, smooth and velvety in texture and retains its shape when whipped.

Double cream (48% fat) Used to increase the flavour of your favourite sauces and your pleasure. It holds its shape without whipping.

Clotted cream (55% fat) Cream is left in a bowl for 12 hours to ripen. The bowl is then put into a shallow dish and placed over a very low heat until the surface of the cream begins to develop small rings or undulations (this takes six to eight hours). It keeps for longer than other types of cream and will form a thick, crusty skin.

Mascarpone (46% fat) This is often erroneously described as cheese. It is, in fact, acid-coagulated cream. Cream is gently heated to 85°C/185°F, then citric and tartaric acid are added while the cream is constantly stirred. The cream gradually thickens and is then cooled for 12 hours. The whey is not poured off, as with cheese, but is absorbed into thefat and protein, producing a versatile, long-life, rich, nutty sweet cream.

Soured and fermented milks

What differentiates these from cheese is that rennet is not used to bring about coagulation and the whey is not removed. Instead the milks thicken as a result of a starter culture similar to that used in cheesemaking, which converts the lactose or milk sugars into lactic acid (ie fermentation).

As the whey is not removed the fat content is significantly lower than that of cheese. The variety of bacteria has a big effect on the taste and texture – a feature overlooked by some commercial producers.

Buttermilk (8-10% fat) Some butter is made by adding a starter culture to allow the cream to ripen, and the liquid released is buttermilk. Used as a substitute for sour milk, buttermilk is also more easily digestible than skimmed milk because of its higher lactic acid content.

Yoghurt (15-30% fat) A starter culture – usually a mixture of two bacteria, *Lactobacillus bulgaricus* and *Streptococcus thermophilius* – is added to full-fat or skimmed milk. Working together, the bacteria achieve a balance of acidity and taste and a soft moist blend of curd and whey. Today, most yoghurt is made from cow's milk, although the demand for sheep's and goat's milk yoghurts is increasing. *Kumiss* from mare's milk and *kefir* from the camel are other types of yoghurt, but they differ in that the bacteria used also produces alcohol during the fermentation.

Sour cream (20-30% fat) This is made from single cream treated with a bacteria culture, giving it a rich, tangy, acidic taste and smooth, wet, thick texture with a relatively low fat content.
Crème fraîche (30-50% fat) Cream is left to mature and naturally sour without any added bacteria starters, becoming nutty rather than acidic. The consistency is of clotted cream: spoonable not pourable. It tolerates higher temperatures in cooking than double cream before it curdles. Ideal for the less attentive chef.

The longevity of life among nomadic races of Africa and Asia has been attributed to their diet of soured and fermented milks. It seems that the bacteria in these milks settle in the intestinal tract, where the milk sugars are broken down into lactic acid, which aids digestion, improves the immune system, reduces cholesterol and offers an antidote to the side effects of antibiotics. It may be decades before irrefutable proof can verify these theories. However, no-one has yet discovered any negative aspects to soured and fermented milks.

*Clockwise from top: **Farmhouse butter:** – fresh, sweet, unsalted. **Greek yoghurt:** drained to give it a thicker texture and higher fat content. **Clotted cream:** thick and buttery; when left will form a thick, dark yellow crust. **Double cream:** always best beaten in a cool, clean bowl. **Crème fraîche:** rich and unctuous; should always hold its shape on a spoon.*

Myths and misconceptions

There are numerous myths and misconceptions about cheese that need to be dispelled. Believe it or not, many people still believe that Edam is British and the rind on Camembert is edible paper.

A lot of these misconceptions came about in a time when knowledge of the cheesemaking process was limited and refrigeration had not been invented. One classic misconception is that Stilton can be enhanced by pouring port into it – a habit that came about when there was no refrigeration and Stilton was served whole in magnificent, deep porcelain jars, at banquets in grand houses. At the bottom the cheese was warm, dark, airless and a veritable haven for those creatures that thrived in this environment. Holes were made in the Stilton and port was poured down to drown the maggots and help prolong the life of the Stilton.

Questions most frequently asked

Fresh
What is the difference between Mozzarella in liquid and the firmer, more supple one, wrapped in plastic?
Fresh Mozzarella in liquid is soft, moist and has a very short shelf life. It is wonderful for salads, as it absorbs the oils and juices of the other ingredients and is soft and light in texture. The less expensive, block-packed Mozzarella, sometimes known as 'pizza cheese' keeps well, slices easily, and has the wonderful stretchy texture that is essential for pizzas.

Soft, white-rind
How do you choose a ripe Camembert?
The closer to the 'best by' date, the softer and more flavoursome the cheese will become.

Why do you sometimes get the chalky centre in Camembert and Brie?
When a Camembert or Brie is young, the curd in the centre has not yet been broken down by the fermentation process into its characteristic soft, mushroomy flavoured texture.

What is the rind on Camembert and Brie? Can you eat it?
The moist rind of these cheeses attracts a beautiful white 'bloom' of penicillin mould that grows like soft velvet. Yes, if you like it, eat it.

Semi-soft
What makes the rind orange?
When the cheeses are rubbed or washed in salt, the growth of an orange-coloured mould is encouraged.

Should they be sticky?
Washed rind cheeses such as Epoisses should be sticky and have a pungent aroma. Those with

waxed or leathery rinds are normally milder, more supple and have a drier, less orange rind.

Hard
Why do some cheeses vary in taste from one week to the next?
This is one of the wonderful things about cheese – that each batch is like a vintage of wine and has its own unique character affected by what the animals eat, the weather, the seasons and the individual skills of the cheesemaker.

Why do Cheddars not have rinds any more?
Only Cheddar wrapped in muslin and allowed to mature in cellars will develop a rind.

How do they make the same cheese mild, medium or tasty?
It is the style of the cheesemaker and the age of a cheese that determines its strength of flavour. Hard cheeses, because of their low moisture content, take a long time to mature compared with softer cheeses.

Blue
What is the blue in blue cheese?
The wonderful blue-green colour does not come from copper wire, as many people believe, but from a harmless penicillin mould that goes blue when exposed to air. When the young cheese is pierced with stainless-steel rods, carbon dioxide escapes and oxygen is let in, causing the mould to turn blue.

*Why does blue cheese smell
so strong?*
It is a combination of the
fermentation process that occurs in
all maturing cheeses, the way it is
stored and the unique type of rind
it grows. The bacteria that eat the
moist curd are similar to those that
like the cosy, moist warmth of your
toes, and consequently they smell
very similar.

Low-fat
*What is low-fat cheese? And how
does this affect the flavour?*
Cheese is generally made from full
or whole milk. However, when
made from skimmed or semi-
skimmed milk, the final fat content
will be lower than normal. It is,
however, the fat in cheese that is
responsible for its rich, full flavour
and texture, and so there is
inevitably a loss of some flavour
and a difference in texture. This is
more noticeable in some cheeses
than in others.

*Where is the best place to
store cheese?*
Store cheese in the fridge wrapped
in waxed paper in a plastic box,
and keep the blues separate from
the rest unless you want
blue Cheddar!

Allergies
*If you have an allergy to
cheese, can you eat goat's or ewe's
milk cheese?*
Many people have found that
although they are allergic to cow's
milk products, they have no
reaction to goat's or ewe's milk
products. It is definitely worth
discussing with your doctor.

HEALTH AND NUTRITION
How healthy is cheese?
We are brought up on mother's milk because milk contains everything we
need to sustain life – calcium for the development of bones and the
prevention of osteoporosis, and minerals, vitamins and fats to help us grow.
If we decide to lose weight, we need to consider cutting back on sugars and
fats, particularly saturated fats. Cheese tends to be one of the first things
we cut down on. Yet many people find that, even by doing without their
favourite cheese, there is little change in their weight. Why?

Look at the chart below and then work out which foods you eat more
of and where the fats you are eating really come from.

NUTRITIONAL VALUES PER 100G

	Calories	Protein (g)	Sugars (g)	Starch (g)	Fat content (g)
Margarine	739 kcal	0.2	1.0	0.0	81.6
Butter	737 kcal	0.5	trace	0.0	81.7
Mayonnaise (5 brands)	691 kcal	1.1	1.2	0.4	75.6
Peanuts roasted/salted	617 kcal	28.3	3.6	3.0	53.0
Potato crisps	540 kcal	5.6	0.7	44.2	37.6
Plain chocolate	528 kcal	4.7	56.7	4.8	29.2
Tomato ketchup	433 kcal	2.1	22.4	1.0	trace
Cheddar	410 kcal	25.0	0.1	0.0	34.4
Edam	331 kcal	25.5	trace	0.0	25.4
Brie	318 kcal	18.9	trace	0.0	26.9
Milk (whole)	66 kcal	3.1	4.6	0.0	3.9

From Food Labelling Data for Manufacturers (Royal Society of Chemists/MAFF) 1992

HEALTHY SUGGESTIONS FOR EATING CHEESE
When cooking, use a stronger cheese as you will need to use less to get a
  good flavour.
Eat soft rather than hard varieties of cheese.
Eat salads with cheese to help you break down and digest the fats.
Don't eat butter with cheese.
Eat bread rather than biscuits with cheese, as biscuits contain more fat.
Avoid drinking tea and coffee with cheese, as the combination can
  give you indigestion.
Red wine helps your body break down the cholesterol in fat and means
  you absorb less of the fat.
Salads, fruit and wine all help break down the fats.
Low fat cheeses are a good alternative to full-fat varieties, but remember
  that when you reduce the normal fat content you also reduce the flavour,
  as fat enhances and increases flavour in cheese.
Use oils high in mono or polyunsaturates instead of butter or margarine
  when cooking. Olive oil is the best.

Glossary of terms

Acid-curd Some cheeses are made using acetic or lactic acid as the coagulant, rather than rennet.

Acidimeter Used to test the acidity of the whey various stages of cheesemaking.

Affineur Specialist who matures cheeses.

Annatto A natural dye obtained from the bright red-orange seeds of the Annatto tree native to South America.

AOC Appellation d'Origine Contrôllée – the regulation in France by law of a particular cheese in terms of where it can be made, the breed of the cow, sheep or goat, the manufacturing methods used and its shape, texture, etc. DO and DOC are (respectively) the Spanish and Italian equivalents.

British Cheese Awards Created by the author in 1994 and sponsored by Tesco, these are an annual event designed to raise the profile of British cheese and provide the consumer with a recognizable symbol of excellence. In 1998 nearly 600 cheeses were entered and the best were awarded gold, sliver or bronze medals. The awards culminate each year with the British Cheese Festival – a national campaign in October to promote all British cheese.

Brine A concentrated mixture of water and salt, used to seal the outside of a cheese and help in the formation of a rind, to expel whey and deter the growth of some bacteria and moulds.

Buttermilk What is left after cream has been churned into butter.

Carotene Deep yellow pro-vitamins found in vegetation, that give colour to milk and cheese. Some is converted into Vitamin A.

Casein The main protein in milk which solidifies during coagulation. The casein in soft cheeses becomes soluble; the casein in hard, cooked cheeses becomes hard.

Coagulation The conversion of the solids in milk (casein) into a mass of curd and whey, the basis of cheesemaking.

Cottage cheese Unlike other washed curd cheeses such as Edam or Gouda, the newly formed curds of cottage cheese are washed and rinsed in cold water to separate the individual curds, leaving them supple, moist and with the taste

of fresh milk rather than cheese. If cream is added the feel is more velvety.

Curds and whey When milk becomes sour it curdles or coagulates, separating out into the solid protein (the curd) and the watery element of milk (the whey).

Enzymes Found in living cells, these cause chemical changes when associated with particular substances (eg rennin enzyme causing coagulation of casein protein in milk).

Esters Fatty acids and glycerides in plants. The aromatic esters give aroma and flavour.

Fat A carrier and enhancer of flavour, it provides that delicious soft, creamy feel in the mouth. If you reduce the fat content of any cheese, you will change its depth of flavour and texture or 'mouth feel'. Low-fat versions of a cheese tend to be drier in texture and lack the depth of flavour of their full-fat counterpart.' Full fat' is the expression used to indicate that the cheese has been made with unskimmed milk – most cheeses are made with full-fat milk.

Fat content This varies in cheese, depending on how much moisture a cheese contains and whether it is made from skimmed or full-fat milk. The more moisture in a cheese, the lower its fat content. A hard cheese has had most of its moisture removed, and therefore has a higher concentration of fat.

Fermentation The process of converting the components in milk by micro-organisms into various acids, aldehydes, ketones and gases, which contribute to the ripening of the cheese and its flavour.

Gruyère Name given in France to all large cheeses: Comté, Beaufort and Emmental. In Switzerland, it is a cheese from the Jura Mountains.

Hoop Cylindrical open-ended cheese mould.

Lactation Milk production, used to describe the period during which a milking animal gives milk – from calving to drying out. Cows have no specific season, and so the herds can be staggered to provide milk all year around. Goat and sheep, however, are influenced by the seasons and generally sheep's milk is

available from autumn to spring; for goat's milk it is from spring to autumn, although modern farming practices allow farmers to adjust their seasons.

Lactic acid Formed when certain bacteria attack the lactose or milk sugars in milk.

Lactose Sugar specific to milk, occurring in the milk of all mammals. Converted to lactic acid by the enzyme action of some micro-organisms in the lactic fermentation.

Mould 1) The container into which the curd is packed after salting, usually called a hoop when open ended, a mould when one end is closed.

2) The microflora that grow on the surface or within cheeses during ripening.

New Zealand Cheese Awards Created by the author in 1994, these are an annual event designed to raise the profile of New Zealand cheese and provide the consumer with a recognizable symbol of excellence. In 1999 nearly 400 cheeses were judged, and the best were awarded gold, sliver or bronze medals. They culminate each year with the New Zealand Cheese Festival in May.

Organic Cheese produced on farms approved by the Soil Association or other similar organizations bear the 'Organic' label, demonstrating their commitment to traditional, 'green' farming practices. The label excludes the use of many sprays and dictates the amount of nitrates spread over the land.

Pasteurization Heat treatment to destroy harmful micro-organisms in milk, which also destroys many beneficial and flavour-enriching micro-organisms.

Pricking Aerating a cheese by piercing with needles to allow the entry and development of mould spores.

Processed cheese (not to be confused with speciality cheese) Cheese subjected to heat-treatment and combined with an emulsifying agent, oil and water, then moulded when hot and immediately sealed in its final pack.

Proteolysis Breakdown of proteins by enzymes, acids, alkalis or heat.

Quark Thought to originate from the fermented milk products of the nomadic tribes of the Middle East. Like a cross between *fromage frais* and yoghurt, it is made from skimmed or semi-skimmed milk, is virtually odourless and has a slightly sour taste and wet, grainy feel.

Raw milk The natural state of milk not subjected to pasteurization or heat treatment.

Rennet The enzyme extracted from the lining of the stomach walls of milk-fed animals and used in cheesemaking to break down the solids in milk into digestible form, helping coagulation.

Ripening 1) (of milk) Natural maturing of milk through rising acidity before the starter or rennet is added.

2) (of cheese) Continuing enzyme action of rennet and completion of bacterial action on curd, and consequent enzyme action.

Scalding The heating of curd during cheesemaking to make it contract and expel more whey.

Serum *See* whey.

Silage Preservation of grasses and legumes by air-free storage, with limited fermentation.

Skimmed milk Milk from which part or all of the cream has been removed.

Starters A milk-based bacterial culture that is added to fresh milk to start the conversion of lactose into lactic acid. The enzymes from starters help break down the milk and contribute to the texture, flavour and aroma of cheese.

Taste The following expressions are commonly used to describe the taste of cheese:

Acidity A positive attribute if not excessive – a refreshing, citrus sensation in the mouth.

Aromatic A sensation of varied and interesting aromas, generally spicy, perfumed, herbaceous or fruity.

Bite A distinct, sharp, intense, initial flavour usually carried through to the finish.

Bitter A characteristic taste of some cheeses; can be a positive attribute, as in a strong Cheddar, or a fault when used to describe a Brie.

Burnt caramel A delicious sweet flavour with just a hint of overcooked, caramelized sugar.

Earthy An aroma of freshly tilled soil.

Finish The taste that remains with you after the last mouthful.

Fruity A flavour reminiscent of both the odour and taste of fresh fruit picked at its optimum stage of ripeness eg pears, apples, melon, mango, etc.

Grassy Characteristic aroma of freshly cut grass – a fresh pleasantly sharp flavour.

Herbaceous The leafy fragrance of wild flowers, herbs, hedgerows and grasses.

Lactic The taste of slightly soured milk.

Lemony As the lactose or milk sugars are converted into lactic acid, the cheese develops a pleasantly refreshing acidity which can be described as lemony or citrus.

Metallic The mould in blue cheeses can be mild and slightly herbaceous, reminiscent of tarragon and thyme, or strong with a distinct sharp mineral or metallic taint.

Nutty Flavour reminiscent of freshly crushed or ground nuts.

Peppery A peppery hot sensation at the back of the throat.

Pungent A forceful, pleasant, sometimes almost bitter flavour, reminiscent of meat, farmyards or smelly socks.

Rich Like a thick, syrupy sweet or savoury sauce.

Spicy A sensation of various spices – cinnamon, nutmeg, pepper, allspice, normally accompanied by a warm to hot feeling in the mouth.

Sweet Normally refers to a sweetness like slightly caramelized milk rather than actual sugar.

Tingle A sensation like fizzy lemonade or over-ripe fruit.

Tangy The sensation in the mouth that causes it to pucker and tingle, usually caused by a tart or acidic flavour, often associated with a mature hard cheeses, such as Cheddar.

Texture The following expressions are commonly used to describe the texture of cheese:

Body The sensation of weight and substance in the mouth.

Dry A feeling of lack of moisture in the mouth.

Elastic A firm but flexible bounce-back feel.

Grainy Slight roughness on the palate

that can be due to whey powder added to fresh cheeses. Can be either unpleasant or a pleasant sense of small particles in crumbly cheeses such as Cheshire, or young Camembert-style cheeses.

Moist Used in contrast to dry.

Rubbery A bouncy, springy feel and texture that rips rather then breaks.

Smooth An absence of any structure – double cream, custard (without lumps!).

Soft Yielding texture, as when you eat mashed potato or cheesecakes.

Supple A rubbery feel but with an underlying structure.

Squeaky When curd is washed it becomes very smooth and feels shiny and 'squeaky' clean.

Velvety A cheese that is soft, smooth and structure-less, a term usually used to described a processed cheese.

Trappist Generic name given to cheeses made in monasteries that follow Trappist practices.

Transhumance A term for the movement of animals in summer to new pastures, normally in the mountains.

Ultrafiltration Involves passing milk through a series of pipes and processes to concentrate rather than coagulate the solids. The extracted whey from ultrafiltration contains virtually no solids, compared with traditional methods, and so the yield is higher.

Vegetarian rennet To meet the needs of the growing number of vegetarians, many cheeses are now made using non-animal rennet. It has no discernible effect on the final taste or texture.

Whey The yellow-green liquid left after most of the solids, including the fats, have been coagulated into the curd.

Whole milk As it comes from the cow.

Yield 1) Milk yield of animals – one cow can produce from 9-27.75 litres/16-40 pints of milk per day; a goat gives one to 1.13-2 litres/2-3 pints three times per day, while sheep give about 4.5-5.7 litres/8-10 pints a day.

2) Ratio of milk to the weight of cheese produced – it takes 2.27 litres/ 4 pints of milk to make an 250g/9oz Camembert, compared with 1,420 litres/ 2,500 pints to make an Emmental cheese.

Index of cheeses by country

Index

Picture credits in source order

FRONT COVER, BACK COVER LEFT AND RIGHT: Octopus Publishing Group Ltd/*Laurie Evans*. BACK COVER CENTRE: Franca Speranza/*Adriiano Bacchella*. B & U International: 12 BOTTOM RIGHT. Anthony Blake Photo Library: 12 TOP LEFT, 13, 165, 172 TOP LEFT. *Gerrit Buntrock*: 10 TOP, 14, 181 CENTRE RIGHT. *John Heseltine*: 181 BOTTOM RIGHT. *Maximilia*: 181 BOTTOM LEFT. *Kieran Scott*: 11 TOP RIGH. *John Sims*: 11 TOP LEFT. Cephas Picture Library/ *Dorothy Burrow*: 108. *Herve Champollion*: 12 BOTTOM LEFT. *Frank B. Higham*: 23. *Pierre Hussenot*: 2. *MJ Kielty*: 167. *Stockfood*: 177, 181 TOP, 181 TOP RIGHT. *Wine Magazine*: 17 BOTTOM RIGHT. Long Clawson: 145, 146. Robert Harding Picture Library: 20. Image Bank/*F. Ruggeri*: 19. Laurie Evans 4, 6, 7. Octopus Publishing Group Ltd: *Joe Cornish*; 1, 11 CENTRE, 173. *Laurie Evans*; 18, 21, 22, 25, 46, 47, 58, 61, 62, 76, 79, 80, 106, 109, 110, 113, 114, 144, 147, 148, 150, 164, 166, 175. *Jason Lowe*; 172 TOP RIGHT, 172 BOTTOM RIGHT. *Richard McConnell*; 10 BOTTOM. *James Murphy*; 176. *Alan Williams*; 9, 11 BOTTOM, 107, 111, 172 BOTTOM LEFT. JA & E Montgomery Ltd: 15, 16, 17. Scope/*Daniel Czap*: 178. *Jean Charles Gesquiere*: 63. *Jacques Guillard*: 12 TOP RIGHT, 49, 59, 60, 77, 78, 81. *Francis Jalain*: 8. *Jean-Luc Barde*: 149. Franca Speranza/*Adriiano Bacchella*: 112. *Dino Fracchia*: 151. *Robert Frerck*: 115. *M. Courtney-Clarke*: 24.

Authors acknowledgements

It is impossible to write a book that spans so many countries and disciplines without the help of wonderful skilled, knowledgeable and generous people, too numerous to mention. A special thanks, however, goes to the following:

My friends Mike and Sue Willis, Carole Thompson and Julie Ogler who gave me the support and confidence to write this book. The patrons of the Tite Inn, my favourite watering hole and sanity check, Jasper for his discerning palate and sense ofaof the ridiculous and the two great cheese men of this century, Patrick Rance and Pierre Androuet, beneath whose shadow I would proudly stand.

To John Campbell and Sandra Ott for their insight into the lives of the shepherds and their families who still practice transhumance and the cheesemakers around the world who shared their time and their cheeses.

The cost of research for this book would have been prohibitive without the support of Food From Spain, Sopexa, Food From Britain, Slow Foods, Avilton Foods (importers of Italian cheese) and Tribillat who have provided invaluable funds, material or information on the many producers and lesser-known cheeses of Europe.

Patricia Michelson at La Fromagerie in London provided some wonderful cheeses for me to taste and for the photography, as did Jeroboams, Neal's Yard, Paxton & Whitfield, Harvey Nichols and Iain Mellis in Scotland. Their shops are an inspiration, as are those of St-Hubert and Marie Cantin in Paris where I make regular sorties in search of the rare and the wonderful.

I would also like to thank Rik Yapp and Barnaby Scott for not being computer geeks, Debra Dickerson (Neal's Yard, US), Karen Kaplin (*Bon Appetit*, US), Nick Haddow (Richmond Hill Café, Australia) and Lucy Bridgers, Fiona Knowles and the team at Mitchell Beazley for driving me mad and getting the best from me.